I dedicate this work
to the memory of the late
CARDINAL WILLIAM CONWAY
1913 –1977
who was Archbishop of Armagh
1963 – 1977

Cardinal Conway was thrilled by the whole phenomenon of space exploration. He was fascinated by the seeming insignificance in the cosmos of planet Earth as seen from outer space, and by the minuscule littleness in that vast universe of the human beings who inhabit the thin, green fringe of the zoosphere, and who yet can find mind and order, meaning and purpose in that vast myriad of galaxies and can find a loving God as their Source and Sustainer, their Alpha and their Omega.

The Cardinal kept in his study a photograph of planet Earth taken from the surface of the moon in July 1969 by the astronauts of Apollo XI. The design on the cover of this book is based on that photograph.

Yet nothing mattered so much to him as

PRAEDICARE EVANGELIUM
To Preach the Gospel. This was his motto; this was his life.
Requiescat in Pace

CONTENTS

Table of Topics   7

Acknowledgements   11

Foreword   13

I   Science and Faith   17

II   The Galileo Case   58

III   Church and World   95

IV   The Christian and Work   135

V   The Minding of Planet Earth (1) and (2)   167

       Appendix: Behold Your God   224

       Notes   232

       Index   247

TABLE OF TOPICS

CHAPTER I: SCIENCE AND FAITH

Myth about the Medievals   19
Historically False   23
The Centrality of the Human   26
'When I Behold the Heavens'   31
Theology as a Preparation for Science   33
Science and Mystery   38
Reason in Nature   41
Christianity and Democracy   46
Filled with the Glory of God   50
'Clothed with Beauty'   55

CHAPTER II: THE GALILEO CASE

Galileo and His Times   58
Copernicanism   60
Galileo's Fervent Faith   62
Dispute Begins   63
Letter to Castelli   63
Foscarini and Cardinal Bellarmine   65
Letter to Christina of Lorraine   67
Copernican System Condemned   69
The Assayer   70
The Dialogue   72
Church Versus Science?   77
After the Condemnation   78
Galileo's Last Years   79
Vindication of Galileo   80

Pope John Paul II and Galileo   83
Developments in Hermeneutics   86
Developments in Science   88
Could There Be Another Galileo Case?   89
Church and Science   93

CHAPTER III: CHURCH AND WORLD
'Other-Worldliness': Nietzsche and Marx   95
Semantic Difficulties   98
Plato   99
Immortality   101
The Last End   102
Eternity is Now   104
Christianity and Time   104
Christ's Coming   106
The Last Things are Now   107
The 'Today' of the Sacraments   109
Contempt for the World?   113
The Imitation   114
Attachment-Detachment   120
Contemplation and Action   123
Science, Politics, Charity   129
Social Justice   131

CHAPTER IV: THE CHRISTIAN AND WORK
The Popes and Labour   135
Vatican II and Trade Unions   140
Pope John Paul II on Work   141
Structures of Sin   146
The Bible and Work   148
'Fill the Earth and Conquer it'   149
Atheistic Theories of Work   149
Christ and Work   150
Baptism and Work   152
Prophets, Kings and Priests   153
Christ's Kingship over Matter   154
Work and Christ's Priesthood   155
Bring Christ's Peace to Others   156
Divine Creation and Human Work   157

The New Creation   158
Work and the New Creation   159
The Transfiguration   163

CHAPTER V: THE MINDING OF PLANET EARTH (1)
Earth: Our Fragile Home   168
Church and Ecology   169
Catholic Teaching   171
World Council of Churches   175
The Orthodox Church   178
Caring for the Earth: John Paul II   179
Science, Technology and Industry   180
The Brandt Report   181
The Thorsson Report   183
World Charter for Nature   184
Global 2000 Report   184
Population Growth and Poverty   190
Individual Responsibility   191
Greed   193

CHAPTER V: THE MINDING OF PLANET EARTH (2)
World Poverty and Human Rights   196
Debt and World Poverty   197
Overseas Development Aid   199
The Arms Trade   202
Disarmament and Development   206
Moral Influence   207
Ireland's Role in the EU   207
Refugees and Asylum-Seekers   208
'Supplement of Soul'   209
Taxation, Tax-Evasion and Greed   210
Change of Lifestyle   211
Covenant and Creation   212
Prayer Inspired by Creation   213
The New Creation   215
The Cross: Symbol of Universal Reconciliation   216
The Eucharist and Ecology   219
St Francis of Assisi and Ecology   219
Ecology and Mary, Mother of the Lord   220

ACKNOWLEDGEMENTS

I have received helpful suggestions and corrections from persons much more competent than I in matters of science. I am very grateful to them all; but I do not name them because I alone am responsible for what is written here and for any errors which still remain.

I thank the surviving members of my family, my brother Patrick with his wife, Barbara, and my sister Rosaleen, together with my nephews and nieces and my whole extended family, for their support in everything concerning my welfare and work. I thank Archbishop Sean Brady, the Archdiocese of Armagh and its Diocesan Office, and Father Eugene Sweeney, Diocesan Secretary, for much help and support. I thank my nephew Dr Gerard Daly and my grand-nephews, John Daly and John Hillan and my grand-niece, Dr Joanna Hillan, for help in accessing books. I thank David Gordon of Queen's University Main Library, Colette Haughey of the Armagh Campus of the Queen's University Library, and Stephanie McLaughlin of the University of Ulster's Magee Campus Library, Derry, for invaluable help with books.

I thank Gerry Powers and Gerry Flood of the staff of the Office of International Justice of the US Conference of Catholic Bishops for much help in connection with matters concerning world debt and related issues which are touched on in Chapter V. I thank also Justin Kilcullen and Eamon Meehan and their staff in Trócaire for great help in connection with international development aid, poverty and world debt reduction and related matters touched on in the same chapter. I thank Martin Long, Director of the Catholic Communications Office; and Brenda Drumm, its Communications Officer, for help, particularly in accessing newspaper files. All of these have been most generous with their time and patience.

I thank Gemma Loughran, my former student, who carefully read the manuscript and made helpful suggestions.

My special thanks go to Alice Warde and Nancy McGarry for their patience and skill in endless re-typing of the manuscript and in preparing the final typescript for the printers. I thank Veritas Publications, Maura Hyland, Director, Helen Carr, Managing Editor, and the staff generally, for their skilled, professional work in editing, proof-reading and all the tasks of seeing the book through its printing and publishing, and for great patience with long delays in my finalising of the typescript. I thank Bill Bolger for the cover design and Gráinne Farren for the index.

FOREWORD

There are a number of fallacies which have, in the post-Enlightenment era, bedevilled authentic dialogue between the Church and the modern world. It is taken for granted, for example, among many scientists and in a large swathe of public opinion that the Church is the enemy of science; that faith is incompatible with reason; that the Christian is so concerned with the 'other world' that he or she neglects to work for the betterment of this world and this planet; that for the Christian all that is really of value is 'the next life', so that the concerns of this life are unimportant; that prayer and resignation to God's Will are the Christians' excuse for inaction and passivity. I touch on some of these issues in this book and I hope to show that we have to do, not with the choice, Church *or* science, etcetera, but with the complementarity, Church *and* science, faith *and* reason, 'other world' *and* this world, 'next life' *and* this life, prayer *and* action. To that extent, my book is a plea for unprejudiced dialogue between the Church and the modern world, and is perhaps a modest contribution to that dialogue.

This is in part what the Second Vatican Council was about, particularly in its Pastoral Constitution on the Church in the Modern World, *Gaudium et Spes*. After the Council, some interpreted this document and indeed the whole Council in such a way as to reverse the Church's then perceived imbalance vis-à-vis the world and to eliminate, as far as possible, all tension between Church and world, giving priority to activism over prayer, and emphasising social justice in this world rather than the Kingdom 'which is not of this world.' Hence came such slogans as: 'First the political Kingdom;' 'The world sets the agenda for the Church.' This book is, in this sense, indirectly and in part an exercise in interpretation of the Second Vatican Council.

Much more remains to be said, and better said than I have managed to do, about all these issues. Furthermore, I am not a scientist; and the warning, *Ne sutor supra crepidam*, roughly translated as, 'the cobbler should stick to his last', is a salutary phrase; it has made me pause and reflect before publishing these chapters. However, as a former teacher of philosophy, I have in my time done some reading and research on the questions raised here, (although, since I left academia, pastoral preoccupations have made it impossible to keep up my reading). Also, as a pastor, I know what an impact, directly or indirectly, these issues have had and continue to have on the prevailing culture in which today's Christian pastors are called to preach the faith and in which today's Christian is called to live and practise his or her faith. I have felt the pain of seeing people reject the faith because of thinking that faith and science, religion and reason, are incompatible with one another. I have felt the pain also of seeing people cut themselves off from the Church without ever having really known its message in the fullness of its truth, its beauty, the sure hope it offers and its sheer goodness and joy. Hence I have put aside my hesitations and I push the boat – and this book – out, in the hope that it might at least stimulate reflection.

There is an intended play on words in the title I have given to the book. 'The Minding of Planet Earth' refers to God's act of creation, done freely, gratuitously, in the fullness of His Wisdom and through the Wisdom of His Son, who is Infinite Reason, Mind, (*Logos*), in person; and whose Mind is reflected in the order of the created world, making it intelligible to human minds. It refers to God's creation of human beings, made in His own image, sharing by their finite minds in His Infinite Reason, and thus empowered to decipher the 'reason' or 'mind' embodied in God's universe and in its workings. It refers to God's giving to human beings of a share in His Providence, which is His 'minding' of the world; and this sharing (which we can call 'prudence') makes humans co-responsible under God for the 'minding' of the earth and makes them accountable to God for its prudent management, for the benefit of present and future generations of human beings, and for the glory of God.

The main thrust of the book could, therefore, be stated in words used by Pope John Paul II in his October 1992 address to the Pontifical Academy of Sciences:

> Einstein used to say: 'What is eternally incomprehensible in the world is that it is comprehensible.' This intelligibility, attested to by the

marvellous discoveries of science and technology, leads us, in the last analysis, to that transcendent and primordial Thought imprinted on all things.

So far as my book is concerned, may I remark that the French have a term for a work which is neither specialist and technical in its field nor simply ignorant of its subject matter. They call it *'vulgarisation'*. They distinguish *'haute vulgarisation'* from its opposite, to which, tactfully, they do not give a name. This book is certainly 'vulgarisation'; whether it be *'haute'* or *'au contraire'* is not for me to judge.

I am happy to see the text completed on the Feast of the Annunciation of the Lord, when Mary the Virgin, giving her consent to God's word, became Theotokos, Mother of the Incarnate Word; and thereby a new creation of the aeons-old cosmos was begun.

✠ Cahal B. Cardinal Daly
Feast of the Annunciation of the Lord,
25 March 2004

Chapter I

SCIENCE AND FAITH

A very common reason given in our time for rejecting Christian faith is that it is incompatible with science. This charge is scarcely thought by its advocates to need proof or to require argument: it is treated as virtually self-evident. Faith and Church and religion generally are simply dismissed as unscientific, irrational, vestigial remnants of a prescientific and superstitious age, having no place in a modern rational society. Richard Dawkins is the best known contemporary exponent of this kind of view, but it is not by any means a recent attitude towards religion. It was commonly shared in the nineteenth century by rationalists such as T.H. Huxley and in the twentieth century by his grandson, Julian Huxley. It was a standard topic for argument in nineteenth and early twentieth-century Britain. It was debated by H.G. Wells and G.K. Chesterton in packed halls up and down England. It was a commonplace in the polemical writings of Betrand Russell.

Indeed, we find it much earlier in the rhetoric of the eighteenth-century 'Enlightenment' in France, when 'reason' was assumed to have discredited and replaced Christian faith, reason being associated with modernity and 'progress' and 'laicité', and faith with 'clericalism', backwardness and superstition. 'Enlightenment' thinkers indeed called their century the 'Age of Reason'. Newspapers in provincial France often have the title, 'Le Progrès', which frequently betokens the 'anti-clerical' origin and orientation of the publication. The name alone subtly suggests that 'laicity' and anti-clericalism represent Progress while religion is associated with backwardness and ignorance, superstition and poverty. This was an unquestioned part of the official public culture in which Thérèse of Lisieux lived and struggled towards sainthood in provincial France towards the end of the nineteenth century. There are signs of its re-emergence in the public culture of Western Europe today – not excluding Ireland.

A British journalist, writing in the *Sunday Times* recently, remarked, quite casually, 'the British like their debates rational, not religious.' There is a *déjà-vu* feeling about a recent heading in an Irish Sunday paper over an article about the debate surrounding genetic cloning; the heading was: 'Progress or Superstition?' and the sub-heading: 'Religion cannot be allowed to hold back the medical advances cloning can bring about.' One of its sentences reads: "'Soul' is a supernatural fantasy that cannot be exposed to scientific analysis ...' The Galileo case, as we shall see, is often adduced as proof of the Church's opposition to science. The article in question alludes to this case when it states:

> The old idea that humanity was at the centre of the universe collapsed into dust in the face of Copernican truths (after a vicious attempt by the unreconstructed Church to stay standing).[1]

Some things apparently have not changed since Voltaire's *'Ecrasez l'infame!'* 'Crush the Infamous Thing,' where the 'thing' to be crushed was everything that was 'irrational,' and primarily the Catholic Church. I wish in this chapter to submit some reasons for rejecting such views of the relations between science and faith. Indeed, here and elsewhere throughout this book, I wish to plead for dialogue between science and faith as complementary ways of attaining truth. I shall argue that both are needed if we are to make sense of our own existence and of the world around us.

In this opening chapter, I propose to ask first whether such views about science and faith are historically true as accounts of the 'copernican revolution'. I shall then try to show that post-copernican science, far from marginalising human beings in the vastness of the non-human universe, actually affirms man's place in the cosmos as revealed by science; for science is the product of the human mind's exploring of the world. I shall argue on a later page that there is a certain 'centrality of the human' involved in the doing of science; there is a certain 'anthropic principle' at work in the scientific enterprise. I shall then attempt to show that, so far from religion's having been discredited and displaced by modern science, Christian faith and Christian theology have as a matter of fact played a vital role in creating the cultural climate in which modern science took root and flourished.

I then put forward some considerations which suggest that science itself, of its very nature, makes a number of assumptions, which it takes as 'givens', but which it cannot itself explain. Science raises questions which it cannot by its own methods answer. There is a realm of 'mystery' within and beyond science, which science itself cannot account for, but which the human mind cannot ignore. There is, as Greek philosophy already showed, a 'meta-physics' in and beyond the science of physics. Science cannot constitute the whole of human knowledge or of human exploration. Science cannot exhaust the remit of reason.

Then, since there seems to be a natural affinity between science and democracy, I look briefly at the role of Christianity in the genesis and the value system of modern democracy. Finally, in this chapter I look at the contribution of religion, and particularly of the Judaeo-Christian Bible, to the appreciation of beauty in the cosmos, and the place of nature's beauty in that praise of God which is the Church's liturgy.

Myth about the Medievals

The view that science is incompatible with faith is often expressed along the following lines. In the Christian centuries before Copernicus and Galileo men and women felt themselves to be comfortably installed in an earth-centred and human-friendly cosmos, whose sun and stars and planets revolved in harmonious circles around the human being, centre and lord of the universe, and revolved precisely for human edification and delight and benefit; and all of this was taking place under the benevolent eye of a God who was Himself man's *Alter Ego*, a projection of man's own image.

Copernicus and then Galileo, so the story continues, shattered this geocentric and anthropocentric complacency. Earth, they showed, is not the centre, and man is not the measure, of the cosmos. Consequently, the main foundation of human self-esteem is at once demolished; the basis of man's sense of his own importance in the cosmos, indeed the basis of his religion, is in principle destroyed. This, it is argued, is the meaning of the copernican revolution. The full force of the destruction was not, indeed, at once perceived. But subsequent progress in astronomy and in science generally has only completed the process begun by Copernicus and Galileo. Science has cut man down to size – the size of a marginal, negligible and expendable accident in an indifferent, inhuman, and above all, irreligious cosmos. Science has, in brief, discredited and disqualified religion.[2] Religion is no longer an option for modern and post-modern human beings, at least for those who wish to retain intellectual integrity.

I wish to quote some of the classic statements of this theory. First, to show how pervasive it has been in the scientific era, I shall quote from David Hume near the beginning, and Sir Bernard Lovell nearer our end, of the modern scientific age.

David Hume, in *Dialogues Concerning Natural Religion (1779)*, asked:

> What peculiar privilege has this little agitation of the brain that we call *thought*, that we must thus make it the model of the whole universe? ... If thought, as we may well suppose, be confined merely to this narrow corner and has even there so limited a sphere of action, with what propriety can we assign it for the original cause of all things? The narrow views of a peasant who makes his domestic economy the rule for the government of Kingdoms is in comparison a pardonable sophism.[3]

Sir Bernard Lovell, giving his BBC Reith Lectures in 1958 on *The Individual and the Universe*, called his first lecture 'Astronomy Breaks Free'; and in it he spoke of the work of Copernicus and Galileo as seeming to upset the long-held unitary conception of the cosmos, thereby having the potential to undermine the existing ethical and moral basis of life. Lovell said:

> The coherence established under the guidance of Aquinas between the ecclesiastical doctrines and the basic idea of the fixed earth and finite universe, provided an organised scheme of great strength which formed the basis for physical and theological teaching in the Middle Ages. Attempts to undermine the central features of this scheme were bound to lead to bitter struggles...[4]

Sir James Jeans, who did not himself share this view, stated it well in his book, *The Mysterious Universe*.[5] But probably the most extreme and the most celebrated of all expressions of this point of view is that found in Bertrand Russell's early (1903) essay, 'A Free Man's Worship'.[6] Russell begins by presenting Goethe's Mephistopheles telling the history of the Creation to Dr Faustus in his study. Creation is God's sadistic jest, a drama conceived in order that he might 'be worshipped by beings whom He tortured'. At the end of the play, God smiled; and seeing that man was not perfect in renunciation and worship, decided to bring down the curtain; so 'he sent another sun through the sky, which crashed into Man's sun; and all returned again to nebula'. 'Yes', God murmured, 'it was a good play; I will have it performed again'.

This, Russell contends, is an imaginative picture remarkably close to what science has shown to be the true picture of the cosmic process and of man's place in it. I quote the Russell passage in full, since it is a classic piece of his early writing:

Such, in outline, but even more purposeless, more void of meaning, is the world which Science presents for our belief. Amid such a world, if anywhere, our ideals henceforward must find a home. That Man is the product of causes which had no prevision of the end they were achieving; that his origin, his growth, his hopes and fears, his loves and his beliefs, are but the outcome of accidental collocations of atoms; that no fire, no heroism, no intensity of thought and feeling, can preserve an individual life beyond the grave; that all the labours of the ages, all the devotion, all the inspiration, all the noonday brightness of human genius, are destined to extinction in the vast death of the solar system, and that the whole temple of man's achievement must inevitably be buried beneath the debris of a universe in ruins – all these things, if not quite beyond dispute, are yet so nearly certain, that no philosophy which rejects them can hope to stand. Only within the scaffolding of these truths, only on the firm foundation of unyielding despair, can the soul's habitation henceforth be safely built.

Brief and powerless is Man's life on earth; on him and all his race the slow, sure doom falls pitiless and dark. Blind to good and evil, reckless of destruction, omnipotent matter rolls on its relentless way; for Man, condemned today to lose his dearest, tomorrow himself to pass through the gate of darkness, it remains only to cherish, ere yet the blow falls, the lofty thoughts that ennoble his little day; disdaining the coward terrors of the slave of Fate, to worship at the shrine that his own hands have built; undismayed by the empire of chance, to preserve a mind free from the wanton tyranny that rules his outward life; proudly defiant of the irresistible forces that tolerate, for a moment, his knowledge and his condemnation, to sustain alone, a weary but unyielding Atlas, the world that his own ideals have fashioned despite the trampling march of unconscious power.[7]

Russell subsequently confessed that he did 'not now think well' of 'A Free Man's Worship'. When he wrote it, he says, 'I was steeped in Milton's prose, and his rolling periods reverberated through the caverns of my mind'.[8] But it is permissible to think that there is more at fault in the essay than the prose style. From such a expert on logic, the argument seems, to borrow a modern euphemism, 'logically challenged'. It may be wondered, for example, how despair, however reinforced with verbal unyieldingness, can provide a 'firm foundation', even for the habitation of something so unsubstantial as a materialist's 'soul', which surely is, like the Emperor Hadrian's, an *animula vagula, blandula, pallidula, frigida, nudula,* 'a fleeting little wisp, pale and wan and cold and naked'. It remains a mystery as great as any how, out of this half-creature, there can emerge a being superior to 'the resistless forces' of matter, because aspiring to and challenged by ideals which 'are not realised in the realm of matter'; indeed 'an ideal of perfection which life does not permit us to attain'. This 'outcome of accidental collocations of atoms', the human being, is yet mysteriously 'free from the petty planet on which our bodies impotently crawl'. 'We must learn, each one of us, that the world was not made for us', cultivating the while, as best we may, 'the pilgrim's heart', indeed meditating, in face of death and pain and the irrevocableness of the past, the 'sacredness ... (the) awe ... (the) feeling of vastness, the depth, the inexhaustible mystery of existence'.

Indeed, we are asked 'to burn with passion for eternal things'; which seems difficult if indeed, as Russell believes, all is 'destined to extinction in the vast death of the solar system' and to burial 'beneath the debris of a universe in ruins'. Chesterton once remarked that we could recognise the nineteenth-century materialist by the *religiousness* of his language about the irreligious cosmos. This seems true of Russell in this essay.

For good measure, I refer to one more statement of this theme, one in which Miltonic melodies and Russellian strains can both be detected: it is a purple page of the late Professor C.E.M. Joad. I hasten to add that Joad stated this doctrine only to criticise and reject it. Nevertheless, his statement of it is still worth quoting:

> Life then, if the materialists are right, is to be regarded, not as the fundamentally significant thing in the universe in terms of which we are to interpret the rest, but as an incidental product thrown up in the haphazard course of evolution, a fortuitous development of matter by means of which matter has become conscious of itself. It is an outside passenger travelling across a fundamentally hostile environment, a passenger, moreover, who will one day finish his journey with as little stir as once in the person of the amoeba he began it. In every direction the material and the brutal underlies and conditions the vital and the spiritual; matter everywhere determines mind, mind nowhere determines matter.

The prospects for humanity in this view are not encouraging, Joad points out. When the sun goes out, ' a catastrophe which is bound to be', mankind will have long since disappeared from the face of the earth. The last inhabitants of the earth will be as destitute, feeble and dull-witted as their prehistoric ancestors. Eventually the last survivor of mankind will

> exhale to an unfriendly sky the last human breath and the globe will go rolling on, bearing with it through the silent fields of space the ashes of humanity, the pictures of Michelangelo and the remnants of the Greek marbles frozen to its icy surface.[9]

Whatever may be thought about an ice age as earth's final future, this view, like that of Russell, is not one which favours or flatters mankind.

Historically False

The theory implied by these statements is coherent, and it offers some comfort to modern readers by stressing their 'progressiveness' as compared to previous generations;[10] but it is not in agreement with the facts. Essentially it rests on a flawed version of history, anachronistically interpreting the events and ideas of the sixteenth and early seventeenth century in the light of the psychology and ideology of people of the nineteenth and twentieth centuries.

The distinguished philosopher and historian of ideas, R. G. Collingwood, discussed the suggestion that copernican astronomy taught mankind for the first time that 'man is only a microscopic parasite on a small speck of cool matter revolving round one of the minor stars'. He dismissed this idea as 'both philosophically foolish and historically false'. He pronounced it philosophically foolish, because the relative importance of persons or things is not measured by 'the relative amount of space they occupy'. The idea is historically false, Collingwood continued, because 'the littleness of man in the world has always been a familiar theme of reflection'. Boethius, who lived in the late fifth and early sixth century had already stated this in his book, *De Consolatione Philosophiae*.

Collingwood quotes from this work, which, he reminds us, was perhaps 'the most widely read book of the Middle Ages'. Boethius wrote:

> Thou hast learnt from astronomical proofs that the whole earth compared with the universe is no greater than a point, that is, compared with the sphere of the heavens, it may be thought of as having no size at all. Then, of this tiny corner it is one-quarter that, according to Ptolemy, is habitable to living things. Take away from the

quarter the seas, marshes, and other desert places, and the space left
for man hardly even deserves the name of infinitesimal.[11]

Collingwood concluded:

> Every educated European for a thousand years before Copernicus
> knew that passage and Copernicus certainly did not risk
> condemnation for heresy by repeating its substance.[12]

C.S. Lewis points out that in the second century AD the astronomer,
Ptolemy, had written a work called *The Almagest*, which was 'the standard
astronomical handbook used all through the Middle Ages'. Ptolemy wrote:

> The earth, in relation to the distance of the fixed stars, has no
> appreciable size and must be treated as a mathematical point.[13]

Ptolemy's message about the infinitesimal smallness of planet earth in
relation to the vastness of the universe would, like the Boethius passage,
have been known, therefore, to every educated European for a thousand
years before Copernicus.

One might add that medieval philosophers were not completely
unfamiliar with the heliocentric hypothesis. This was recognised as a
conceivable – though hypothetical – alternative to the geocentric system. St
Thomas Aquinas, in the *Summa Theologica,* distinguishes between hypothesis
and proof in astronomy. He writes:

> There are two sorts of explanation possible in respect of any given
> subject-matter. First there is an explanation which adequately proves
> the truth of the initial hypothesis; an example would be the proof, in
> natural science, of the uniform velocity of the movement of the
> heavenly bodies. A second type of explanation is one which does not
> amount to a proof of the initial hypothesis, but, on the assumption
> that the hypothesis is true, shows that observed consequences agree
> with what would be expected to follow on this assumption. An
> example of this would be, in astronomy, the hypothesis of eccentric
> cycles and epicycles: this hypothesis is justified by the fact that, if we
> make this assumption, then the observed phenomena of motion of
> the heavenly bodies can be accounted for. But this does not amount to

a proof of the hypothesis; for it is possible that these phenomena could be accounted for equally well by other hypotheses.[14]

This distinction is later to figure prominently in the Galileo controversy. Cardinal Bellarmine, in his efforts to persuade Galileo to treat copernicanism as a hypothesis, is indebted to Aquinas for his conception of the role of hypothesis in science. It is interesting to note that the manner in which Bellarmine, following Aquinas, treats of scientific hypothesis has some parallels in the hypothetico-deductive method often used by modern science. (This is the method whereby a scientist offers a formula or a mathematical equation as a possible explanation of a given phenomenon, and then deduces from this the effects which would be expected if the hypothesis were correct, and finally sets up experiments to determine whether these effects are verified in reality.) Speaking of Bellarmine's reply to Galileo, James Brodrick suggested that, as a piece of scriptural exegesis, Galileo's views were much superior to Bellarmine's, whereas, 'as an essay in scientific method', Bellarmine's views are 'far sounder and more modern than Galileo's'.[15] The resemblances, however, are superficial. Bellarmine, like Aquinas, had no conception of the experimental method characteristic of modern science. Brodrick's interpretation of Bellarmine is in this respect mistaken.

On the other hand, Sir Bernard Lovell was in error when he made his Aquinas ground his 'ecclesiastical doctrines' on 'the basic idea … [of a] finite universe'. Aquinas indeed argues that a body cannot be of infinite magnitude; but he admits that his arguments are not conclusive or necessitating.[16] Clearly, his difficulties about spatial infinity are contingent, not conceptual, much less theological. But on the question of temporal infinity, he is explicit: there is no conceptual and no theological impossibility for him in the hypothesis of a temporally infinite duration of the cosmos.[17] Time, Aquinas teaches, is a measure of events in a world which is contingent and therefore necessarily a world of change. Time is continuous with the duration of the world; it is 'co-created' with the world. When there is a world, and for so long as there is a world, there is time. Apart from the world, there is no time: the world 'begins' therefore *with* time, but not *in* time. The 'beginning' of the world, so far as human reason and philosophy are concerned, is an aspect of its existence as dependent totally on God, rather than a determinable date in its duration. Aquinas formally and repeatedly refuses to base the truth of creation or the proof for the existence of God, on the assumption of a temporal origin of the cosmic process. 'The world exists', he declares, 'for as long as God wills it to exist, for the being of the world depends on God's will as its cause.'[18] Hence, whether the duration of the world be infinite or finite, can be known, not from the nature of the cosmos, but only from the Revelation of God.[19]

When Aquinas, in his 'five ways for proving God's existence', repeats that 'one cannot regress to infinity' (*non est procedere in infinitum*), this has nothing to do with a 'walled-in universe'.[20] It has nothing to do with a five-thousand-year time-scale since 'the morning of creation'. Aquinas explicitly shows that he means, not that it is physically impossible to proceed backwards in an infinity of astronomical time, but that it is metaphysically useless to do so, so far as accounting for the existence of the cosmos is concerned.[21] The point for Aquinas is that the cosmos, in all its being, depends totally on God. Its creation, philosophically speaking, is its absolute ontological dependence, not its chronological beginning.

In the next chapter I deal more extensively with the 'Galileo case', which demands special attention because of its role in shaping modern attitudes to the relationship of science and faith. Here, I simply remark that only a very slight acquaintance with medieval literature or art is needed to convince us that medieval man, with his spatially finite, geocentric cosmos and his Infinite God, felt far more humble, more little, more insignificant, more dependent, than does modern secular man, with his infinite universe and no God. If the medieval cosmos is walled-in, it is not by its defective cosmology and astronomy, but by its awe before the mystery of the universe and the mystery of God, before divine majesty, before the certainty of eternal judgement. Medieval religious art illustrates this vividly: as, for example, in Fra Angelico's Last Judgement scene. It could plausibly be claimed in a 1965 broadcast on 'Dante's relevance today' that, though 'Dante is seven hundred years old this summer, yet he is still the most topical poet for a cosmonaut floating in space to read.'[22] The medieval sense of mystery can still retain all of its power for a contemporary scientist.

The Centrality of the Human
The idea that the human being's importance or significance in the cosmos is a function of relative size or of spatio-temporal location, is, as Collingwood declared, philosophically foolish. Bertrand Russell once criticised traditional philosophy for beginning with the problem of how we know. This, he held, is a mistake:

It tends to give to knowing a cosmic importance which it by no means deserves, and thus prepares the philosophical student for the belief that mind has some kind of supremacy over the non-mental universe ... I accept without qualification the view that results from astronomy and geology, from which it would appear that there is no evidence of anything mental except in a tiny fragment of space-time, and that the great processes of nebular and stellar evolution proceed according to laws in which mind plays no part.[23]

But surely the sciences of astronomy and geology which reveal these 'great processes' are themselves discoveries of the human mind and show its supremacy over the non-mental universe. The existence of these sciences is possible only because the processes of the non-mental universe are intelligible to human minds, and therefore have some relationship with human thinking. One cannot discredit the human intellect in the name of science, which is itself one of the greatest products of the human intellect.[24]

Science is the thinking of humans on the earth, it is what Hume's Philo called 'the little agitation of the brain that we call thought'. But science is the measurer of the entire cosmos throughout all its 'mind-less' space and 'human-free' time. The possibility of science proves that mind and nature have between them some kind of 'pre-established harmony'; for science is the discovery by the human mind of a pre-existing pattern in nature, which is responsive to the postulates of thought, warp to the weft of the workings of mind; and yet is not mind-made. The human body is ludicrously puny in comparison with the cosmos; but in mind a human being spans the cosmos, reaching out to its farthest horizons of space and back to its uttermost aeons of time. The human mind arrived in the cosmos very late in evolutionary terms; but the cosmos has forever been mysteriously shaped for understanding by the human mind. The cosmos had, one may say, been long 'waiting' for man's arrival with 'mind-friendly' features, which only the human mind when it eventually came could recognise.

In another sense too the cosmos can be said to have been 'waiting' for the arrival of the human species long before *homo sapiens* came into being. The environmental elements and combinations of elements which are consistent with the appearance of human life in the cosmos and capable of sustaining it are extremely complex. Aeons of astronomical and geological time were required to bring them into being. We are now only beginning to understand how fragile and vulnerable this combination of elements is. How and why did this come about? How and why did conditions come to be which were suited to the appearance of the precise kind of creature which is the human being? It is as though the universe, in this sense, was 'waiting' for the arrival of mankind. What I have called the human-friendly nature of the universe has been termed the 'Anthropic Principle'. It is completely at variance with the Russellian picture of the universe as alien and indeed hostile to human life. It is in agreement with the theistic concept of the universe as having been created by an infinitely wise and good Creator and so arranged as to be able to contain a planet suitable to the existence of the human being and capable of being understood by the human mind. As the scientist and theologian John Polkinghorne puts it, this theistic concept of the universe offers, at the very least, an 'insightful account of what is going on'.[25]

Many modern cosmologists, such as Gold and Bondi, adhered to the hypothesis of the endless duration of the cosmos; an hypothesis according to which 'continuous creation' of matter is balancing cosmic expansion in such a way as to keep the universe in a constant 'steady state'. Thus, at any given point of endless time or boundless space the broad-scale features of the universe remain the same for any observer. Bondi and Gold subscribed to the 'Perfect Cosmological Principle', formulated by Bondi in these words:

> The large-scale aspect of the universe is always the same, irrespective of position and time … If the universe looks the same from all places at all times, then our physics is universally valid. Location in space and time is irrelevant.[26]

Many of these cosmologists and astronomers would perhaps accept as indisputably true the Russellian story which I have been calling a myth. But they should surely see that their Perfect Cosmological Principle assumed that the cosmos has for ever been attuned to man's mind and man's mind to the cosmos in a manner to which 'location in space and time is irrelevant'. The 'Steady State' theory seems to have been excluded by contrary evidence of an evolving universe. However, one may ask whether science is not committed to a different kind of 'perfect cosmological principle', one which assumes the accessibility of all matter throughout all space and all time to man's scientific intellect and indeed to man's mathematics. We shall see in the next chapter how one of the founders of modern science, Galileo, declared that 'this grand book, the universe, … cannot be understood unless one first learns to comprehend the language and to read the alphabet in which it is composed'; and went on to say that it 'is written in the language of mathematics', its characters being 'triangles, circles and other geometric figures'.

Three centuries later, Fred Hoyle wrote:

> What Einstein's principle of 'relativity' states is that whatever your environment, the same mathematical equations will suffice to describe your observations.[27]

What is this but a postulate of what can be called scientific 'anthropocentricity'? In thought, in science, man *is* the centre of the cosmos. It has been fashionable to accuse metaphysics and religion of a naive and pre-scientific anthropocentricity and anthropomorphism.[28] But in truth there *is* an unavoidable dimension of a certain kind of 'anthropocentricity' and 'anthropomorphism' about all human thinking. To avoid ambiguity, one should perhaps speak of an 'anthropic' dimension, rather than an 'anthropocentric' one; for the latter term suggests 'anthropomorphic'. Human thinking is by definition 'anthropo-thinking', the thinking of *anthropos*. Scientific thinking is, in that sense, no less and no more man-based and man-shaped than metaphysical and religious and theological thinking. Copernican astronomy is, in this epistemological sense, no less 'geocentric' and 'anthropocentric' than aristotelian astronomy. Astronomy is knowledge on the part of anthropos-man on the earth. There is, *in this specific sense*, no non-anthropocentric science, no non-geocentric astronomy. All human thought and knowledge, including science, are by definition anthropic. And yet there is no 'ego-centric predicament'. Humans can think only human thoughts; but it is a well-known epistemological fallacy to conclude that they are therefore only thinking thoughts, not knowing things. F.H. Bradley scornfully wrote of the theory of the 'relativity of knowledge':

> 'I know what I know', 'I experience what I experience'. 'I want what I want', indeed, 'here be truths'; much the same as 'I am what I am'; but it is a poor neighbourhood where such truths can be considered as making the fortune of a philosopher.[29]

It is only through and for earth-bound anthropos-man that the scientific picture of the cosmos exists. It is only for human beings that the universe becomes a cosmos with a logos. Without man, without human beings, there is no cosmology – but only a chaos which does not even have a name. The implication of science is in this sense one with the message of Genesis:

> And the Lord God, having formed out of the ground all the beasts of the earth, and all the fowls of the air, brought them to Adam to see what he would call them: for whatsoever Adam called any living creature, the same is its name. (Genesis 2: 18-20)

And this in turn is the same truth which Heidegger and Sartre utter when they say that man is the being through whom meaning comes into the world. Indeed the universe's infinities of quantity are themselves revealed as infinitesimals of worth in comparison with the mind that knows them. None better than Pascal felt the awful immensities of astronomical space, yet took its spiritual measure.

> When I consider the short duration of my life, swallowed up in the eternity before and after, the little space which I fill, and even can see, engulfed in the infinite immensity of spaces of which I am ignorant, and which know me not, I am frightened, and am astonished at being here rather than there; for there is no reason why here rather than there, why now rather than then. Who has put me here? By whose order and direction have this place and time been allotted to me? *Memoria hospitis unius diei praetereuntis* ..... The eternal silence of these infinite spaces frightens me.....[30]

But Pascal goes on:

> Thought constitutes the greatness of man ... Man is but a reed, the most feeble thing in nature; but he is a thinking reed. The entire universe need not arm itself to crush him. A vapour, a drop of water suffices to kill him. But, if the universe were to crush him, man would still be more noble than that which killed him, because he knows that he dies and the advantage which the universe has over him; the universe knows nothing of this.
>
> All our dignity consists, then, in thought. By it we must elevate ourselves, and not by space and time which we cannot fill. Let us endeavour, then, to think well; this is the principle of morality .....
>
> *A thinking reed.* It is not from space that I must seek my dignity, but from the government of my thought. I shall have no more if I possess

worlds. By space the universe encompasses and swallows me up like an atom; by thought I comprehend the world.[31]

That 'I comprehend the world' is itself a metaphysics encapsulated in a word: to 'comprehend' is to understand and explain, and, therefore, also to exceed, to transcend, the comprehended. Also, it remains as true in the age of science as it was for Ecclesiastes:

> All things are hard: man cannot explain them by word. The eye is not filled with seeing, neither is the ear filled by hearing. (Ecclesiastes 1:8)

Opus scientificum semper imperfectum; the work of science is perpetually incomplete. Science can never exhaust or fully satisfy man's need to know. Man aspires insatiably beyond the limits of all possible science, beyond the infinities of boundlessness to the Infinite of Perfection, beyond inference and hypothesis to Vision. Science reveals the truth of Browning's lines:

> And thus I know this earth is not my sphere,
> For I cannot so narrow me but that
> I still exceed it.

'When I Behold the Heavens'

It seems sometimes to be assumed that it was science which first revealed to human beings the immensity of space and time. This is not so. I have already referred to Boethius and to Ptolemy's *Almagest*. Furthermore the sense of distance and of antiquity is as much a matter of existential impact as of mathematical computation. Medieval humans, for whom travel shared one word with travail, had perhaps a greater sense of distance and of human lostness in it, than have we who live in the age of supersonic speed and space travel and light-years and the telecommunications revolution. The sense of time is psychological as much as chronometric. Medieval man, whose historical time was less packed with known data, whose lived time was less filled with change, than ours, may have had as strong a sense of the remoteness of the 'In the Beginning' of the Book of Genesis as we with our geological and astronomical timescales.

This is particularly true of the sense of awe aroused by the immensity of the heavens. The two sources of the sense of awe for Kant were the 'contemplation of the starry heavens above and of the moral law within'. But to have the sense of awe beneath the heavens it is necessary to look up; and ancient man and medieval man did this as much as, or more than, modern man does. There can be as great a sense of cosmic immensity to be derived from long gazing at a star-filled sky as from looking through a telescope or watching spacecraft launchings on a television screen. It is only such looking that will translate the unimaginable milliards of astronomical calculations into felt immensities. And this was done perhaps more often in the past by religious men and women than in the present by non-religious scientific men and women. Yet even so, the solar eclipse of August 1999 and the landing on the surface of Mars of the probe Rover in January 2004 evoked in many people a sense of awe which can truly be described as in some sense religious.

Nearly three thousand years ago a Hebrew went out into the night to gaze at the heavens, and was suddenly overwhelmed by the sense of his own insignificance beneath the stars and cried out:

> When I behold the Heavens, the work of your hands,
> the moon and the stars which you arranged, –
> What is man...? (Psalm 8)

Modern astronomers have scarcely conveyed the sense of planetary and human insignificance better than Isaiah:

> Have you not understood how the earth was founded:
> He lives above the circle of the earth,
> its inhabitants look like grasshoppers
> He has stretched out the heavens like a cloth
> spread them like a tent for people to live in ...
> Scarcely are they planted, scarcely sown,
> scarcely has their stem taken root in the earth
> than He blows on them. Then they wither
> and the storm carries them off like straw.
> (Isaiah 40: 21-4)

This is from the section of Isaiah known as the 'Book of the Consolation of Israel'. The consolation consists in Israel's knowing by faith that this Almighty God loves His tiny creature, man, with an unconditional love and that His almighty power is manifested above all in His pity and His mercy.

Is it not, incidentally, ironical that the same writers who condemn religion for making men proud and possessive towards the cosmos, as filling them with emotional reassurance and security, are found in nearby pages castigating religion for making men humble and self-distrustful, for filling them with fear and guilt and shame?[32] Little wonder that Chesterton concluded:

> What again could this astonishing thing be like which people are so anxious to contradict, that in doing so they did not mind contradicting themselves? … Such hostile horrors might be combined in one thing, but that thing must be very strange and solitary.[33]

The whole story about religion having a vested interest in a reassuring and consoling cosmos is, of course, contradicted by the alternative story coming from the same sources suggesting that religion results from pre-scientific fear of cosmic unknowns. What science understands and controls, we are told, man ceases to hold in religious awe and fear; therefore, as science advances, and man's knowledge and power increase, religion withers! The truth is that some of modern humans' greatest fears actually are fears of what science, uncontrolled by ethics, is capable of doing.

Theology as a Preparation for Science

In spite of the unfortunate historical conflicts between science and Christianity, a number of scholars have concluded that Christian Revelation and Christian theology in fact provided indispensable intellectual foundations for modern science.

Some have argued that it is an historical puzzle why science arose in Western Europe and not in other cultures, such as the Chinese or the Indian, which were just as philosophically sophisticated and as intellectually developed as the European. Several scholars, among them historians of science, have argued that the explanation lies in that which specifically differentiated European culture from other cultures, namely its Christian faith.

The late Professor Trevor-Roper is one of those historians who raised the question. In a series of broadcast lectures on 'The Rise of Christian Europe' in November 1963, he said:

> The Byzantines invented clockwork of a kind – and how did they use it? To levitate the emperor in order to dazzle the ambassadors of barbarian Europe. The Tibetans discovered turbine movement; but they were satisfied to exploit it for the rotation of prayer-wheels. Something existed, or something happened, in those mature societies to render their own achievements, from that point onwards, barren. The ideas were there, but the social structure was too soft to sustain

them, or too rigid to pursue them in the cause of further discovery.

Anyway why should it be Western Europe? Is it not, when we examine the question, rather extraordinary?[34]

Trevor-Roper did not answer the question. But an answer has been given by thinkers as diverse in background, temperament, and outlook as M.B. Foster, R.G. Collingwood and A.N. Whitehead. Their answer is in terms of Christian theology.

A.N. Whitehead, began his *Science and the Modern World*,[35] with a chapter on 'The Origins of Modern Science'. In the course of it he wrote (and I apologise for the length of the quotations, but feel that it is better to express Whitehead's thesis as far as possible in his own words):

> There have been great civilisations in which the peculiar balance of mind required for science has only fitfully appeared and has produced the feeblest of results. For example, the more we know of Chinese art, of Chinese literature, and of the Chinese philosophy of life, the more we admire the heights to which that civilisation attained …. There is no reason to believe that China if left to herself would have ever produced any progress in science. The same may be said of India. Furthermore, if the Persians had enslaved the Greeks, there is no definite ground for belief that science would have flourished in Europe. The Romans showed no particular originality in that line. Even as it was, the Greeks, though they founded the movement, did not sustain it with the concentrated interest which modern Europe has shown.

He pointed to a number of ways in which medieval Christian thought predisposed people to think scientifically. He says that the Middle Ages formed 'one long training of the intellect of Western Europe in the sense of order'. It was pre-eminently an epoch of orderly thought, rationalist through and through. Whitehead maintains that it was the 'long dominance of scholastic logic and scholastic divinity' which implanted in the European mind the 'habit of definite exact thought'. More importantly still, medievalism contributed to the scientific movement 'the inexpungable belief that every detailed occurrence can be correlated with its antecedents in a perfectly definite manner exemplifying general principles'. This tone of thought is, Whitehead holds, peculiar to European civilisation as compared to other cultures. It can be explained, he says, only:

from the medieval insistence on the rationality of God, conceived as with a personal energy of Jehovah and with the rationality of a Greek philosopher.

This 'instinctive tone of thought' was the result of 'the impress on the European mind arising from the unquestioned faith of centuries'.

Whitehead contrasts this with the religions traditions of Asia. In these, the divine being tended to be seen as impersonal, as acting arbitrarily; any occurrence might be due 'to the fiat of an irrational despot' or might come from some 'impersonal, inscrutable, origin of things'. Hence, he concludes that:

> the faith in the possibility of science, generated antecedently to the development of modern scientific theory, is an unconscious derivative from medieval theology.

Whitehead refers also to the influence of the canon law of the Church and the civil law of the medieval State. These, codified by Justinian's lawyers, established in the Western mind the principle of a rational ordering of society and a 'rationally adjusted system of organisation'.

Finally, Whitehead argues that Christianity contributed to Europe 'a sense of the importance of practical application of knowledge'. He points to the influence of two outstanding men, St Benedict and St Gregory. Both of these were 'practical men, with an eye for the importance of ordinary things'. St Benedict's monasteries were 'homes of practical agriculturists as well as of saints and artists and men of learning'. They thereby helped to form the mentality which allied science with technology, whereby learning 'is kept in contact with irreducible and stubborn facts'. The rise of Naturalism in the later Middle Ages was a further contribution to the rise of modern science, emphasising as it did the 'interest in natural things and natural occurrences for their own sakes'.[36]

All of this is in refreshing contrast to the dismissive attitude towards the medieval period which has been dominant in the Western world since the Enlightenment. The Middle Ages have long been regarded as equivalently 'the dark ages', and the very term 'medieval' has been used as a term of disparagement. Chesterton and Belloc and Christopher Dawson were among the Catholic writers and historians who tried hard in the last century to change this attitude, though without great success. Such an attitude to the medieval period, let it be said in passing, is presently being revised by theologians and philosophers of the 'Radical Orthodoxy' movement, associated mainly with Cambridge University.

The importance of the Christian faith and of medieval theology in the genesis of modern science is emphasised also by R. G. Collingwood.

Collingwood gave an idiosyncratic twist to the same thesis in a chapter of his *Essay on Metaphysics*. Curiously entitled *Quicumque Vult*, from the opening words of the Athanasian Creed, the chapter argues that the articles of this Creed really represent the 'absolute presuppositions' of modern science. He summarises these presuppositions thus:

I   That *there is one God*; in other words, that there is one world of nature with one system of laws running all through it, and one natural science which investigates it.

II   That *God created the world*.

III   That *there are many modes of God's activity*, in other words, that the oneness of nature does not preclude, it logically implies the distinction of many realms within nature ..... This solves the 'problem of the one and the many'. The solution in terms of religion ..... can only be found in a monotheism which regards the one activity of the one God as a self-differentiating activity.

IV   *That the creative activity of God is the source of motion in the world of nature*.[37]

Collingwood's enterprise in interpreting the Blessed Trinity and the Incarnation in terms of philosophy of science, is surely a solecism which we must disregard; but this does not disqualify his main argument. His conclusion is interesting in our present context:

> The presuppositions that go to make up this 'Catholic Faith', preserved for many centuries by the religious institutions of Christendom, have as a matter of historical fact been the main or fundamental presuppositions of natural science ever since.[38]

One can certainly query the use of the term 'presuppositions'. Science takes as given the existence of the world and its intelligibility and rationality. It is neither necessary nor even possible for science as such to examine or to validate these 'givens'. Science can legitimately take them for granted and proceed with its own explanations of the universe, using its own methods.

The successes of science serve indeed as further validation of the 'givens'. It remains true, however, that Christian belief in God as Supreme Reason and as Creator of an ordered and rational universe, helped to shape a culture congenial to the formation and development of modern science. This is the core of truth in Collingwood's thesis.

Finally we come to M.B. Foster, an Anglican, who died young, to the grave loss of philosophy in Britain.[39] He wrote an article in 1934 on 'The Christian Doctrine of Creation and the Rise of Modern Natural Science'.[40] He saw modern natural science as specified precisely by its 'un-Greek elements', and these in turn as deriving from the Christian Revelation and, in particular, from the Christian doctrine of creation. It is the doctrine of creation *ex nihilo*, and of God's freedom in creating – notions utterly foreign to Greek thought – which provided modern science with the conviction of the contingency of the world of nature, and therefore with the imperative to investigate nature empirically, not deductively.

> Modern natural science could begin only when the modern presuppositions about nature displaced the Greek ...; but this displacement itself was possible only when the Christian conception of God had displaced the Pagan as the object ... of systematic understanding. To achieve this primary displacement was the work of medieval theology, which thus laid the foundations both of much else in the modern world which is specifically modern, and of modern natural science.[41]

Foster was certainly and seriously at fault in downplaying the importance of Greek thought in the genesis of modern science. But this need not invalidate his argument about the importance of Christian thought and indeed medieval theology in that genesis.

It was repeatedly being argued, in the aftermath of logical positivism, that religious statements, not being empirically verifiable, cannot be known to be true and cannot be statements about the world. But if religious statements about the world are a preparation for man's belief in the very attainability of truth by empirical verification, this argument can scarcely be sustained. If religion is, historically, psychologically and logically, a formative part of the culture in which science in fact developed, one surely needs to re-examine the tendency to dismiss religion as anti-scientific.

Science and Mystery

I have claimed that there are propositions whose truth science takes for granted, and must take for granted, if its own enterprise is to be even begun, if its methods are to work and its operations to succeed. These propositions lie beyond the scope of investigation by science, but, unless their truth be assumed, science could not proceed.

Science must take for granted the existence of the world, the rationality of the world, the uniformity of nature. But human reason must ask the fundamental questions: Why is there a world at all? Why have humans come into existence at all? Why should humans, having come into existence on this planet, find the planet and the world intelligible in terms of their concepts, amenable to explanation by their logic, their reasoning, their mathematics? Let us recall Einstein's saying: 'the most incomprehensible thing is that nature is comprehensible'. The above questions are certainly meta-scientific; they are surely not unscientific or anti-scientific. They are beyond the scope of scientific reasoning; but they are not thereby irrational. We must revisit the tendency to grant science a monopoly on the terms 'reason' and 'rational'. We must, in the name of reason, defend the rationality of metaphysics.[42]

Richard Dawkins dismisses rather summarily such 'why questions' and the sense of mystery which they evoke and the use of such questions as pointers to the existence of God. He suggests that 'that which we don't understand' is sometimes regarded as a name for 'God'; (the quotation marks are his); whereas, Dawkins says, the words may simply mean 'that which we don't *yet* understand'. What I am saying, however, is that certain assumptions have to be made, certain realities taken for granted or taken as 'given', before science begins and before understanding is possible. One must take as given, for example, that the world exists, when it might well not have existed; and one must ask 'Why?' One must take as given that this world is ordered and intelligible, when it might instead have been 'unorderly', chaotic, arbitrary and absurd; and we must ask 'Why?' One must take as given that the human mind can attain to objective truth, when instead all truth claims might be subjective perception or illusion; and one must ask 'Why?'

These questions are not questions that science can hope one day to answer or things that science can hope eventually to explain. They are of their nature questions that lie beyond scientific understanding and explanation; for these questions are, if I may use the term, 'begged' in the very doing of science. But human beings cannot evade the task of confronting these questions. They have been confronted by the great philosophers of all the ages of human history. For there has to be a different way of understanding and explaining than the way of science; this way, the way of philosophy, the way of metaphysics, has its own norms of argument and proof and its own criteria of validity, different from those of science. Yet this way of knowledge is rational, resting on rational arguments and appealing to rational evidence and leading to rational conviction. Theistic philosophers are led by argument and by evidence to the conclusion that only the postulate of an All-wise and All-good and Almighty God as Creator of the universe can give a reasoned explanation of all the facts and a rationally satisfying answer to the sorts of question I have listed.

If belief in a rational Creator-God makes possible the rational understanding by humans of the created universe, such belief can scarcely be itself irrational. It is beyond scientific reason, but is surely not contrary to reason. If Christian belief in a rational God can, as we have argued, be shown to have historically prepared the way for modern science, that belief can hardly be itself contrary to scientific truth.

Medieval philosophers spoke of God as creating the world according to 'number, weight and measure'. They claimed biblical authority for this, though they were almost certainly using a certain freedom in so interpreting their biblical text. They were, however, thus unconsciously providing a bridge between medieval philosophy of nature and modern science. The Austrian National Library in Vienna has a thirteenth-century manuscript of the Old Testament with a drawing which represents the Creator at the moment of creation as measuring the universe with callipers, as scientists were later to do with their compasses. It is a fitting counterpart to the later drawing of Galileo studying the heavens with a telescope, which is reproduced in a recent newspaper article featuring extracts from Dawkins' writings.[43]

A more reasonable Dawkins makes an appearance briefly in the last chapter of his book, *A Devil's Chaplain*, when he urges a little girl to look for evidence for whatever she believes:

> Next time somebody tells you that something is true, why not say to them: 'What kind of evidence is there for that?'[44]

This is a perfectly reasonable demand; but scientific evidence is not the only kind of evidence there is. The religious, and specifically the Christian, believer appeals, as I have said above, to evidence of a rational, philosophical kind for the existence of God as Creator of the universe and as Ultimate Author of moral law and Supreme Good and Final End of all human striving. Philosophers, many of them outside the Christian tradition, have advanced proofs for the existence of an infinite Creator from the finite or contingent and time-conditioned nature of the world; proofs of a supremely intelligent Creator from the signs of order and the patterns of uniformity and 'laws of nature' in the world; proofs of a supremely good Creator from the aspirations after moral perfection of human beings and the hunger for ideal and unending happiness in human hearts. These and similar arguments are based on reason and logic; they are rational; they are even 'scientific', unless we are to identify 'rational' with the experimental and empirical sciences; but to do this would be to make a decision about lexicography, not to prove one's case.

Christians furthermore appeal to evidence from many domains – historical, textual, linguistic, hermeneutic and palaeographical – for the authenticity and reliability of the founding texts of Christianity. A separate book would be needed to examine the wide-ranging evidence for the historical veracity of the gospels, the historicity of the figure of Jesus Christ and of His claim to divinity, the continuity of the Christian Church and its teaching with the historical Jesus. There is not space to develop these matters here.

It may be claimed for science, as I have hinted above, that its successes are sufficient to prove its truth. I am far from questioning the successes of science. They have been spectacular. They have contributed hugely to human knowledge and life and health and well-being and happiness. But so too has faith; and faith, though it comes from God's grace, also has its reasons. It is not a question of either/or, but of both/and. Science tells us how the world works; it cannot tell us why the world is. Reason itself is not satisfied until both questions are answered. Science does not exclude faith; faith does not dispense with science. Both are needed for a full view of reality, within ourselves, around ourselves and beyond ourselves. We need dialogue between the two, not diatribe. I return to this point later on in this chapter and elsewhere in this book.

Dawkins does not help his case by his gratuitous insults of those who believe in miracles like the Virgin Birth and the Resurrection, dismissing them as part of a 'non-intellectual mass audience', susceptible to being 'swayed by religious propaganda' like any audience of 'unsophisticates and children'. Such jibes have no place in any rational debate and are not helpful to attempts at dialogue between science and religion – or even to attempts to discredit such dialogue.

Reason in Nature

Nature is comprehensible not only in general, but in the highly specific way in which science both finds it and renders it comprehensible, in terms namely of mathematical formulation and explication. The very existence of the term 'mathematical physics' incorporates a mystery, the meeting of mind with matter in physical nature. There is something dramatic in the scientist's power to predict the observable, deduce the physical, with the aid of mathematical formulae.

A classic instance of this was the discovery of the planet Neptune through mathematical calculations carried out independently and almost simultaneously by Adams in Cambridge and Leverrier in France in the year 1846, each of them working on extensive observations by Tycho Brahe, Kepler and others. After Uranus was discovered by Herschel, it was found that the 'new' planet did not travel exactly on the lines indicated by Newton's Law of Gravity. Assuming the invariability of the latter, and the general validity of Newtonian physics, the 'errant' behaviour of Uranus suggested the hypothesis that another planet, hitherto unobserved, existed which was gravitationally pulling Uranus off its Newtonian course. The story is described in a popular history of science:

> It was a mathematical problem the like of which had never been attempted. Here was Uranus being pulled out of its path by an absolutely invisible agent, and Adams had got to find the size and whereabouts of the latter just with a pencil and paper. Well, he did it. Then he wrote to the Astronomer Royal and told him that if he pointed his telescope at such and such a point in the sky, at such and such a time, he would see the new planet which was upsetting Uranus.....
>
> In the meantime, a young French astronomer, Leverrier, was at work on the same problem, and he also solved it successfully. Eight months after receiving Adams' letter, the same Astronomer Royal of England received a letter from Leverrier, giving a position for the new planet within 1° of that given by Adams ... In the meantime, Leverrier had also communicated with the observatory in Berlin, where a first-rate map of the heavens had just been completed. The head of this observatory pointed his telescope in the direction advised by Leverrier, and with the aid of his map was at once able to pick out the new planet, which was not a mere point like the other stars, but appeared as a small disc .....

The new planet was called Neptune, and was found to take third place among the others in size.....[45]

But, as though to prove that there is an irreducible physics hyphenated with her mathematics, Nature 'played a trick' on the mathematicians when they tried to stage a repeat performance. Neptune in turn showed aberrations; but, though mathematics directed the Mount Wilson Observatory's telescopes towards yet another new star, Pluto, it was found that it was not Pluto after all that was disturbing Neptune.

Another theme for reflection on Nature's mysterious 'mindfulness' is the import of Einstein's equation '$E = mc^2$', (where 'e' stands for energy, 'm' for mass and 'c' for the speed of light), an equation which ushered in the 'Age of the Atom' and of the atomic bomb. What secrets have been unlocked in nature, what forces captured for man's good or evil purposes, what abysses opened in human history, by this apparently innocent, aseptic mathematical formula!

The Cambridge astronomer, Fred Hoyle, although no religious believer, used strangely religious language about this situation. In his 1950 broadcast lectures, *The Nature of the Universe*, he described the method of physical science in these terms:

> It consists of two steps. The first is to guess by some sort of inspiration a set of mathematical equations. The second step is to associate the symbols used in the equations with measurable physical quantities. Then the connections that are observed to occur between various physical quantities can be obtained theoretically as the solutions of the mathematical equations. This process has two important advantages. It not only makes it possible to condense an enormously complicated mass of experimental information into a few comparatively simple equations, but it also brings out new previously unsuspected relations between the physical quantities.[46]

In 1957, in *Man and Materialism*, Hoyle reflected upon the implications of this method. He talked about the remarkable successes achieved by science, giving, as examples, the ability to predict eclipses of the sun in advance by calculations based on Newton's theory of gravitation; or the prediction from Maxwell's theory of light of all the properties of radio, long before radio was discovered experimentally; the prediction from Einstein's theory that light passing near the sun would be deflected in its path; or the prediction from Dirac's theory of electron that a new type of particle would be discovered, namely the positron. Hoyle concluded:

> Now what is so striking about all these cases is the way in which it was found possible to describe a vast range of physical phenomena in terms of a quite small number of mathematical equations. Not only this, but in each of the cases just mentioned, first a group of physical phenomena was discovered experimentally, second it was found that the observations could be completely represented by mathematical equations, third the mathematical equations turned out to have wider implications than the original observations on which they were based, and fourth, these wider implications were used with complete success to predict new phenomena not known to exist up to then, and indeed not even suspected to exist. It is no exaggeration to describe this correspondence between observations and mathematics as completely astounding. The element of mystery in it never wears off, no matter how familiar we may become with the details. We cease to wonder at an ordinary conjuring trick once we know how it is done. In contrast, the more we know of how the scientific conjuring trick is done, the more we continue to be amazed by it.....[47]

Professor William Reville, associate professor of biochemistry and director of microscopy at NUI, Cork, gives a good description, not unlike Hoyle's, of the methodology of science. Scientists tend to build a model of the phenomenon they are studying, then use mathematical equations to describe the behaviour of the model. They then test the model to see to what extent its behaviour corresponds to observable conditions in the real world. Thus they can increase their knowledge about the phenomenon in question with the help of the model and of their mathematics. An added, if surprising, feature is that the correct mathematical equations are invariably those that the mathematicians recognise as being, in their terms, the most beautiful. 'And so', Reville goes on, 'physicists consciously seek out beautiful equations when building their models'.

Reville concludes:

> The world is rational and transparent and seems everywhere to bear the fingerprint of Mind ... Perhaps the explanation of the harmony between the reason of our minds and the reason found in the

structure of the outside world is that they both have a common origin in the reason of the creator.[48]

In an age and a culture so enriched by science, in an age when time itself is so scarce, we must take 'time out' to reflect on the great mysteries which lie behind and beyond science. I list some of these again: How is science possible? How and why can the human mind and the non-human universe intersect so as to make science possible? Why is there a universe at all, and how does it have a pattern of order and rationality such as to make science possible? What kind of beings are we humans who can understand and to some extent control the workings of Nature? We diminish our stature as humans and we fail the nature given into our charge, and we do less than justice to science itself when we neglect to take time to wonder, to question, to reflect; and, the Christian will add, to praise and to pray. As Plato remarked, the unexamined life is not worth living.

The sense of awe before the mystery of nature is characteristic of the great scientist. Einstein wrote, in *The World As I See It*:

> The fairest thing we can experience is the mysterious. It is the fundamental emotion which stands at the cradle of true art and true science. He who knows it not and can no longer wonder, no longer feels amazement, is as good as dead, a snuffed-out candle. It was the experience of mystery – even if mixed with fear – that engendered religion. A knowledge of the existence of something we cannot penetrate, of the manifestations of the profoundest reason and the most radiant beauty, which are only accessible to our reason in their most elementary forms – it is this knowledge and this emotion that constitute the truly religious attitude; in this sense, and this alone, I am a deeply religious man.....[49]

Newton, shortly before he died, declared:

> I do not know what I may appear to the world, but to myself I seem to have been like a boy playing on the sea-shore and diverting himself in now and then finding a smoother pebble or a prettier shell than ordinary, whilst the great ocean of truth lay undiscovered before me.[50]

Surely one is justified in comparing these words with the famous words in which St Augustine recalls walking along the sea-shore, reflecting on the mystery of the Blessed Trinity, when he saw a child busily carrying water in a shell from the sea to a hole in the sand. When asked what he was doing, the child said he was trying to empty the sea. St Augustine applied the incident to his own reflections, and remarks that one might as well try to empty the ocean with a shell as to probe the mystery of the Blessed Trinity with the human intellect.

The sense of mystery in science is not unconnected with the sense of religious mystery. Gabriel Marcel distinguishes 'problem' from 'mystery' and strives valiantly to open the mind of modern man to the mystery that lies around and stretches infinitely beyond the bounds of man's problem-solving science and technology.

This sense of mystery, of questions raised by doing science, but not fully answerable by science, is associated also with Erwin Schrödinger, one of the fathers of quantum physics. Schrödinger, exiled from Austria because of Nazi occupation and anti-Jewish pogrom, was invited by Eamon de Valera to come to Ireland and join the new Dublin Institute of Advanced Studies. Schrödinger wrote:

> You may ask: What, then, is in your opinion the value of natural science? I answer: Its scope, aim and value is the same as that of any other branch of human knowledge. Nay, none of them alone, only the union of all of them, has any scope or value at all, and that is simply enough described: it is to obey the command of the Delphic deity, *Gnóthi seauton*, ('Know thyself') ... Or, to put it in the brief, impressive rhetoric of Plotinus: '*Tines de Hémeis*'; 'And we, who are we anyhow'? ... The isolated knowledge obtained by a group of specialists in a narrow field has in itself no value whatsoever, but only in its synthesis with all the rest of knowledge, and only inasmuch as it really contributes in this synthesis something towards answering the demand ... 'Who are we?'[51]

A painting, entitled 'Schrödinger in the Hand of God' was executed by John Lighton Synge, a nephew of John Millington Synge. Professor Jim Malone, medical physics professor at Trinity College, Dublin, wrote an article on this painting, in which he reflects on the dimensions of beauty, of inspiration and of 'the mystical' which are found in science. He points to 'the exceptional beauty of Schrödinger's formulation of wave mechanics'; and speaks of how the painting 'intrigues' him because of its 'numinous evocation of mystery and the mystical at a defining moment in science'.

Professor Malone refers to the parallels between 'scientific insight' and 'mystical experience and artistic creation'. He finds 'a sense of the 'other' and the numinous at the fringes of science'.[52] This recalls earlier references in this chapter to beauty in science and to the fact that science raises questions which underlie science itself and which science cannot answer. And beyond these lies the still more profound question: 'What or Who makes all this possible?'

The only satisfying answer is that found in the Book of Wisdom, where we read of the Divine Wisdom who was 'present when (God) made the world.' It is God who in His creative Wisdom made the world, who alone can 'give us true knowledge' (through science) of all that is and can 'teach us the structure of the world and the properties of the elements'; for Wisdom 'deploys her strength from one end of the earth to the other, ordering all things for good'. Hence the writer of the Book of Wisdom, writing in the name of King Solomon, says:

> I fell in love with her beauty ...
> when life is shared with her there is not pain;
> gladness only and joy.[53]

It is surely reasonable to conclude, as theists do, that science exists because God made nature and nature bears upon it the pattern of His mind. God made nature 'mind-full'; and this is why humans can find a mental-mathematical structure in it. God made the human mind also, in the image of His own, and made it thereby capable of understanding and explaining nature, and of being 're-minded' by nature of the God who made it. And therefore also science can be part of humans' 'minding' of nature and shaping of it more and more to the mind of its Maker and the purpose of its making.

Christianity and Democracy

There is little doubt but that modern science has close links with modern democracy. What has proved beneficial for democracy has been beneficial for science and vice versa. Science in general has been stunted and often distorted in dictatorial regimes, whether of the marxist-leninist left or the nazi-fascist right. The only sciences to flourish in these regimes were those linked to the military complex or to the genocidal extermination of the 'unfit', as in the Holocaust. Even in democratic regimes, however, there is a worrying tendency for both State and private-sector funding to be directed by preference towards military-orientated scientific development. Nevertheless, historically, the links between science and democracy have been mutually beneficial. It is not irrelevant to the theme of the present chapter, therefore, to refer briefly to the influence of Christian teaching on the genesis and development of democracy.

The influence of Greek civilisation on the idea and the politics of democracy has undeniably been immense. But the influence of Christianity has been less acknowledged. One of the thinkers who has studied this phenomenon in depth is the late A. D. Lindsay.[54] Lindsay argued that 'the Christian contributions to our (democratic) political heritage were far-reaching and important'. First among these he lists 'the doctrine of human equality'. This equality transcends all discriminations and divisions, of race or tribe, of ethnicity or continent or country, 'civilised' or 'barbarian', slave or serf; it is 'an equality which overshadows but does not deny their differences'.[55]

Another important Christian contribution to democracy is the teaching that 'the rights and authority of power can only come from its service to the community'. It is significant that the members of a democratic government are usually called 'ministers'; they are expected, as Christian ministers of religion are expected, to be servants of their people. Furthermore, the existence, alongside the State but independent of it, of another society, the Church, with an alternative understanding of authority and of power, introduced a completely new situation into the imperial world of Rome.

I add a note on the political significance of the fact that Rome called its Emperor, Caesar (from which are derived the words 'Kaiser' and 'Czar') or, in Greek, 'Kurios'. But the early Christians called Christ *Kurios*, thereby exalting his authority as, not just equal to, but superior to, the authority of the August Emperor. Thereby, Christians exalted the rights of conscience as superior to the authority of the temporal power. Christians were expected to 'obey God rather than man', even when the man was Caesar Augustus. This was inevitably seen by the Roman power as treason, deserving of death. The contemporary account of the martyrdom of St Cyprian, which took place in the year 258 AD, ends with these words:

> The most blessed martyr Cyprian suffered on the fourteenth day of September under the Emperors Valerian and Gallienus, but in the reign of our Lord Jesus Christ, to whom is honour and glory for ever and ever. Amen.[56]

Sadly, the Church itself began later to introduce terminologies and attitudes which aped rather than challenged the temporal power; but this does not negate the Christian principle of the freedom and supremacy of God's law and conscience vis-à-vis the State. Gradually, Lindsay points out, the Christian Church became a society which could stand up to and challenge the State.

Finally, Lindsay comes to what he calls 'the most important perhaps of all the contributions of Christianity to western political thought'. He states this as the:

> teaching of the perfection of the moral ideal and the consequent imperfection and inadequacy of any existing social standards.[57]

Plato and Aristotle had supposed that it was possible to draft a constitution which would produce the best possible State; and they urged legislators to take all possible steps to resist any change of that constitution. Christianity, on the other hand, by stressing the *ideal* of perfection and the *reality* of human imperfection and of sin, taught that therefore 'no historical moral standard can be final' (where the word 'historical' is the important word). This was in effect a call to continuous change, to meet new situations and new needs and to approximate ever more closely to the ideal, which always challenged the less good by the standards of the ideal better. The call on Christians for a 'spiritual revolution'[58] had for its consequence a readiness for ever-renewed social and moral progress.

In a small but challenging book on *The Moral Teaching of Jesus*, Lindsay speaks of the political implications of the distinctive prayer of Christians, the Lord's Prayer, or the 'Our Father'. 'Father' calls us to fellowship, equality, fraternity, respect for one another. 'Our' expects community, sharing, solidarity. 'Thy Kingdom come' and 'Thy Will be done', call for the creation of a society reflecting the values of God's kingdom of love and justice; and demand the placing of moral principle above State or party, and the placing of conscience above conformity and popularity.[59] Reflecting on the Sermon on the Mount, Lindsay stresses the importance for life in the society, and for law-abiding citizenship, of the call to gospel perfection. He writes:

> We are asked to be better than our own selfish desires, our ambitions, our own self-importance, our cowardice, our laziness; and we shall continuously, in spite of our best efforts, find this self of ours catching

us out. If ever we stop being dissatisfied, it can only be because we have become insensitive.[60]

The Sermon on the Mount, therefore, becomes 'a leaven and a ferment' in society. It becomes a force for continual political effort in the direction of a more just and more equal and more caring and more honest society.[61]

Lindsay sums up his consideration of the contribution of Christianity to democracy in a quotation which he makes his own. This asserts that authority 'has in itself some element that never is and never can be merely human'; that, therefore, the exercise of power is a source less of rights than of duties, and obedience is due less to men than to moral principle, and authority should be subservient 'to the divine order of justice which alone can legitimate political rule'. The quotation concludes:

> Such principles, which medieval thinkers were to develop from the original sources of Christian experience, have become outstanding landmarks of Christian political thought and must remain such, unless Christianity abdicates all hopes of constructive political action and takes refuge in a passive acceptance of the powers that be.[62]

The great Enlightenment movement of the eighteenth century is often held to have begun the overthrow of Christianity, and modern science is held to be the child of the Enlightenment. I hope that evidence has been produced in this chapter to show that things are much more complex than that and that science has roots much deeper than the Enlightenment. Indeed, many of the leading concepts of the Enlightenment – such as reason, liberty, equality, fraternity – are also key concepts of Christianity. There is a strange paradox in the fact that the Paris revolutionaries erected a statue of the goddess Reason above the High Altar in Notre Dame, an altar dedicated to the worship of Jesus Christ, whom Christians believe to be the Incarnate Reason (*Logos*) of God Himself, the Word through whom all things came to be (John 1:1). When the French Revolution – a true child of the Enlightenment – overthrew the monarchy, wrongly thought to be synonymous with Christianity, it thought it was overthrowing Christianity itself. Cardinal de Lubac wrote:

> Every time people abandon a system of thought, they imagine they are losing God.[63]

We could say the same about a people's change of an economic system or of a political regime or of a public culture.

The many-sided Christian contribution to modern democracy has also, as a consequence, been a contribution to the progress of modern science. At the same time, the dramatic progress being made today in all the sciences, and particularly in the domain of the 'creation' of human life, human fertilisation, experimentation on embryos, cloning, makes the need for moral and ethical principles for the guidance of scientists more imperative and urgent than ever.

In the context of the current debate about a Constitution for the European Union, and about the inclusion therein of a reference to God and to Europe's Christian tradition and to the moral values which Europe received from that tradition, a respected journalist has recently written that 'socialism and social democracy are secular forms of Christianity, whose insistence on justice, fairness and equality have palpable Christian roots'; while Christian Democrats' 'embrace of market capitalism is qualified by the Catholic commitment to a just wage, just price and just profits', and to the Catholic insistence 'that work should be a source of human dignity'.[64]

Underpinning all these Christian contributions to modern secular Europe is the Christian teaching on human dignity and human rights, the human right to life, and the sacredness of human life. If these principles are violated, then science becomes an agent of moral regression rather than of moral and human progress. It must never be forgotten that the pioneers of genetic experimentation and genetic engineering in the twentieth century were the Nazis. The mutual and mutually beneficial relationships between modern science and modern democracy are many; and Christianity made an important contribution to the development of both. Christianity itself, of course, has benefited greatly from both modern science and modern democracy, just as it has benefited from the Enlightenment, which was the forerunner of both.

Filled with the Glory of God

To conclude this chapter, I would like to suggest that Christianity is also a great inspirer of that love of nature's beauty which impassions alike the scientist, the artist, the poet, and indeed the mystic. The idea is prevalent in some quarters that Christianity is the enemy of the world of nature and of natural beauty, that it is world-hating, world-denying, and nature-scorning. Such a view of the world would surely be ruled out of

Christian belief by the very first pages of God's self-revelation in the
Book of Genesis. There we read of how, having completed the work of
creation,

> God saw all that He had made
> and indeed it was very good.

The fatherly – and motherly – love, and indeed 'contentment' with which
God looks upon creation seems to me to be beautifully caught in Seamus
Heaney's translation of Beowulf:

> The Almighty had made the earth
> a gleaming plain girdled with waters;
> in His splendour He set the sun and the moon
> to be earth's lamplight, lanterns for men
> and filled the broad lap of the world
> with branches and leaves, and quickened life
> in every other thing that moved.[65]

In this passage from Beowulf there are echoes of the Bible. A theme which
recurs frequently in the Bible is that of praise and thanksgiving to God for the
glory and beauty and order and stability of earth and the heavens. This is
particularly true of the Book of Psalms. Here the stability of earth, the
regularity of the seasons, the fruitfulness of the fields and the olive groves and
the vineyard, are seen as reflecting the love and goodness and generosity of
God. Archbishop Robinson chose as motto for the new observatory he founded
in Armagh the opening lines of Psalm 18:

> The heavens proclaim the glory of God
> and the firmament shows forth
> the work of his hands.

God's care of the earth, and God's fidelity to His promises, become
themes for songs of praise. Psalm 64 is one such song. In it, the psalmist
praises God, who 'crowns the year with His goodness', who 'cares for the
earth, gives it water, fills it with riches, blesses its growth'. Paul Claudel,
among his collections of translations of the psalms into French verse, gives
one collection a title taken from the Latin version of a phrase from Psalm
64, *Corona Anni Benignitatis*, 'The Crown of the Year of (God's) goodness'.

This psalm is full of the joys of spring, turned into a song of joyful praise of God:

> The hills are girded with joy …
> They shout for joy, yes, they sing.

The same note of joy is sounded in Psalm 95:

> Let the heavens rejoice and earth be glad
> let the sea and all within it thunder praise,
> let the land and all it bears rejoice,
> all the trees of the wood shout for joy.

Psalm 97 in the Grail version is given the title, 'Orchestra of Praise to God, King of the World'. Earth and sea and sky play their part in this cosmic orchestra:

> Let the sea and all within it thunder;
> the world and all its peoples.
> Let the rivers clap their hands
> and the hills ring out their joy
> at the presence of the Lord.

God's boundless care for creation is hymned in Psalm 103:

> Lord God, how great you are
> clothed in majesty and glory
> wrapped in light as in a robe.

The psalmist acknowledges that, were it not for God's constant breathing into the world and all the living things in it of the breath of his own Spirit, all this would vanish into dust and nothingness. Earth and sea, fish and fishermen alike, and all living creatures, look to God for food and for life:

> All of these look to you
> to give them their food in due season.
> You give it, they gather it up.
> You open your hand, they have their fill.
> You hide your face, they are dismayed,

you take up your spirit, they die,
returning to the dust from which they came.
You send forth your spirit, they are created,
and you renew the face of the earth.

This is the biblical expression of that continuous creation of the world, that total dependence of the world on God for its continuance in being, of which Aquinas speaks. It is also the source of Hopkins' image of the Holy Ghost as 'hovering over the bent world with warm breast', surely a beautiful expression of God's motherly caring and shielding and sheltering of the world.

The greatest of Israel's songs of praise is Psalm 135, the last of the group known as the Hallel Psalms, which were sung at the annual Passover Meal (psalms 112-7 and 135). This was known as the Great Hallel. The refrain running through the psalm is: 'Great is His love, love without end'. God's love is seen at work first in the creation of the world: God 'whose wisdom it was made the skies ... who fixed the earth firmly on the seas', for 'great is His love, love without end'.

It was He who made the great lights ...
the sun to rule in the day ...
the moon and the stars in the night...;

Each line, each act of creation, is followed by the refrain:

Great is His love, love without end.

The next manifestation of God's love is in His deliverance of His people, Israel, from slavery in Egypt at the Exodus and His protection of them throughout history. The psalm ends with a return to God's love in creation:

He gives food to all living things,
great is His love, love without end.
To the God of heaven give thanks,
great is His love, love without end.

This psalm has particular significance for Christians, for it would have been the last prayer of Jesus with his disciples after the Last Supper, before they left the Upper Room and crossed the brook Kedron, on the way to Gethsemane and the Agony and Passion.

The cosmic music of the Great Hallel reaches a new climax in the song of the three young men flung into the fiery furnace by Nebuchadnezzar. Undaunted by the flames, the three 'began to sing, glorifying and praising God'. They call on each part of creation in turn to 'give glory and eternal praise to God' so that His 'glorious and holy name may be praised and extolled for ever' (Daniel 3:51-90). It is as though the three see their vocation as being to give voice to creatures and to express in words the glory and praise which creatures can express only by existing and by being the kind of creatures God made them to be and fulfilling the function God gave them to perform. This is how a human being becomes 'nature's priest', bringing to God in words of prayer the praise that creatures would give if they could speak. This, of course, Christians do pre-eminently through the Eucharist, where they bring to God the bread and the wine which 'earth has given and human hands have made' by their work, to have these changed into Christ's own perfect sacrifice of praise.

In the chapter on 'The Christian and Work', I hope to show how the great biblical hymn of cosmic praise of the creator is raised to a new plane by faith in Christ as the image of the unseen God, the One in whom the world is created in the beginning and by whom it is redeemed and reconciled in a new creation, and, at the end of time, in whose transfigured glory it is itself transformed, thus achieving, as Aquinas puts it, 'a kind of resplendence in its own way', because touched by God's glory, the glory on the face of Christ.[66]

Aquinas, prince of Christian philosophers, turns poetical in reflection on the theme 'that the consideration of creatures is useful for the instruction of faith':

> If therefore the goodness, beauty and delightfulness of creatures are so alluring to the minds of men and women, the fountainhead of God's own goodness, compared with the rivulets of goodness found in creatures, will draw the enkindled hearts of all wholly to itself ..... Consideration (of creatures) endows men with a certain likeness to God's perfection ..... It is therefore evident that the consideration of creatures has its part to play in building the Christian faith.[67]

Elsewhere, however, he reminds us that if the consideration of creatures is important and satisfying, incomparably more important and more satisfying is the consideration of God in Himself, who is the Creator and Source of the 'goodness, beauty and delightfulness' of creatures. Simone Weil says that 'love of the order of the world' is an 'implicit form of the love of God'.[68] It must, however, be recognised that it can become a substitute for the love of God. There are many 'spiritualities' in favour nowadays, including 'Nature spirituality', 'Earth spirituality', and so on. These can serve as prelude to the love and worship of the Person who is God. Indeed, they point beyond themselves to God who created them and who made them reflections of His own goodness and beauty. Isolated from their Creator and Source, however, they cannot fulfil the human need for the True, the Good and the Beautiful. As St Augustine so memorably put it, they cannot satisfy the restlessness of the human heart.

I have quoted the scientist, William Reville, about the significance and beauty of the mathematical equations used in scientific explanation of the world. There is beauty also, at the microscopic level, in the 'double helix' pattern found in the constitution of the human cell, which has strange resemblances to the interweaving lines found in the Celtic artwork of the High Crosses and illuminated manuscripts of the Irish monks. Could all this be connected with the Beauty of the Creator, who 'clothed with beauty' the world which He created?

'Clothed with Beauty'

I take the phrase, 'clothed with beauty', from one of the greatest of Christian mystics, St John of the Cross. He, if anyone, should verify the modern stereotype of monk and mystic and should be the world-evading despiser of nature's beauty. But here is how he speaks of creatures in the *Spiritual Canticle*:

> O woods and thickets
> Planted by the hand of the Beloved.
> O meadow of verdure
> Enamelled with flowers,
> Say if he has passed you by
>
> *Answer of the Creatures*
> Scattering a thousand graces
> He passed through these groves in haste,
> And, looking upon them as he went,
> Left them by his glance alone
> Clothed with beauty

Bride
All those that serve
Relate to me a thousand graces of thee
And all wound me the more,
And something they are stammering
Leaves me dying [69]

In his commentary on these stanzas, St John of the Cross says:

> To pass through the groves is to create the elements ..... Through these, the Bride says, He passed, scattering a thousand graces, because He adorned them with all the creatures, which are full of grace ..... And she says that He passed, because the creatures are, as it were, a trace of the passing of God, whereby are revealed His greatness, power, wisdom, and other Divine virtues. [70]

One wonders if the beauty of creatures was ever more transcendently hymned than by hailing them 'full of grace', finding in them trace of the passing of their Creator, God.

The Spiritual Canticle is the poetry of the *Gloria* and the *Sanctus*, in the Mass in which theologian and philosopher, scientist, artist, and poet, all join to give glory and honour to the Almighty Father through Christ and with Christ and in Christ who is the Splendour of His Glory. Russell's Mephistopheles was wrong. The cosmic process is not an Ionesco play. Aquinas, by a fascinating coincidence, discusses the question whether the universe may not be compared to a theatrical play, since it is to be destroyed like the stage at the end of the performance. But he answers:

> The object of the play is the play itself. But in the process whereby God moves material creatures, the object in view is something other than the process itself: it is the completion of the number of the elect; and when that number is complete, the movement, though not the substance, of the world will cease ..... The whole process of mutation in mundane bodies is in a sense ordered towards the multiplying of souls..... [71]

And the multiplying of souls and the mustering of the elect are ordered in the end towards an eternal *Sanctus*, the everlasting singing of the praise of

the glory of nature's God, as we find this expressed in the Book of
Revelation (4: 8, 11):

> Holy, Holy, Holy,
> is the Lord God, the Almighty,
> He was, He is and He is to come ...
>
> You are our Lord and our God,
> you are worthy of glory and honour and power,
> because you made all the universe
> and it was only by your will
> that everything was made and exists.

Chapter II

THE GALILEO CASE

It is necessary to dwell at some length on the case of Galileo, because of its importance in shaping subsequent attitudes and because of the role which it played in seeming to pit science against religion throughout much of modern history. The conflict between Galileo and the Catholic Inquisition, leading to the condemnation and the silencing of Galileo in 1633, has long been presented as a paradigm case of the conflict between Church and science.

Galileo and His Times

Galileo Galilei was born in Pisa in 1564 in the same year and the same month of February as that in which Michelangelo died. He himself died in Arcetri in 1641. He did not marry, but had a long extra-marital liaison with Marina Gamba of Venice, with whom he had three children. The two daughters became nuns in the enclosed Poor Clare Monastery in Arcetri. Daughters born out of wedlock would have had poor marriage prospects, and this may have had a bearing on Galileo's decision to place them at an early age in the care of the nuns, whose community they later joined. The son, Vincenzio, was 'legitimised' by decree of the Grand Duke of Tuscany, Don Cosimo de Medici, once a private pupil and later the patron of Galileo. One of the girls, his elder and favourite daughter, Virginia, took the name in religion of Sister Maria Celeste. A collection of letters written by her to her father have survived and are now preserved in the Central National Library in Florence. A recent book, *Galileo's Daughter*,[1] based on these letters, gives a new insight into Galileo the man and the father. It reveals Galileo's tender love for and pride in his daughter, whom he calls 'a woman of exquisite mind, singular goodness and most tenderly attached to me'. The daughter responds with filial love, with admiration for his learning, his fame and his Christian and Catholic faith, and with concern for his health and his peace of mind. Something of an amateur apothecary, she prepared pills, ointments, powders and herbal potions for his various ailments. She is solicitous to shelter him and defend him from all criticism. She is concerned about his garden and fruit trees, his cellar and his grapes and wines, and with everything concerning his welfare. Her affection and her admiration for her revered father are very touching. Her letters reveal aspects of Galileo's life in which later history was not interested, as well as giving us valuable information about contemporary social history in Galileo's time.

Galileo was certainly a towering figure in the history of science. He was a brilliant mathematician, a pioneering astronomer, a physicist. He made important discoveries in the science of mechanics. He is author of the celebrated saying that, 'the Book of Nature is written in the language of mathematics'. He was a founder of the experimental method in science. He perfected the telescope, and with its aid he identified irregularities in the surface of the moon and observed Saturn and the satellites of Jupiter and the phases of Venus. Einstein called him 'the father of modern physics, indeed of modern science altogether'. He himself thanked God 'for being so kind as to make him alone the first observer of marvels hidden in obscurity for all previous centuries'. He was a master stylist, a gifted writer, and an important figure in the history of the Italian language.

Galileo was regarded in his own time as one of the outstanding figures of the Renaissance, to be ranked alongside Michelangelo Buonarrotti in that scintillating period. After his death, his fame continued to grow. He gradually became seen as a hero of science, a martyr for the cause of science. Although he was, and remained through all his life, a convinced Catholic, he became for the Enlightenment a martyr in the struggle against the 'obscurantism' of religion. Voltaire held him as a martyr of the Inquisition, and scornfully declared that 'if Newton had been in Portugal and any Dominican had discovered a heresy in his inverse ratio of the squares of the distances' he would have been immediately burned as a sacrifice acceptable to God at an 'auto-da-fé'! In Protestant circles, Galileo became a martyr of conscience of a different kind, a standard-bearer for private interpretation of Holy Scripture. John Milton, who paid him a visit in his home in Arcetri, set the fashion in this regard. In his prose work, *Areopagitica*, published in 1644, Milton has some derogatory words about the 'servile conditions' of learning and writing in Italy, contrasted with the freedom of thought in England, and reports that, while in that country, he had 'visited the famous Galileo, grown old, a prisoner of the Inquisition.'[2] For Marxists and for many secular humanists, Galileo became a kind of prometheus-figure, part of the 'promethean myth' of modern science. In this case, 'Galileo-Prometheus' was presented as bravely scaling the ramparts of the Inquisition to set science free from the dungeons of the Church Inquisition, and thereby freeing mankind from superstition.

Much of this, I hope to show, represents a 'mythologisation' of Galileo, and a degree of demythologisation is called for. It is, in this connection, interesting to note that Doctor F. Sherwood Taylor, once Curator of the Museum of the History of Science at Oxford, became a Catholic, partly as a result of his research into the case of Galileo, undertaken at the request of the Rationalist Press Association. He wrote:

> As I studied the documents and detailed histories, I became aware that the usually accepted Galileo legend was full of deliberate distortions of anti-Catholic and so-called Rationalist writers. The Catholic Church did not, it was true, play a very admirable part therein but it was quite clear that she had been wickedly traduced. I came to think that, if the assertions of her opposition to science were so ill-founded, so also might all those stories of her wickedness, deceit and superstition, which my Protestant and rationalist reading had put into my mind.[3]

Copernicanism

When Galileo began, as a mathematics professor in Padua, to question the aristotelian world system and to argue for the rival copernican system, he immediately aroused the ire of the 'scientific establishment' of the time, all of them aristotelians and passionate defenders of the geocentric system. They were also the 'philosophical establishment' of the time, science not yet having been demarcated as a discipline in its own right, distinct from philosophy; it was still called 'natural philosophy'. The majority of contemporary theologians in Galileo's time were formed in this aristotelian system. Interestingly Galileo wrote scornfully in 1612 about 'persons whose philosophy is badly upset by this new arrangement of the universe.'[4] It has been pointed out that the first use of the word 'science' as we now understand it was (so the OED informs us), in 1725 and the first use of the word 'scientist' in 1840.

The aristotelian system of the heavenly bodies had been significantly modified by Ptolemy, who was active about 130 AD. While still espousing the centrality and the immobility of the earth, Ptolemy brought the movements of the sun and the other heavenly bodies more into line with observations and with mathematical measurements by means of a theory of eccentric motions, epicycles and what he called the Principle of the Equant. This Ptolemaic system became universally accepted and remained, it has been said, 'for more than 1400 years, the Alpha and the Omega of theoretical astronomy.'

The great Polish astronomer, Copernik or Copernicus (1473-1543), in his *De Revolutionibus Orbium Coelestium*, 'On the movements of the heavenly orbs', was revolutionary in that, while retaining many elements of the Ptolemaic system, he placed the sun at the centre of the heavenly bodies and postulated the movement of the earth as necessary to account for the motions of the heavenly bodies. This was literally an 'earth-moving' development. It inaugurated the great heliocentric versus geocentric conflict in which Galileo became the leading protagonist. The Catholic Church authorities did not immediately react to Copernicus' book, in contrast to Luther, who called its author a 'mad man' who wanted to 'turn upside down all astronomical knowledge' and to subvert the clear teaching of the Holy Scripture. The silence of the Catholic Church until 1616, however, was probably due to the preoccupation of the Pope and the Cardinals with the theological problems posed by the Protestant Reformers and with the debates of the Council of Trent, rather than with any disposition to look with favour on the copernican position. Galileo entitled his great work, *Dialogue Concerning Two Chief Systems of the World, Ptolemaic and Copernican*; where the debate fundamentally was between the heliocentric system, advanced by Copernicus, and the geocentric system, as modified by Ptolemy and supported, as I have said, by the Aristotelian-trained 'natural philosophers' and most of the theologians of the time.

The conflict between Galileo's copernican 'system of the world' (placing the sun and not the earth at the centre of the system) and the Ptolemaic system backed by Aristotelians, on the one hand, and the Congregation of the Holy Office (or the Inquisition, as it was then known) and the Pope, on the other, passed through several phases. The conflict cannot be properly understood without taking account of its gradual development. I attempt an account, however summary, of this development here. In what follows, I rely heavily upon on what I believe will long be the definitive study of Galileo, that by Annibale Fantoli.[5] This is a very detailed and remarkably balanced study, putting the Galileo 'Affair' in its historical context and bringing its history right up to its latest phase in the papacy of Pope John Paul II. Galileo emerges as a decisive figure, not simply in an historical conflict between science and religion, but also, and paradoxically, in the process towards greater mutual respect and understanding between the Church and science. Hence the sub-title of Fantoli's work: *For Copernicanism and for the Church*. For Galileo, it was never a question of choosing between copernican science and the Christian and Catholic faith; he remained, to the end of his life, deeply committed to both. Indeed, Galileo, particularly by his reflections on the interpretation of Holy Scripture, hoped to bring about a reconciliation between faith and science. A man of unwavering faith in the truth of divine revelation, he also believed strongly in the unity of truth and was convinced that what was proved true by science could not conflict with the truth revealed in Holy Scripture correctly understood; and this, of course, is a profoundly Catholic position.[6]

Galileo's scepticism about the aristotelian 'world system' began at an early stage of his academic life and developed through his mathematical studies and through his experiments with the telescope, an instrument which, though not invented by him, was greatly refined by him. Through the telescope, he became the first to observe mountains on the moon, the first to detect the Milky Way, made up of myriads of stars, and the first to identify four planets revolving around Jupiter. Finally, he discovered sun spots, and established, to his own satisfaction, that they were indeed 'spots' on the surface of the sun. These discoveries made Aristotle's theory of the heavenly spheres increasingly implausible, postulating, as this theory did, that the spheres were immutable, incorruptible, 'superlunary', essentially different from 'sublunary bodies', and with the earth at their centre. The copernican system, putting the sun at the centre, seemed to Galileo more and more to be incontrovertible. In fact, he came to feel a sense of divine mission to demonstrate copernicanism as the true 'system of the world', and to convince philosophers and theologians of the truth of the copernican system. In this, as in all his scientific work, Galileo declared that he had 'no other aim but the honour of the Holy Church' and did not 'direct (his) small labours to any other goal.'[7]

Galileo's Fervent Faith

Galileo's fervour as a Catholic is clear from Sister Celeste's letters; one expression of it was the pilgrimage he made in 1618 to the Holy House of Loreto, supposed to be the residence of the Blessed Virgin Mary, and held to have been miraculously transferred there from the Holy Land. A convinced, faithful and devout Catholic all his life, he saw his work as an academic, a mathematician and a scientist, as a way of giving glory to God and a cause for giving thanks to God. He speaks of a particular telescope which he invented as due to his receiving 'the illumination of divine grace'. He spoke of his treatise on the causes of the tides as being interrupted by 'a voice from heaven [which] aroused me and diffused all my confused and tangled fantasies in mist'; three years later, he recorded that this treatise was satisfactorily completed when 'with God's grace [he found] the right line'. His discoveries about the movement of the tides were in fact for him the conclusive proof of the truth of copernicanism.

Dispute Begins

Meanwhile, Galileo's espousal of the copernican system was becoming more widely known, and the aristotelian philosophers, as well as many theologians, were alarmed. Their counter-attack was based partly on the principles of aristotelian philosophy, which seemed to be corroborated by common sense experience of the movement of the heavenly bodies. Their critique of copernicanism, however, relied much more on Holy Scripture, which, they argued, spoke clearly of the motion of the sun and the immobility of the earth. In particular, they cited scriptural passages (such as Joshua 10:12-13; Job 9:6; Judges 5:31; Isaiah 38:8) as indisputably and infallibly asserting the movement of the sun and the motionlessness of the earth. In the hope of defending himself, Galileo made a visit to Rome in the year 1611. Here he was given every mark of respect by ecclesiastics of note, and even by the Pope, Paul V. He also met Cardinal Robert Bellarmine, undoubtedly the greatest theologian of the time, and the question of copernicanism was raised during these conversations. We are not informed as to the content of the conversations, but we know that Bellarmine saw copernicanism as one of the great questions emerging at the time, and was worried about the compatibility of the copernican theory with Holy Scripture. Bellarmine, however, also questioned the competence of Galileo, as a lay person, to pronounce on theological questions, and particularly on the interpretation of Holy Scripture. As a consultor to the Holy Office, Bellarmine was later to play a vital role in the dispute with Galileo.

Letter to Castelli

When Galileo left Rome he was in no doubt that the interpretation of scripture was a vital issue for his defence of the copernican system. He developed his own thinking on this issue in his celebrated *Letter to Castelli* in 1614. Benedetto Castelli was a pupil and a devoted disciple of Galileo, who later became a Benedictine monk. In the letter, Galileo declared his conviction that scripture could not err, but immediately added that its interpreters could err. He argued that they would most certainly err if they always insisted on the literal meaning of the words used in the Bible. If they did so, they would, he argued, be attributing all kinds of obviously human attributes and feelings to God, and this would clearly be incompatible with the transcendent nature of God. Galileo went on to declare that the same mistake would be made if the literal meaning of Holy Scripture was to be invoked in disputes about scientific matters. When 'sense experience' or 'necessary demonstrations' are in conflict with the literal interpretation of Holy Scripture, then it is the literal interpretation which must be called in question. God most certainly reveals Himself in Holy Scripture, but He also reveals Himself in the Book of Nature; and these two truths cannot contradict one another; both come from the same Divine Word. Galileo declared:

> Apart from articles concerning salvation and the establishment of the Faith, against the solidity of which there is no danger that anyone may ever raise a more valid and efficacious doctrine, it would perhaps be a very good counsel never to add more (articles of Faith), without necessity.

He concluded:

> I would believe that the authority of Holy Writ had only the aim of persuading men of those articles and propositions, which, being necessary for our salvation, and over-riding all human reason, could not be made credible by any other science, or by other means than the mouth of the Holy Ghost. But I do not think it necessary that the same God who has given us our senses, reason and intelligence, wishes us to abandon their use, giving us by some other means the information that we could gain through them – and especially in matters of which only a minimal part, and impartial conclusion, is to be read in Scripture. Surely if the intentions of the sacred writers had been to teach the people astronomy, they would not have passed over the subject so completely.[8]

Foscarini and Cardinal Bellarmine

Help for Galileo came from an unexpected source, a Carmelite theologian called Antonio Foscarini. In a published paper dealing with the copernican systems and its compatibility with Holy Scripture, Foscarini dealt sympathetically with Galileo's discoveries and with the copernican theory which Galileo favoured, although realising that Galileo's arguments fell short of proof. Foscarini suggested ways in which, supposing the copernican hypotheses were eventually proven, the relevant scripture passages could be reconciled with that position. He sent a copy of his paper to Cardinal Bellarmine. In view of Bellarmine's role in the later evolution of the 'Galileo Affair', a rather extensive quotation from Bellarmine's reply (dated 12 April 1615) seems justified. I quote from Brodrick's translation:

> My very Reverend Father, as you ask for my opinion I will give it as briefly as possible because, at the moment, you will have very little time for reading and I have very little time for writing.
>
> First. It seems to me that your Reverence and Signor Galileo would act prudently were you to content yourselves with speaking hypothetically and not absolutely, as I have always believed that Copernicus spoke. To say that on the supposition of the earth's movement and the sun's immobility all the celestial appearances are explained better than by the theory of eccentrics and epicycles, is to speak with excellent good sense and to run no risk whatever. Such a manner of speaking is enough for a mathematician. But to want to affirm that the sun, in very truth, is at the centre of the universe and only rotates on its axis without going from east to west, and that the earth is situated in the third sphere and revolves very swiftly around the sun, is a very dangerous attitude and one calculated not only to annoy all scholastic philosophers and theologians but also to injure our holy faith in contradicting the scriptures.
>
> ....
>
> Third. If there were a real proof that the sun is the centre of the universe, that the earth is in the third sphere, and that the sun does not go round the earth but the earth round the sun, then we should have to proceed with great circumspection in explaining passages of Scripture which appear to teach the contrary, and rather admit that we did not understand them than declare an opinion to be false which is proved to be true. But as for myself, I shall not believe that there are such proofs

until they are shown me. Nor is it a proof that, if the sun be supposed at the centre of the universe and the earth in the third sphere, the celestial appearances are thereby explained, equivalent to a proof that the sun actually is in the centre and the earth in the third sphere. The first kind of proof might, I believe, be found, but as for the second kind, I have the very gravest doubts, and in the case of doubt we ought not to abandon the interpretation of the sacred text as given by the Holy Fathers.[9]

Bellarmine, therefore, did allow that copernicanism could be maintained as a mere mathematical hypothesis, and he cautioned Galileo and his supporters to limit themselves to so doing. This suggestion was to feature prominently in the subsequent debate. A young curial friend of Galileo, Father Giovanni Ciampole, was one of those who urged Galileo to follow this safer line. He wrote to him saying:

> Cardinal Del Monte told us that he had discussed the question of copernicanism at great length with Cardinal Bellarmine and that they had concluded as follows: If you treat the system of Copernicus and set forth its proofs without bringing in the scriptures, the interpretation of which is the business of qualified theologians, then you should not be opposed in any way whatever.[10]

Galileo, however, consistently refused to treat copernicanism as a mere mathematical hypothesis; he was convinced that it was objectively true and could be proven to be true. He claimed to have himself provided proofs of the truth. His proofs, however, were found by critics to be inconclusive. His theory of the tides, which he believed to be the strongest proof, was in fact mistaken, since he rejected Kepler's invoking of the influence of the moon, believing this to be a mystical or mythical theory, rather than a scientific fact. This was a weakness for Galileo's case in terms of the contemporary debate. In fact, however, the case against the aristotelian system had by now grown in strength to a point where aristotelian cosmology could no longer be credibly sustained. The aristotelians nevertheless, together with most theologians, defended the aristotelian system to the bitter end. Since, as we have remarked, aristotelian science at this time constituted what might be called the 'scientific establishment', it could be claimed that science itself, as understood by very many at the time, as well as theology and Holy

Scripture, were all opposed to Galileo. In contemporary terms the debate was in part a debate between scientists (who were then called natural philosophers) and not simply a dispute between science and faith.

Letter to Christina of Lorraine

More and more, the question of copernicanism came to centre on the interpretation of Holy Scripture. A discussion on these matters took place in the Court of the Grand Duke of Tuscany, Cosimo II, who was Galileo's patron and protector. The Grand Duke's mother, Countess Christina, who was a very influential person at the court, was present at this discussion. Galileo decided to write to her in order to defend his position. In his famous *Letter to Christina* (dating probably from June 1615), Galileo notes that his opponents have largely ceased to depend upon philosophical arguments in favour of the aristotelian system, and are now concentrating on scriptural arguments. He says that they are donning 'the mantle of pretended religion and the authority of the Bible'. As in the letter to Castelli, Galileo points out that the Bible manifestly cannot be always understood in its literal sense; otherwise, all kinds of human features and frailties would be attributed to God. It follows, Galileo goes on, that:

> In disputes about natural phenomena, one must begin, not with the authority of scriptural passages, but with sensory experience and necessary demonstrations.

Hence, the discoveries of the natural sciences are a great help to 'the correct interpretation of Scripture'. Tellingly, Galileo points out that his opinion on this matter is in fact the opinion of St Augustine. He quotes Augustine:

> We do not read in the gospels that the Lord said: 'I will send you the Paraclete to teach you how the sun and moon move,' because he wished to make them Christians, not mathematicians.

Augustine, Galileo continues, tells us that the sacred writers did not set out to teach us about 'the form and figure of the heavens', or other such astronomical questions, because these 'were not useful for salvation.'

Galileo states that this conclusion is in agreement with 'what I heard from an ecclesiastical person in a very eminent position, namely that the intention of the Holy Spirit is to teach us how one goes to heaven, and not how heaven goes: *quomodo ad coelum eatur, non quomodo coelum gradiatur*'.

Galileo concludes, (and obviously he has theologians and perhaps the Holy Office in mind) that:

> It would be very prudent not to allow anyone to commit and in a way to oblige scriptural passages to have to maintain the truth of physical conclusions, whose contrary could ever be proved to us by the senses and demonstrative and necessary reasons.[11]

Pervading this *Letter to Christina* is the conviction, which is a constant with Galileo, that 'a truth from scripture cannot contradict the truth from our knowledge of nature'. He even quotes the Council of Trent in support of this position. Trent, he says, quoting the Fourth Session of the Council, forbade any 'tampering in ways contrary to the interpretation of the Holy Church or the collective consensus of the Fathers, with those propositions which are articles of faith or involve morals and pertain to edification according to Christian doctrine'. However, the mobility or stability of the Earth or the Sun are not questions of faith or morals, and 'none of those who uphold the mobility of the Earth has ever wished to abuse the sacred texts by appealing to them in support of his own opinion'. Although copernicanism may not as yet be demonstratively proven, he goes on, nevertheless, it remains possible to prove it; in the meantime, therefore, the case for and the case against copernicanism must be left to future demonstration, and it cannot be pre-empted by citing Holy Scripture. Fantoli sees in these passages 'an indirect but firm warning directed to Pope Paul V himself'. Galileo acknowledges that scientific certainty about the truth of copernicanism does not yet exist; but it still remains possible in the future. Consequently, theologians and Church authorities 'are respectfully, but firmly, invited to be prudent'.[12] Fantoli comments:

> It has to be admitted, however, that Galileo is not always respectful to his opponents, either in the *Letter to Christina*, or in his other writings. He is at times dismissive, scornful, even contemptuous of them. There are occasional hints of arrogance in his polemical writing. This was not calculated to win favour from critics of his positions.[13]

The *Letter to Christina*, and other studies by Galileo, make him an important figure in the field of scripture studies, as well as in science. His views on the interpretation of scripture were fundamentally derived from St Augustine; but his restatement and development of Augustine's teaching were destined to be influential in the future. Galileo's views, expounded in the *Letter to Castelli*, and his *Letter to Christina* and elsewhere, are in fact close to those expounded three centuries later by Pope Leo XIII, who, in his 1893 encyclical on the divine inspiration of Holy Scripture, citing St Augustine, declared:

> The sacred writers ... did not wish to teach people these truths [that is, the inward constitution of visible objects], which would not help any to salvation; [but they use] language to some extent figurative, or as the common manner of speech in use at the period required.[14]

This teaching, as we shall point out later, was repeated by Pope Pius XII and later by the Second Vatican Council, and is now standard Catholic teaching.

Copernican System Condemned

However, rumours adverse to Galileo continued to spread. A Dominican called Tommaso Caccini formally denounced him to the Holy Office, as teaching propositions which are 'repugnant to the divine Scripture', thereby rendering himself 'suspect in matters of faith'. Galileo felt the need to visit Rome again to defend himself and to defend copernicanism. He hoped that his visit would have the result of 'at least showing my affection for the Holy Church.' The visit took place in late 1615 and early 1616. At Rome, Galileo met with many influential persons. His conversations convinced him that the trend of influential opinion in Rome was in his favour. In this, he was sadly mistaken. Two propositions were cited as expressing the copernican position: (a) the centrality of the sun and its immobility; and (b) the motion of the earth round the sun. These propositions were submitted to the consultors of the Holy Office for examination on 19 February 1616.[15] Five days later the consultors agreed that the first proposition was 'foolish and absurd in philosophy and formally heretical', since it contradicted Holy Scripture; and that the second proposition was equally to be censured in philosophy and was 'at least erroneous in faith.' On 25 February 1616, Galileo was summoned to appear before the Holy Office, and was solemnly 'commanded and enjoined ... to relinquish altogether the said opinion ... nor further to hold, teach, or defend it in any way whatsoever, verbally or in writing.' Despite the report of the consultors, however, the Holy Office stopped short of declaring copernicanism heretical.[16] The minute of this fateful meeting concluded with the words: 'The said Galileo acquiesced in the injunction and promised to obey'.[17]

The Congregation of the Index met on 5 March 1616, and issued its notorious Decree, ordering that the book of Nicolaus Copernicus on the movement of the heavenly bodies 'be suspended until [it] be corrected', and that the work of Foscarini (referred to above) 'be altogether prohibited and condemned.' Fantoli concludes his account of the injunction of the Holy Office and the Decree of the Congregation of the Index (often, though inaccurately, called the 'first Trial of Galileo'), with the words:

> This 'abuse of power', both doctrinal and disciplinary, will have its inevitable sequel in the trial and condemnation of Galileo in 1633, and will continue for centuries to weigh heavily upon the relationship of the Church to modern culture.[18]

Galileo himself bore this calamity with admirable restraint. He wrote to a friend that he felt himself that 'a saint would not have handled (this affair) either with greater reverence or with greater zeal towards the Holy Church'. He took heart from the fact that the proposition referring to the motion of the earth had not been declared formally heretical. A few important ecclesiastics in Rome were eager to show that they held Galileo personally in great respect and were convinced by his sincerity. The Pope himself, Paul V, arranged a meeting in audience with Galileo, and spent a considerable time in his company, assuring him of the Pope's belief in his integrity and sincerity. Cardinal Bellarmine issued a statement repudiating slanderous reports that Galileo had abjured his beliefs or had penances imposed upon him. Other Cardinals publicly declared that Galileo left Rome with his reputation intact, that he enjoyed the esteem of all who had dealt with him in Rome; and they deplored the fact that his enemies had spread calumnious reports about him.[18] Bellarmine himself, who had such an important role throughout this whole process, died in 1621. It is worth noticing that William Shakespeare died in 1616, the year of what is often called Galileo's 'First Trial.'

The Assayer

Galileo did not abandon hope that the Church would eventually change its mind concerning copernicanism; he read the Decree of the Congregation of the Index, not as formally and finally condemning copernicanism, but as requiring that, if defended at all, it be defended as merely an hypothesis. Meanwhile, Galileo decided to turn his mind to other scientific questions, notably his experiments on motion and his astronomical observations. Meanwhile, in 1623, Cardinal Maffeo Barberini was elected Pope, taking the name Urban VIII. He was a cultured and learned man. He was personally well-disposed towards Galileo, whom he admired, and was regarded as holding a moderate position in respect of copernicanism. There are suggestions indeed, that he may have intervened with the Holy Office in 1616 to prevent copernicanism from being pronounced heretical.

Galileo's studies resulted in the publication, in 1623, of the book entitled, *The Assayer*, which Galileo dedicated to the new Pope. The title is derived from the instrument of measurement employed by Galileo in his experiments; it was the most precise measuring instrument of its kind known at the time. The book is polemical in tone, since Galileo had been the butt of much hostile criticism. *The Assayer* is one of the landmark documents in the history of science. It opens with a splendid paragraph, which is often cited. It deserves being cited again, for it is a kind of charter for modern science:

> Philosophy is written in the grand book, the universe, which stands continually open to our gaze. But the book cannot be understood unless one first learns to comprehend the language and to read the letters in which it is composed. It is written in the language of mathematics and its characters are triangles, circles, and other geometric figures, without which it is humanly impossible to understand a single word of it.[19]

Thus a way was opened for an understanding of science and a practice of science which has been used by scientists ever since. It can be summed up in the slogan: 'Measure what is measurable and make measurable what is not measurable yet'.

In *The Assayer* Galileo responds vigorously to critics, revealing an aspect of his character which contrasts with his many admirable qualities and which earned him enemies. I refer to what Annibale Fantoli calls his vanity, his 'self-esteem as well as his fiery temperament', his 'excessive susceptibility', his occasionally polemical style. *The Assayer* has been called 'a stupendous masterpiece of polemical literature.'[20] During Galileo's visit to Rome in 1616, the Tuscan Ambassador, at whose villa Galileo was staying, had expressed concern to the Grand Duke about his guest's intensive and widespread lobbying in the cause of copernicanism. He spoke of how 'passionately involved' Galileo was in his campaign, saying that he was 'vehement and stubborn and very worked up in this matter.' The Ambassador warned the Duke that Galileo would 'be tripped up and will get himself into trouble'. These qualities of Galileo unfortunately had some part in the events which were to follow the publication in the *Dialogue*.

On the other hand, in reference to copernicanism, Galileo, in *The Assayer*, writes with extreme caution. He holds this theory as superior to its alternative, when considered as an hypothesis, but declares that 'as a pious and Catholic person' he is willing at all times to be prepared for 'every decree [of his ecclesiastical] superiors'. Indeed, the book was highly appreciated by the new Pope, who, we are told, had such esteem for it that he chose it for reading at table.[21]

The Dialogue

Hoping to build on the esteem manifested towards him by the new Pope, Galileo decided to visit Rome once more. This he did in April 1624. During this visit he had six meetings with Pope Urban, and used the opportunity prudently to try to influence the Pope towards a reappraisal of copernicanism. His efforts, however, had little success. The Pope could countenance copernicanism only as a mathematical hypothesis, but was convinced that it neither was proven nor ever could be proven to be true. Indeed, his personal opinion was that no astronomer, now or in the future, would ever be able to penetrate the mysteries of the heavenly bodies and their movements, mysteries known only to God. Science, still known as 'philosophy,' could never explore the secrets of the universe. This personal opinion of the Pope had an important bearing on the later condemnation of Galileo. A complicating factor was that, from his conversations with Galileo, the Pope had formed the impression that Galileo shared his view and would not again attempt to assert the truth of the copernican 'hypothesis'.

Galileo, however, felt that he could safely continue to defend copernicanism at the level of mathematics and science, leaving the theological and scriptural problems to be resolved elsewhere. He felt that one of his strongest arguments in favour of the earth's motion was based on the ebb and flow of the tides. To this question he now turned his attention. His health, never robust, continued to deteriorate; and increasingly his daughter, Sister Maria Celeste, was worried about him and continued to ply him with the healing potions in which she specialised. In spite of his failing health, Galileo decided to make yet another visit to Rome, his fifth. This was in 1630. His intention this time was to prepare the way for the favourable reception in Rome of his new book, *On the Ebb and Flow of the Sea*. Galileo felt at the same time that the omens were favourable for revisiting the question of Copernicanism. Indeed, and ironically, it seems that the Pope may have suggested the title, *Dialogue on the Chief Systems of the World* or something similar; his hope obviously being that this title would underline the tentative and 'hypothetical' nature of Galileo's position on earth's motion. Indeed, the Pope's views and hopes were conveyed to Galileo by an intermediary: namely, that Galileo's book would assert the 'hypothetical truth' of copernicanism as 'saving the appearances' of nature, but would not claim 'absolute truth' for the copernican system, since this truth claim could come only from Holy Scripture.[22]

The Pope's negative reaction to the *Dialogue* when it was published owed much to his belief that Galileo had agreed with the Pope's own views about the matter. It was in this atmosphere of misunderstanding and confusion that the book was published in 1632. The title chosen by Galileo was *Dialogue Concerning the two Chief Systems of the World, Ptolemaic and Copernican*. There were three participants in this fictitious dialogue, and the names can be read as also code-words. The first is Salviati, a deceased friend of Galileo who in the *Dialogue* reflects Galileo's own views. In the *Dialogue*, Salviati vigorously defends Copernicanism. Sagredo, another deceased friend of Galileo, is a detached, but well-informed, arbiter of the debate. Simplicius is the name of a celebrated sixth-century commentator on Aristotle, a name still frequently invoked in scholarly discussion and writing at the time; he defends the ptolemaic-aristotelian view. The choice of name, however, suggests 'simpleton', and Galileo may not have been unaware of this association. The name was not likely to please Pope Urban!

The setting for the *Dialogue* is Venice, and the 'conversation' is prolonged over four days. Although in the end copernicanism was technically left an open question, the dialogue was clearly intended to present the aristotelian system as discredited and the copernican system as the only credible 'world system'. Salviati argues that a variety of facts provide 'strong evidence in favour of the copernican system' (he instances particularly the observed movements of the planets, the revolution of the sun upon itself, the sun spots, the ebbing and flowing of the tides); and concludes that, if they do not prove copernicanism, they 'absolutely favour it, and greatly'.[23] As though to soften his blows Salviati occasionally interjects such comments as might imply that he is open to persuasion that he may after all be mistaken, and copernicanism may in the end prove to be 'a most foolish hallucination and a majestic paradox'. Simplicius seems to 'make a bow' in the direction of Pope Urban and his personal convictions, by saying that 'God's infinite power and wisdom' can do things 'which are unthinkable to our minds'.[24] That views corresponding to those of the Pope should be put in the mouth of a person named 'Simplicius', and should be treated somewhat frivolously, was not likely to please the Pope, particularly since he almost certainly felt also that Galileo had deceived him. His conversations with Galileo, as we have seen, had convinced the Pope that Galileo was in agreement with him.

Meanwhile, Galileo's enemies and rivals were busy denouncing the *Dialogue*. The Cardinals of the Congregation of the Holy Office met with the Pope and decided that Galileo had been 'deceitfully silent' about the injunction of the Holy Office in 1616, which forbade him to 'hold and teach and defend, in word or in writing' the copernican opinion. Galileo was consequently summoned to present himself in Rome within a month. Galileo pleaded to be given exemption or postponement, because of his 'advanced age' (he was seventy) and 'his many bodily ills'. A further difficulty was the fact that, because of a plague then raging, a quarantine was in force at the time for travellers between the Grand Duchy of Tuscany and the Papal States.

Eventually, Galileo reached Rome in February 1633. He spent two months there in virtual seclusion, during which time the *Dialogue* was being subjected to critical examination. Eventually, in April 1633, Galileo was summoned before the Congregation of the Holy Office. Confronted with the charge that he had disobeyed the injunction of the Congregation against his holding or teaching the copernican view, Galileo pleaded that his *Dialogue* was not in fact in contravention of that injunction, but, on the contrary, showed that the arguments of the Copernicans were weak and inconclusive. Galileo even humbled himself to the point of saying:

> My error has been – and I confess it – one of vainglorious ambition and of pure ignorance and inadvertence.[25]

At one point, Galileo pleaded for more time in which, as proof of his belief that copernicanism was not regarded by him as definitively proved to be true, he might be allowed to add further 'days' to the *Dialogue*, in which he would 'refute' the pro-copernican case. He was perhaps exhausted and even confused at the time, and wanted more time in which to try to retrieve his position. He pleaded 'ten months of constant mental anxiety', together with the fatigue of his long journey. He kept hoping for a favourable response.[26] His hopes were in vain. The Holy Office decided that Galileo be interrogated and, if he persist in his view, that he be declared to be under vehement suspicion of heresy, and be required to abjure and ordered not to reoffend; he is to be imprisoned at the pleasure of the Congregation and the

Dialogue is to be prohibited. The Pope, in a message intended for Galileo's patron, the Grand Duke, undertook to do everything possible to 'cause the least pain and least affliction to him.' The date, 21 June 1633, was fixed for the 'interrogation'.

Galileo faced his interrogators as one who knew that the die was already cast against him. Accused of disobeying the Holy Office and of defending an opinion condemned by it, Galileo declared that, following the decision of the Holy Office, he now held 'as most true and indisputable' the opinion of the stability of the earth and the mobility of the sun; that he held the arguments to the contrary as inconclusive; and that, due to 'the decisions of higher teaching' he affirmed 'on his conscience' that he did not now hold the condemned opinion and did not hold it since the decision of the Authorities'.[27] His declaration did not convince the Holy Office. He was detained overnight and brought to face the Congregation again the next day.

Wednesday 22 June 1633 was the fatal day. It is a day which can be recalled now only with deep embarrassment and sadness. Galileo, in accordance with the rules of the Holy Office concerning offenders, was obliged to dress in the white robe of a penitent and to ride to his appointment on 'the mule of the Inquisition'. The meeting of the Congregation took place in the Dominican Convent of Santa Maria Sopra Minerva. It was a plenary session of the Holy Office. He was ordered to kneel down while his sentence of condemnation was solemnly read:

> We say, pronounce, sentence and declare, that ... you have rendered yourself vehemently suspected of heresy, namely of having believed and held the doctrine which is false and contrary to the Sacred and Divine Scriptures [that is, the Copernican doctrine]. ... from which we are content that you be absolved provided that first, with a sincere heart and unfeigned faith, you abjure, curse, and detest before us the aforesaid errors heresies and every other error and heresy, contrary to the Catholic and Apostolic Roman Church in the form prescribed by us for you.
>
> And ... we ordain that the book of the *Dialogue of Galileo Galilei*, be prohibited by public edict.
>
> We condemn you to the formal prison of this Holy Office during our pleasure, and by way of salutary penance we enjoin that for three years to come you repeat once a week the seven penitential Psalms.

Galileo then read, as ordered, the prescribed formula. As the text required, he acknowledged that he had written the *Dialogue* and, thereby:

> I have been pronounced by the Holy Office to be vehemently suspected of heresy, that is, of having held and believed that the sun is the centre of the world and is unmovable, and that the earth is not the centre and moves. ... Therefore, with sincere heart and unfeigned faith I abjure, curse, detest the aforesaid errors and heresies and I will never again say or assert verbally or in writing, anything that might furnish occasion for a similar suspicion regarding me.[28]

Fantoli rightly describes all this as 'an abuse of power, both on the doctrinal plane and with respect to Galileo's personal conscience.' He speaks of 'myopic authoritarism' and of 'an institutionalised abuse of power which can never be sufficiently deprecated.' He says that the 'judges' of the Holy Office passed into history as the true 'accused' in the affair.[29] The remark attributed to Galileo as he left the tribunal, *'eppur si muove'*, 'and yet it [the earth] does move', is almost certainly fictional, but the words have long stood as a slogan for the independence of science vis-à-vis all authority, and particularly Church authority.

Nevertheless, we must not misrepresent the nature of the sentence pronounced by the Holy Office. Fantoli shows that the terms 'heresy' and 'heretical' were used, in the technical language of the Holy Office, to include infractions of the precepts of the Inquisition. There is no doubt but that one of their concerns was the effect which Galileo's action in publishing the *Dialogue* would have on the authority of the Papacy and of its agency, the Holy Office, or Inquisition. In the post-Reformation period, with a deeply divided Europe, the so-called 'Catholic powers', partly out of self-interest, supported papal authority in the doctrinal area and frowned upon any apparent weakening of that authority. Galileo's views on the interpretation of scripture would have been seen at the time as dangerously close to the Protestant view on private interpretation of scripture independently of Church authority. Catholic theologians felt obliged, therefore, to emphasise the God-given right and responsibility of the Church's pastors, and supremely the successor of Peter, as the authoritative interpreters of holy scripture. Furthermore, the Pope felt that he had been personally led by Galileo to expect a different kind of book than the *Dialogue* turned out to be; and he also felt slighted by the way in which his own views, as he saw it, were presented. Given the ideology of the time, and given the principles and the methods upon which the Inquisition operated at the time, Fantoli concludes that the Holy Office 'could not do otherwise than issue a sentence of condemnation of Galileo'.[30]

It has to be remembered that the paramount concern of the Pope and of the Holy Office was the defence of the authority of Holy Scripture. Protestant leaders like Luther and Melanchthon condemned copernicanism on the same grounds. Cardinal Bellarmine, as we have seen, in his *Letter to Foscarini*, stressed that Holy Scripture, as interpreted by the Holy Fathers of the Church, must be decisive in matters of faith and doctrine. If copernicanism were ever demonstrated as true, an event which he thought extremely unlikely, Bellarmine said that extreme caution would have to be observed in interpreting the words of scripture in this context in any other than their literal meaning.

Church Versus Science?

Clearly, the course taken by the Galileo case and its outcome made it easy and almost plausible in later generations to present the affair as proof that the Church's whole ecclesiastical and theological system depended on the assumption of a fixed earth and an earth-centred world, and that Galileo was condemned on grounds of teaching a cosmology which conflicted with this view. This was how, in fact, it soon came to be presented and perceived, the inference being that Christian faith and science are irreconcilable.

This, however, is a gross oversimplification of the facts. If the new cosmology had the dogma-demolishing effect which it was alleged to have, this would have loomed large in contemporary discussion. But such is not the case. One over-riding reason keeps repeatedly being adduced for condemning the Copernican-Galilean astronomy, namely that, as Cardinal Bellarmine stated, 'it injures our holy faith by contradicting the scriptures'. It was on scriptural, not primarily on cosmological, grounds that Copernicus and later Galileo were condemned. Copernicus' teaching was condemned by the Inquisition because his teaching,

> explicitly contradicts in many places the sense of the Holy Scriptures according to the literal meaning of the words and according to the common interpretation and understanding of the Holy Fathers and the doctors of theology.[31]

The latter part of this sentence is a key point for the understanding of the whole affair. The Catholic Church was still shaken by the seismic shock of the Protestant Reformation. The role of Holy Scripture and its interpretation were obviously central elements in the Catholic/Protestant dispute. The core question was: can any Christian interpret Scripture by the light of his or her own conscience, or has the Church the right and duty to decide on the true interpretation of Scripture? The Catholic response was that, while Scripture was most certainly the touchstone of faith, Scripture itself taught that Christ instituted the Church as the guardian and transmitter of His teaching, and specifically entrusted the Apostles, with Peter as their leader and head, with the interpretation of the Scriptures. This responsibility was handed on by the Apostles to their successors, the bishops of the Church, with their leader and head, the Pope, as the ultimate guarantor of communion in faith and in consensus regarding the meaning of Holy Scripture, both across the centuries (and this is the basis meaning of the appeal to Tradition) and across the whole worldwide Church. It was the authority of God as author of Scripture which the theologians held to be ultimate and decisive; they felt themselves, as much as any member of the Church, to be bound by this divine authority. The Galileo case was seen by the theologians of the time as primarily a conflict between divine authority and private opinion. In fact, however, as we shall see later, it was Galileo who proved in the end to be the more faithful exponent of the Church's tradition in this regard.

Papal infallibility was not involved and was not seen at the time to be involved in the issuing of the Decree of the Holy Office. The Decree did not formally invoke or engage the authority of the Pope as teacher of the universal Church, nor did it fulfil the conditions postulated by the later definition of the prerogative of infallibility laid down in 1870 by the First Vatican Council. Descartes, a contemporary, himself a committed Catholic, commented that 'this censure has not been confirmed either by a Council or by the Pope' and could some time be withdrawn.[32] Cardinal Bellarmine discussed the question of the infallibility of 'Pontifical decisions and Decrees', and wrote that the Pope, 'even as Pope and supported by his usual advisors, might make a mistake in such matters which chiefly depend on the information and testimony of men'.[33]

After the Condemnation
Galileo's condemnation included a formal notice of his being condemned to imprisonment at the discretion of the Holy Office. On the day after his condemnation and abjuration this sentence was mitigated by his being confined to the rooms and grounds of the Tuscan Embassy in Rome. A

week later this was again mitigated to his being confined to the hospitality of his friend, Archbishop Ascanio Piccolomini, the Archbishop of Siena. After six months, through the intervention of the Grand Duke, he was allowed to live for the last years of his life in his own Villa at Arcetri near Florence. He remained to the end under 'house arrest', being forbidden to invite or to receive guests. This prohibition was, however, not strictly enforced; it was here, for example, that he received the visit of John Milton. The Holy Office gave permission for a visit to Galileo in his last months by his good friend, Father Benedetto Castelli. This priest offered Mass for Galileo every morning from then until his own death in 1643,[34] one year after Galileo's death.

Galileo's Last Years

Galileo's last years were remarkably productive in terms of his scientific observations and his writing. Fantoli indeed says that Galileo 'was never so great as he was in those final years'. His physical sufferings, however, were severe, the greatest trial of all being the decline of his eyesight. Even this was surpassed by the death in 1634, a year after the 'Trial', and following a short illness, of his devoted daughter, Sister Maria Celeste. During Sister Maria Celeste's illness, Galileo walked over from his villa the short distance to the convent to be by his daughter's side. Her death, at the early age of thirty-four, left Galileo distraught and desolate. He wrote to a friend:

> I feel immense sadness and melancholy, together with extreme inappetite; I am hateful to myself and continually hear my beloved daughter calling to me. ... In addition to all this (mourning and sadness), a perpetual sleeplessness makes me afraid.[35]

His only solace was the reading of religious poems and dialogue. Total blindness supervened three years later and was a source of great distress. In one of his last letters, written in 1637, he tells

> how afflicted I am as I think about that sky, that world and that universe, which I, with my marvellous observations and clear demonstrations, had opened up hundreds and thousands of times more than had been commonly seen by the sages of all bygone centuries; now for me it is as diminished and limited that it is not greater than the space I occupy.[36]

His many afflictions and infirmities did not deter Galileo from pursuing his researches. He concentrated on dynamics, and presented his results in a new book, entitled *Discourses and Mathematical Demonstrations About Two New Sciences Belonging to Mechanics and Local Motions*, (commonly referred to as *The Discourses*, or *The Two New Sciences*). This was published in 1638, and it further established Galileo as one of the great founding fathers of modern science. It immediately formed the basis for a new 'natural philosophy', which quickly superseded the old aristotelian natural philosophy, and further contributed to making copernicanism universally accepted. Newton's *Principia* whose full title was, *Philosophiae Naturalis Principia Mathematica*, published in 1687, marked the final replacement of the old aristotelian 'physics'.

Galileo died, aged seventy-seven, on 8 January 1642. His disciple and later biographer, Vincenzio Viviani, wrote that 'with philosophical and Christian constancy he rendered his soul to his Creator'. It is interesting to note that Isaac Newton was born on Christmas Day in the same year. Two years earlier, Galileo, at what he called the 'decrepit age' of seventy-five years, had written to a colleague that he would spend what remained of his life 'satisfying himself with the discoveries of other pilgrim minds.'[37] He would undoubtedly have wished to be remembered as a man of deep Christian faith and a scientist of 'pilgrim mind'.

Vindication of Galileo

It was not until 1757 that the Decree of 1616 condemning copernicanism was at last omitted from the Index of Prohibited books, although the books of Copernicus and those of Galileo remained on the Index until the edition of 1835. All this was held to be justified, in the eyes of the Roman authorities, by the need to protect the 'good name' of the Congregation of the Holy Office and of the Index, and indeed of the Church itself, and avoid the embarrassment of having to admit an error of judgement. By then, Galileo, though he had remained a loyal son of the Church, a committed and devout Catholic, until his death, had already been turned into a symbol of anti-Catholic polemic, a hero of laicism and of anti-clericalism. This did undoubtedly make it difficult for the Church authorities to acknowledge that he had been right on the substantive issues all along. Studies by Catholics purporting to justify the judgements of the Holy Office and of the Congregation of the Index continued to be published right up to the earlier half of the twentieth century. However efforts were made by intellectuals, including Catholic intellectuals, to persuade Pope Benedict XIV (Pope from 1740-1758), seen as a friend of scientists, to order 'the Inquisitors' to recognise their error in condemning Galileo; but what Fantoli calls the 'inertial forces' of 'central Church agencies' thwarted such hopes.[38]

In 1936, Pope Pius XI established the Pontifical Academy of Sciences, with a view to promoting the reconciliation of faith with modern science. In 1941, this Academy took the initiative of setting up a new Commission to prepare a biography of Galileo to mark the occurrence in 1942 of the 300th anniversary of Galileo's death. The President of the Academy, Father Agustino Gemelli, himself a distinguished scholar, entrusted this task to Monsignor Pio Paschini, Rector of the Lateran University in Rome and Professor of Church History there. Three years later Paschini had completed his work and the book was ready for publication. The Roman authorities, however, judged the book to be too favourable to Galileo, and decided that it was inopportune that it be published in its original form. The book was eventually cleared for publication only in 1965, when the author, Paschini, was already two years dead. Even then, alterations were made to the text and a considerable number of the changes were such as substantially to alter the conclusions arrived at by Paschini himself. No acknowledgement of the changes was made in the text of the work, when it was published in 1965, with the title *Vita e Opere Di Galileo Galilei* by Pio Paschini.[39]

The Second Vatican Council was confronted by the 'Galileo question', particularly in the course of the drafting and debating of the Pastoral Constitution on the Church in the Modern World, *Gaudium et Spes*. In its concluding session in 1965, Monsignor Elchinger, the auxiliary Bishop of Strasbourg, proposed a specific declaration on Galileo. A petition in the name of many distinguished European intellectuals and scientists was sent to Pope Paul VI, asking for 'a solemn rehabilitation of "Galileo".'[40]

A much milder version of Monsignor Elchinger's declaration was drafted, admitting that the condemnation of Galileo was in error, and this text was debated by the Council itself. After further debate, however, the specific reference to Galileo was deleted and a generalised paragraph was approved. This paragraph read:

> At this point, may we be permitted to deplore certain mental attitudes, sometimes found among Christians, which come from not having sufficiently understood the legitimate autonomy of science, and which, giving rise to misunderstandings and controversies, draw

many spirits to a point where they hold that science and faith are opposed to one another.[41]

In a later paragraph of the same Pastoral Constitution, *Gaudium et Spes*, the Council says:

> This Sacred Synod, recalling the teaching of the First Vatican Council, declares that there are 'two orders of knowledge' which are distinct, namely faith and reason. It declares that the Church does not forbid that 'when the human arts and sciences are practised they use their own principles and their proper method, each in its own domain'. Hence, 'acknowledging this just liberty', this Sacred Synod affirms the legitimate authority of human culture and especially of the sciences.[42]

Shortly after the Council, Pope Paul VI followed the matter up by paying a striking tribute to Galileo's faith as well as to his genius. On 10 June 1965, during Mass in the Square in front of the Cathedral in Galileo's native Pisa, he asked the people of Tuscany to 'love the Christian Faith of your saints and your geniuses, whose immortal memory we celebrate today as yesterday, Galileo, Michelangelo and Dante'.

Pope John Paul II went much further. On 10 November 1979, the second year of his pontificate, on the occasion of the first centenary of the birth of Albert Einstein, in an address to the Pontifical Academy of Sciences, the Pope acknowledged that Galileo 'had to suffer a great deal – we cannot conceal the fact – at the hands of men and organisms of the Church'. He pointed out that the Vatican Council had recognised and deplored this. He expressed the hope that in order to 'go beyond this stand taken by the Council':

> theologians, scholars and historians ... will study the Galileo case more deeply, and in frank recognition of wrongs, from whatever side they come, dispel the mistrust that still opposes in many minds a fruitful concord between science and faith, between the Church and the world.

He added: 'I give all my support to this task, which will be able to honour the truth of faith and of science and open the door to future collaboration.'[43]

The Pope's initiative led over the following years to the publication of a considerable body of Galilean studies. In particular the Papal initiative led to the setting up in 1981 of a Commission dedicated to a re-examination of the whole Galileo affair and, in the Pope's own words, 'to explore the difficult relations of Galileo with the Church'. The occasion was the 340th anniversary of Galileo's death. This can be fittingly called 'the Galileo Commission'. There were four sections: exegetical, cultural, scientific-epistemological and historical-juridical. This Commission was clearly intended to bring definitive 'closure', from the Church's point of view, to this painful episode. The Commission's work was declared completed in 1990; its conclusions were formally presented to the Pope on 31 October 1992 at a plenary session of the Pontifical Academy of Science. The session included a discourse by Cardinal Poupard and an address by Pope John Paul II.[44]

Fantoli, in his paper on the Galileo Commission, calls attention to discrepancies between elements of Cardinal Poupard's evaluation of the positions of Galileo and Cardinal Bellarmine, respectively, and the 'overall judgment' of the majority of the publications emanating from the Commission itself. He expresses himself 'truly perplexed' by what he sees as a tendency to place responsibility for the debacle disproportionately on Galileo and his arguments.[45] In general, Fantoli finds in the history of the Commission and its closure even at this recent date, a regrettable defensiveness, on the part of people working in the service of the Church, which, he says, leaves 'deluded' those who had expected 'a loyal recognition of wrongs from whatever side they come', as the Pope had sought in 1979.

Pope John Paul II and Galileo

All this makes us admire all the more the courage and determination of Pope John Paul II, who persisted, in the face of all the difficulties and resistances, in his determination to complete, before and during the Year of Jubilee 2000, his programme of expressing 'profound regret for the weaknesses of so many of [the Church's] sons and daughters' in many instances, including the Galileo affair.[46] In his address to the Pontifical Academy of Sciences on 31 October, 1992, Pope John Paul II pointed out that 'the underlying problems of this case concern both the nature of science and the question of faith'. Questions both about the epistemology of science and about hermeneutics or biblical interpretation were at issue. The Pope pointed out that Galileo, like most of his contemporaries, did not distinguish between science and philosophy; they expected the same quality of proof from both.

Pope John Paul connects the Galileo case with the wider question of 'complexity' in science, which, he says, rules out 'a universal model of order' in the disciplines of science, philosophy and theology, and calls for 'recourse to a number of different models, in order to account for the rich variety of reality'. This observation of the Pope is highly important in the whole area of the relationship between science and theology, science and faith, science and the Bible, and indeed, the relationship of the sciences with one another. One way of putting this, which is applicable at least to some areas of scientific enquiry, is to say that science asks and answers 'how' questions about how things work, while faith and theology ask and answer 'why' questions, like why things exist, why science is possible, why man exists. Both sets of questions must be addressed if we are to make sense of ourselves and our world. It is becoming more and more clear that 'different models' are indeed necessary, and that explanations of reality given by the scientific, the philosophical, and the religious worldviews need not be contradictory, but complementary, that each can be valid in its own sphere and for its own purposes, and that each of these different explanations benefits from being supplemented by the others.[47]

On the other hand, the Pope went on, theologians in the time of Galileo also erred in not seeing that, in the light of copernicanism, they needed to examine their own criteria of scriptural interpretation. 'Most of them', the Pope comments, 'did not know how to do so'. The geocentric system seemed at the time to be postulated by ordinary observation. More importantly, it was held to be required by the literal meaning of those Scripture passages which spoke of the sun's motion. Hence, the geocentric system was believed to be true on the authority of God as the Divine Author of Holy Scripture. This, the Pope said, was the main source of the calamitous misunderstanding which led to Galileo's condemnation. There were faults on both sides. The sad consequence is that 'a tragic mutual incomprehension' led to what has been seen as 'a fundamental opposition between science and faith'. In fact, the Pope goes on, a certain myth developed around the Galileo affair, in which the historical facts became obscured. As a result, the Pope continued:

> The Galileo case [became] a symbol of the Church's supposed rejection of scientific progress, or of 'dogmatic' obscurantism opposed to the free search for truth. This myth has played a considerable cultural role.

The Pope points out that, paradoxically, Galileo

> showed himself to be more perceptive ... than the theologians who
> opposed him. 'If Scripture cannot err', Galileo wrote to Benedetto
> Castelli, 'certain of its interpreters and commentators can and do so in
> many ways.'

The Pope observes that Cardinal Bellarmine had earlier argued that, if it
could be scientifically *proved* that the earth orbited round the sun, then every
biblical passage, which 'seemed to affirm that the earth is immobile [should
be] interpreted with great circumspection', and we should

> say that we do not understand, rather than affirm that what has been
> demonstrated is false.[48]

The Pope also observes that, many centuries before, St Augustine had
anticipated Bellarmine in saying:

> If it happens that the authority of sacred Scripture is set in opposition
> to clear and certain reasoning, this must mean that the person who
> [interprets Scripture] does not understand it correctly. It is not the
> meaning of Scripture which is opposed to the truth, but the meaning
> that he has wanted to give to it. That which is opposed to Scripture is
> not what is in Scripture, but what he has placed there himself.[49]

Pope John Paul II also quotes, as Galileo himself did, the celebrated quip
attributed to Baronius:

> *Spiritui Sancto mentem fuisse nos docere quomodo ad coelum eatur, non*
> *quomodo coelum gradiatur;*
> the intention of the Holy Spirit was to teach us how to go to heaven,
> not how the heavens go.

The Pope further reminds theologians of their 'duty to keep themselves
regularly informed about scientific advances'. He declares:

> The underlying problem [of the Galileo case] concerns both the
> nature of science and the message of faith. It is, therefore, not to be
> excluded that one day we shall find ourselves in a similar situation,

one which will require both sides to have an informed awareness of the field and of the limits of their own competencies.

He expresses his confidence, however, that:

> the clarifications furnished by recent historical studies enable us to state that this sad misunderstanding now belongs to the past.[50]

With Pope John Paul II, we can therefore confidently hope that the Galileo episode may henceforth be discussed, on all sides, in a more measured and dispassionate manner, free of the passions and partisanship of the past; and that it may instead play a constructive part in the dialogue between Church and world for which the Pope pleaded in 1994, when he heralded an

> open and respectful and cordial dialogue, yet accompanied by careful discernment and courageous witness to the truth.[51]

Developments in Hermeneutics

It has to be kept in mind that great developments have taken place both in the sciences and in biblical hermeneutics since the Galileo case. For Catholics the year 1943 marks a significant date, with the publication of Pope Pius XII's *Divino Afflante Spiritu* on biblical inspiration and interpretation. This was a watershed in Catholic biblical scholarship; rumour has it that Father (later Cardinal) Augustine Bea had an important advisory role in the preparation of this document, as he was later to have in the Second Vatican Council. A further, and still more significant, date was the promulgation in 1964 of the Vatican Council's Dogmatic Constitution, *Dei Verbum*, which, with the Constitution on the Church, *Lumen Gentium*, contains the most important doctrinal teaching of the Council. *Dei Verbum* states:

> Truth is professed and expressed in a variety of ways, depending on whether a text is history of one kind or another, or whether its form is that of prophecy, poetry, or some other type of speech. The interpreter must investigate what meaning the sacred writer intended to express and actually expressed in particular circumstances as he used contemporary literary forms in accordance with the situation of his own time and culture. For the correct understanding of what the sacred author wanted to assert, due attention must be paid to the

customary and characteristic styles of perceiving, speaking and narrating which prevailed at the time of the sacred writer, and to the customs people normally followed at that point in their everyday dealings with one another.

Echoing Pope Leo XIII, the same Constitution declared that:

> the books of Scripture must be acknowledged as teaching firmly, faithfully and without error that truth which God wanted put into the sacred writings for the sake of our salvation.[52]

This Constitution owes much, of course, to the great work of Catholic biblical scholars since the beginning of the century, beginning perhaps with Jean Louis Lagrange and including Cardinal Bea. If the theologians who advised the Inquisition and who opposed Galileo could have had the benefit of the Vatican Council's teaching, there might never have been a Galileo case. Indeed, if they could have had the benefit of Cardinal Newman's thinking, there might never have been a Galileo case. For, in 1855, Cardinal Newman, in two of his lectures in Dublin on 'university subjects', dealt with the general question of the relationship between Christian faith and empirical science. In the second of these, a lecture on 'Christianity and Scientific Investigation', given to the School of Science of the Catholic University, he makes what has become a classical statement about this relationship. He writes:

> He who believes Revelation with that absolute faith which is the prerogative of the Catholic ... is sure and nothing should make him doubt, that if anything seems to be proved by astronomer, or geologist, or chronologist, or antiquarian, or ethnologist, in contradiction to the dogmas of faith, that point will eventually turn out, first *not* to be proved, or, secondly, not *contradictory* to any thing *really revealed* but to something which has been confused with revelation. And if, at the moment, it appears to be contradictory, then he is content to wait...[53]

I have to add that if Galileo's own principles of scriptural interpretation as set out in his *Letter to Castelli* and his *Letter to Christina* had been followed by the theologians of the time, there might never have been a Galileo case.

Developments in Science

So far as science is concerned, it is sometimes forgotten that science too has undergone fundamental changes since Galileo's time. As I have pointed out above, science and philosophy were not yet clearly distinguished in Galileo's time and Aristotle's thinking still permeated what we can call the 'scientific establishment' of the time. Contemporary 'scientists' were opposed to Galileo as much as were contemporary scriptural exegetes. Furthermore there is now much greater diversity within the broad category of science, diversity both of disciplines and of methodologies. The human and the social sciences are, in some sense, more analogous with the physical sciences than homogenous with them. The human and social sciences apply differently the scientific motto: 'measure what is measurable and make measurable what is not measurable yet'. We distinguish now between 'the exact sciences' and the human and social sciences. Errors have arisen in the psychological and sociological sciences through claims for them of a rigorous exactitude like that of the physical and chemical sciences. The sciences themselves can no longer be said to share precisely the same methodology, or to employ the same criteria of proof, or to offer the same degree of certitude. As Pope John Paul has pointed out, the principle of complexity has now to be recognised, and a plurality of models of science has to be admitted.

The conflict between science and religion has habitually been represented as a series of rearguard actions vainly fought by the Church against the irresistible onward rush of triumphant science. In fact, the response of the Church to science has also sometimes resulted in a more modest and more self-critical and more nuanced version of science. While there are still doctrinaire atheistic darwinians, there are also some evolutionary biologists who see no opposition between themselves and those who believe in the creation of the world and of life by God. The Catholic Church, as Pope John Paul has recently affirmed, now sees no opposition between its teaching and the theory of evolution, while firmly insisting on the special creation of each human being and the unique dignity and inalienable rights of the human person. It is not a question of creation *or* evolution, but of creation *and* evolution; God the Creator using evolution as His instrument in creation.

Scientists are rather less likely nowadays to be ideological and to enunciate, in the name of science, doctrinaire worldviews. Philosophies alleged to be founded on science – such as logical positivism or marxism – have few adherents now, and fewer scientists would agree that the alleged 'scientific principles' formulated by positivists or marxists or some darwinians are either the principles to which they adhere, or are the principles on which science works. Indeed both positivism and doctrinaire empiricism and marxism have been subjected to comprehensive philosophical rebuttal.

Meanwhile, some philosophers of science and historians of science have suggested that scientific modes of thinking are not as fundamentally different from thinking in other domains, such as philosophy, poetry and art, as has usually been supposed.[54] Indeed, the limitation of the terms 'reason' and 'proof' to scientific thinking and proof, as if science alone was 'rational', and science alone could 'prove' a truth, seems much less plausible than was the case a few decades ago. The enlargement of the term 'reason' to include other forms of knowledge than scientific knowledge is a feature of the thinking of not a few philosophers of modern times. This seems to me to be one of the great challenges facing modern philosophy.

In spite of all this, popular understanding of what science means and of its alleged opposition to religion has not changed correspondingly. The 'myth' persists in many quarters that a scientific view of the world and the religious view of the world are irreconcilable and that science and faith are simply incompatible. That is why it is still necessary to challenge those views, as expressed, in the name of science, by people like the late Bertrand Russell, or the contemporary Richard Dawkins.

Could There Be Another Galileo Case?
Could another 'Galileo case' arise in the future? Pope John Paul does not exclude the possibility of conflicts between science and faith in the years to come. He asks that dialogue should take place between scientists and theologians, and that each side should be well informed about what their critics are really saying, instead of accepting caricatures of their views, as often happens; and that at the same time, they should accept the limits of their own respective competencies. The possibility of conflict is clearly present; faith and science exist in the same world and relate to the same empirical and historical events. Jesus Christ can be examined as a person in history. He is also an object of faith. It would be a foolish scientist who would reject the Virgin Birth of Christ because parthenogenesis contradicts the laws of science. It would be a foolish Christian who would dream of confirmation of faith in the Virgin Birth by some future research in biogenetics. The Incarnation is a unique event, uniting human nature with God and uniting time with eternity in one single person; and, of its nature, it can have no precedent in the past and no repetition in the future. The

resurrection of the dead is scientifically impossible; yet the Christian knows it is true. Christian faith knows many examples of objects of faith which could also, at the same time, be the object of scientific research. Theoretically, it would be possible to subject the consecrated Bread of the Eucharist to scientific tests, and to demonstrate by experiment that it is, in scientific terms, ordinary bread. This would not disturb the faith of a well-informed Catholic, who knows, by divine revelation, that the Risen Body of Christ is outside the laws and limits of space and time and therefore, as present in the Eucharist, is, by definition, beyond the limits of science.

Conflicts between science and faith in the past sometimes arose because some scientists put forward a scientific explanation of phenomena as replacing and indeed excluding a philosophical or theological explanation. Believers were confronted with a choice: evolution *or* creation, brain cells *or* soul; whereas both are required for an adequate account of reality and the true accounts are complementary, not contradictory.

There will not be conflict between science and divine revelation so long as science knows and respects the limits of its own competence, and so long as theologians and pastors know clearly what is divinely revealed, and can distinguish this from merely human interpretations of what is revealed.

Two of the contributors to the *Cambridge Companion to Galileo* believe that new 'Galileo cases' could arise in the future. Richard Blackwell entitles his chapter, 'Could there be another Galileo case?'[55] He suggests that evolution and the origin of the human species is one possible locus for such a case, and he instances the Holy Office's interdiction from publishing placed on Teilhard de Chardin as a form of 'Galileo case'. He points to reductionist theories of mind as another possible area of contradiction. Finally, he points to the case of Monsignor Pio Paschini's officially commissioned study of Galileo's life and works, which was rejected by the Holy Office as 'inopportune' for publication in 1944, and was eventually published in 1965, after Paschini's death, but in substantially altered form. These cases he suggests, may be taken as an indication that 'intellectual honesty and freedom of thought may still not be strong enough in the Church to prevent the recurrence of another clash between science and religion, one similar to the Galileo affair'.

I cannot disagree with the comments made about Paschini and the changes made posthumously to his text before its publication. This behaviour was entirely reprehensible. It is acutely embarrassing to find persons working in the service of the Church who fall short of the ethical standards universally accepted by their counterparts who work in the secular world. I do suggest, however, that the phrases, 'intellectual honesty' and 'freedom of thought' are inappropriately used in this context. I should think that what Fantoli calls inertial forces and reluctance to admit errors on the part of one's institution were the relevant factors. As for Teilhard de Chardin, I suggest that it was his theology and especially his christology, rather than his science, which may have caused concern to the Holy Office at the time. I also venture my own opinion that Teilhard was as much poet, or even mystic, as he was either scientist or theologian; his language was often rhetorical and imprecise and his works, brilliant and inspirational *tours de force* though they often were, frequently failed to convince either scientists or theologians. Nevertheless, the robust defence of the orthodoxy of Teilhard by Father (later Cardinal) de Lubac should not be forgotten.

In a chapter in the *Cambridge Companion* book, entitled, 'The gods of theologians and the gods of astronomers',[56] Marcello Pera suggests four areas where, in his view, science and faith could in future clash. They are:

1 The universe is finite in time
2 Life in the universe stems from inorganic matter.
3 Life originated in more than one place.
4 Psychical life is reducible to biological and social conditions.

With respect, taking each point in turn, I would, by way of reply, comment as follows. The question of the finitude of the universe demands clarity about language on the part of philosophers and theologians and Scripture scholars, on the one hand, and on the part of scientists on the other. Eternity is not temporal infinitude; it is, in the literal meaning of the term, time-less-ness; it is totality-of-being-in-simultaneity, though such a state is beyond our human ability to express adequately in words or even to imagine. As we have already noted, Aquinas had no philosophical or conceptual difficulty about a created but nevertheless temporally non-finite universe. From this point of view, 'beginning' can be a way of describing time-conditioned, as distinct from eternal, being. Where there is time, there is world, and when there is world, there is time. A sufficient Cause of the world is necessarily outside of time. Creation, as divinely revealed, is not the same reality as 'creation' in scientific usage. Creation, as philosophers in the thomistic tradition understand it, is the total dependence of the universe for the totality of its being, throughout the totality of its duration, be that limited or unlimited in time, on the creating and sustaining power of God. I have already quoted relevant passages from

Aquinas in this regard. Creation in faith terms cannot be either demonstrated or refuted by astronomy. Creation, as faith knows it, is in principle compatible either with 'big bang' theories or 'continuous creation' or other possible scientific theories of the universe.

As regards Pera's propositions 2 and 3, I suggest that a real clash between science and faith could arise only from confusion about language and methodology, whether in interpreting the Bible or in interpreting science. Due attention by both scientists and theologians to Pope John Paul II's exhortation to observe the limits of their respective competencies would, I believe, go far towards resolving, to the satisfaction of both sides, any apparent conflicts which might arise.

There certainly will continue to be conflicts between science and faith in the field of biogenetics; but these, I believe, will be primarily moral and ethical conflicts; and objections on moral and ethical grounds to some biogenetic experiments and to some of the applications of biogenetic research will come, not only from the Catholic Church, but also from many outside the Catholic or the Christian tradition and will come even from within the scientific community itself. The basic philosophical question, indeed the fundamental human question, still is and will remain the old question of the Greek philosopher – mystic, Plotinus: 'hémeis de, tines de hémeis'; 'we humans, who are we anyhow?' The scientist, Erwin Schrödinger, as I have pointed out, said that this is the question which underlies science itself. Perhaps the basic moral question is: 'what or who is to count as a human being?' The answer to these questions appertains to philosophy, to morality and to religion. Science has its contribution to make, but cannot of itself give a final and definitive answer except in cooperation with philosophy and faith. Catholicism never asks us to choose between science and faith; as Pope John Paul II puts it in the opening words of his encyclical *Fides et Ratio*:

> Faith and reason are like two wings on which the human spirit rises to the contemplation of truth.[57]

With regard to proposition 4, it seems to me that the Pope's words about 'complexity', and about the need for 'different models' to account for 'the rich variety of reality' are much more meaningful for and acceptable to today's scientists, and especially to today's neurophysicists, than they may have been in the past. These different models are complementary to one another, and scientific 'models', properly understood, are compatible with the religious and spiritual 'models'. Indeed, many scientists believe that scientific models need to be complemented by the religious model, in order to give a full account of reality in its inexhaustible variety and complexity. I believe that complementarity, rather than conflict, will be the way forward for science and for faith in the future. Wittgenstein expressed a profound truth when he wrote:

> When all possible scientific questions have been answered, the questions of life have not been touched at all.[58]

Church and Science
It was a bad day for the Church when Galileo was obliged to declare that:

> I … abandon completely the false opinion that the sun is at the centre of the world and does not move, and that the earth is not the centre of the world and moves.

However, it would be a sad day for science to misrepresent important aspects of this story, replacing fact with myth and reading Galileo as if he were a nineteenth- or twentieth-century scientist, and as if the theologians of the Inquisition were mere 'flat-earthers', determined, at all costs, to uphold the centrality and immobility of our human planet, believing that otherwise the whole edifice of Christian faith would crumble. We have repeated frequently that, after, as before, his condemnation by the Inquisition, Galileo remained a convinced and devout Catholic, and a devoted and loyal son of the Church; and many Catholic intellectuals continued to hold his scientific work in admiration and to hold his person in high esteem.

My review of the Galileo case is a summary one and depends entirely on the work of others. I conclude it by repeating that it was not primarily Galileo's astronomy which created problems for the Catholic Church at the time. The prime reason which keeps being repeatedly adduced for the condemnation of Galileo was that, in the words of Cardinal Bellarmine 'it injures our holy faith by contradicting the Scriptures'.

In the teaching of the Second Vatican Council, and in the resolute implementation of its renewal programme by Pope Paul VI, and Pope John Paul II, a whole new future for relationships between the Church and science, and indeed between the Church and modern culture, is presaged. Pope Paul VI, the Pope of the Council and of conciliar renewal, led the way. In this whole context, the courage, commitment and intellectual integrity by which

Pope John Paul II pursues his own vision for the Church in the third millennium – a vision based on the Gospel and on the Second Vatican Council's teaching – provide an excellent augury for that future. As I have said earlier, in his advance preparation for the Great Jubilee of the year 2000, Pope John Paul II spoke of the need for the Church to acknowledge and openly admit and repent of 'past errors and instances of infidelity, inconsistency and slowness to act'. 'Acknowledging the weaknesses of the past,' he declared, 'is an act of honesty and courage' which strengthens the faith and enables the Church to face the new problems of the present and the future more effectively.[59] The thoroughgoing way in which he personally has done this in the case of Galileo has few precedents. It is surely a firm commitment that such 'errors' and such 'slowness to act' in correcting them will never occur again.

The 'Galileo Affair' remains, as Fantoli remarks in the concluding sentence of his book, 'a severe lesson in humility to the Church and a warning, no less rigorous, to the Church, not to wish to repeat in the present or in the future the errors of the past, even the most recent past'. That such words, and a book about Galileo so frank and so honest as his, could be published by the Vatican Observatory and printed by the Vatican Press, is one further augury, promising a new era of constructive and mutually enriching dialogue between the Church and science.

Chapter III

CHURCH AND WORLD

The debate between faith and science, often coterminous with the debate between faith and reason, is at many points beclouded by preconceived ideas about Christian faith which have become deeply imbedded in modern secular culture. Christianity is often accused of being 'otherworldly' because it allegedly gives prior, if not sole, value to 'another world' than this one. It is accused of despising the body and caring only for the soul; of neglecting life and work in time because its focus is on eternity; of disparaging reason because it regards faith alone as the source of truth; of dispensing with evidence and relying only on authority. Christianity is challenged by critics to choose between incompatible opposites: this world *or* the next; the mortal body *or* the immortal soul; reason *or* faith; time *or* eternity; evidence *or* authority; evolution *or* creation. I wish in this chapter to look at some of these challenges and to suggest that it is not a question of 'either/or' but of 'both/and'; sometimes, indeed, of cherishing the first-named reality in each couplet all the more because of the priority given to the second.

'Other-Worldliness': Nietzsche and Marx

It has long been charged against Christianity that it is world-evading, world-denying, other-worldly, escapist. Since Nietzsche and especially since Marx, this has become a cliché of atheist and secular humanist literature. Here are some of Nietzsche's aphorisms on this theme, from *Thus Spake Zarathustra*. I quote from the Tille/Bozman translation in the Everyman's Library, which brings out the quasi-biblical style of Nietzsche's writing:

> Thus speak I to other-worldlings.
> Suffering and impotence created all such other worlds; and
> that brief illusion of happiness which only the most
> wretched can know.

★★★

A weariness that, with a single leap – a death-leap, –
desireth to reach the Ultimate, a poor, ignorant weariness
that willeth not any more to will; this created all gods and
otherworlds.

★★★

Believe me, my brethren, it was the body when it despaired
of the body that groped with the fingers of a besotted mind
at the ultimate barriers.

★★★

Believe me, my brethren, it was the body which despaired of
earth that heard the womb of Being call upon it.

Then it sought, with its head, and not with its head only,
to break through the ultimate barriers – beyond, into 'the
other world'.

★★★

But this 'other world' is well hidden from mankind, this dehumanized
inhuman world that is a celestial nothingness: and the womb of Being
speaketh not unto man, save as man …
    Yea, this I, with its contradiction and confusion reporteth most truly
of its being – this creating, willing, valuing I that is the measure and
the value of things …

★★★

A new pride have I been taught by mine I; and this I teach to man: no
more to bury the head in the sand of heavenly things, but freely to
carry it, a head of earth, giving meaning to the earth … The sickly
and the dying have despised the body and the earth and have invented
heavenly things and redeeming blood-drops … They sought escape
from their misery, and the stars were too remote from them. Then
they sighed: 'Would there were heavenly paths by which to steal into
another life, another happiness' – and they invented for themselves
their bypaths and their little sips of blood! …

Too well I know what they themselves must believe. Verily, not in
otherworlds nor in redeeming blood-drops: but even they believe
most in the body, and their own body is for them the absolute thing.

Yet a sickly thing they find it: and fain would they slough their skin. Therefore they hearken to the preachers of death and themselves preach otherworlds.

***

Hearken ye, rather, my brethren, to the voice of the healthy body: it is a truer and a purer voice.

***

More truly and purely the healthy body speaketh, the perfect the foursquare, and it speaketh of the meaning of this earth.[1]

Much of modern atheistic humanism is expressed here. Its charge against religion is that it is sick; infected by a death-wish; compensating for inadequacy on earth by dreams of fulfilment in heaven; excusing passivity and indolence and inaction in this life by the alibi of life abounding in the next; resigned to suffering, evil and injustice in this world by the conviction that good can triumph only in the other world. Nietzsche speaks of 'contemners of life, moribund and themselves poisoned.'[2]

Nietzsche-inspired modern atheism still tries to force us to a choice: *either* this life *or* the next life; *either* this world *or* the other world; *either* time *or* eternity; *either* man *or* God. Sartre, in some respects a Nietzsche *redivivus*, re-echoes Nietzsche distinctly when, in *Le diable et le bon Dieu*, he makes Goetz say: 'If God exists, man does not exist. If man exists …' Sartre does not complete the sentence; he obviously sees no need to do so.

The accents of Nietzsche are, of course, very similar to those of Karl Marx. Nietzsche, in support of his charge that Christianity substitutes resignation for struggle, had cited the Lutheran formula, 'faith without good works'. So, in his turn, does Marx. In *The German Ideology*, Marx finds the essence of Christianity in the text from the Letter to the Romans (3: 28) which he quotes in the form: 'Therefore is a man justified by faith without deeds.' Christianity is therefore, Marx argues, an alibi for inertia; a folding of hands in defeatist prayer when they should be used instead for work, for struggle, for revolt. For Marx, Christianity is a sanctimonious blessing pronounced upon the iniquities of the world in the name of the paralysing persuasion that since God is in His heaven, nothing on earth ultimately matters. The Christian cherishes his consoling, pious thoughts, nurses his delicate but beautiful soul; and the worse the world gets, the more he withdraws from it, for fear lest action disturb contemplation, or human effort take the place of prayer, or revolution replace God. Thus, Marx contends:

> The transference of the adjustment of all earthly infamies to heaven justifies the further existence of those infamies ... The struggle against religion is mediately the fight against *the other world*, of which religion is the spiritual *aroma*.
>
> Religious distress is at the same time the *expression* of real distress and the *protest* against real distress. Religion is the sign of the oppressed creature, the heart of a heartless world, just as it is the spirit of a spiritless situation. It is the *opium* of the people.
>
> The abolition of religion as the illusory happiness of mankind is required for their real happiness. The demand to give up the illusions about its condition is the *demand to give up a situation which needs illusions*. The criticism of religion is therefore in *embryo the criticism of the vale of woe*, the *halo* of which is religion.[3]

I have quoted Nietzsche and Marx at some length, because their attitudes have become so much a standard part of the modern secular mentality, and indeed have had such influence on contemporary mass culture. They are part of the vocabulary of modern mass media in every Western country, including our own. Christianity today has to be preached, defended, lived in face of the challenge of these ideas. It is these preconceptions, in fact, that form the unstated but ever-present background to the Second Vatican Council's Pastoral Constitution on *The Church in the Modern World*. It is some of these preconceptions that I here propose to examine, drawing, wherever relevant, upon the conciliar document to which I have just referred.

Semantic Difficulties

First, I want to try to point out the possibility of semantic ambivalence in Christian, or in general, metaphysical terminology, which, if misunderstood, can lend a certain plausibility to this sort of charge. We do speak of 'the after-life', or 'the next-life'; 'the other world'; we stress the distinction between soul and body, the tension between flesh and spirit; we preach the mortification of the senses and detachment from the things of this world. But it is imperative not to misunderstand this terminology.

Let me remark, in passing, that Christianity bears the burden of an immense weight of history, much of which it has moulded, but by much of which it has been distorted. Christian thought and terminology have been used by so many, abused by so many, reinterpreted by so many; made to serve so many philosophical, ideological or political or economic systems; it has been given so many secularised renditions, it has been distorted to so many secular uses, that Christianity is made responsible for the mistakes of bad metaphysicians and arraigned for the errors of even unbelieving philosophers, not to say blamed for much of the conflicts and hates of history and of today's world, all the way from the Congo to Kosovo, from Belfast to Baghdad.

Even the best metaphysicians, however, have to struggle with the limitations of human language, and, as a consequence, they express their thought at best imperfectly and with analogies that can mislead. This is particularly true of the spatial and temporal metaphors which we are constrained to use in order to describe the ontological and moral heights and depths, priorities and ultimates of our experience. It is not only metaphysicians who have this difficulty; it is a feature of everyday speech as well. No-one is deceived, no-one thinks of applying measures of distance, time or weight, when we say that human life is 'higher' than matter; duty 'prior' to pleasure; the person of greater 'worth' than many sparrows; or goodness something 'beyond' riches or success; and integrity of greater 'weight' than popularity in assessing an artist's work. Such words properly belong to the world of space, time and matter, but such are the only words we have to describe differences in kind and value within reality. Why should it be only in respect of God that such terms arouse the taunt of a 'three-decker universe' or of an anthropomorphising of non-human reality?

Plato

Let us take the language of immortality as a case in point. Plato is said to have spoken, in this connection, of the soul's 'pre-existence' in a 'separate world of forms', before its 'imprisonment' in the body and in time. Plato is regarded as the classic dualist and the originator and model of the whole degenerate 'other-worldly' tradition in metaphysics and religion. Indeed, Nietzsche called Christianity 'the Platonism of the people'!

I am convinced that Plato is being travestied here, through a misunderstanding of unavoidable but imperfect spatio-temporal images. What Plato is describing is not an 'earlier' or an 'after' life, but the praeter-temporal aspects of this life. What he is pointing to is not a separate 'other world', but the trans-physical, metempirical dimensions of this world. It is human experience, human knowledge, human love and aspiration, here and now, in this body, in this life, but seen in their totality, that Plato is striving to encompass. He is maintaining that these aspects of human experience of life here and now in this world cannot be exhaustively described, or adequately accounted for, in terms of time and space and matter alone.

Plato's point of departure was the same as Nietzsche's – 'this creating, willing, valuing I'. Like Socrates, he held 'know thyself' to be the starting point of all philosophy. But self-reflection convinced him that in its 'creating, willing, valuing', the self is subject to standards of truth, of rightness, of goodness, which it did not invent, but discovers, of which it is not the measure, but by which it is measured. These standards, which are in me, but not of me, can be accounted for ultimately, Plato held, only as the reflection in me of the reason and will of an Other whom people call God. Plato would have accepted the first phrase of Pope's couplet: 'Know then thyself'; but he would have rejected the rest (namely, 'presume not God to scan, the proper study of mankind is man'), as evasion of the reality of the self. For to know the self fully is to know the self as God-reflecting and God-dependent; thus the proper study of mankind is God, and to 'scan' oneself completely is to discover traces of God. This is why St Augustine could find in Plato a propaedutic to the Gospel of Christ.

This, I believe, is the heart of Plato's metaphysics; it is certainly the heart of all good metaphysics. It is not, as is so often charged by contemporary critics, an impossible and self-contradictory attempt to get *outside* human experience or *outside* human language so as to enter and describe a super-human sphere of super-natural entities. It is the supra-natural in the natural, the spiritual in the material, the eternal in the temporal, the transcendent in the human, that metaphysics is concerned with. Metaphysics is a quest for wholeness of experience, for adequacy of description and for ultimacy of meaning. Theistic metaphysics is concerned with vindicating the claim that God is the indispensable condition of this wholeness, this adequacy, this ultimacy.

We humans, are, of course, often and legitimately concerned with limited ends and problems and pursuits. For these, limited views and partial explanations will suffice and indeed are necessary. This is how we come to abstract certain aspects of reality and call these 'science'; to select certain areas of awareness, and call these 'experience' of 'empirical data'; we concentrate on certain functions or fulfilments, and call these 'the world', or 'this life', or 'the healthy body', or 'the meaning of the earth'. Metaphysics is an attempt to loosen the grip of these abstractions, think to a deeper level and see farther than these verbal routines. St Augustine in the Confessions puts it in his inimitable fashion:

[God] raised me up so that I could see that there was something to be seen, but that I was not yet fit to see it.[4]

As Malebranche put it:

No. I will not bring you into a strange country; but I will perhaps teach you that you are a stranger in your own country.

Immortality

Immortality, for example, is not 'another life', or an 'after-life', to follow on 'after' this one. It is regrettable to speak of it as the 'problem of survival' and to suppose it could be tested by psychic research or verified by some sort of apparatus which might pick up spirit-radiations from spirit-space. Immortality is the depth and height and wholeness of the human life we are living now – the 'earlier part' being what we are content to call 'this life'. (We might recall in passing that, in Latin, 'depth' and 'height' shared the same word, '*altus*'.) Our life now, seen in its wholeness, cannot be destroyed by the separation of soul and body, which is physical death. It is not that we *will be* immortal when we die: we *are* immortal now. The 'next life' is begun *in this life*: the 'other world' is *also* here below. Eternity is experienced *also* in time.

It is not, of course, that we either adequately know or fully possess the 'next life' or the 'other world', or eternity, now. We have only an impoverished knowledge of it and an intermittent grasp on its reality. But eternity's relationship to time, immortality's relationship to mortality, are less imperfectly apprehended if we see them as englobing and interpenetrating time and this life, than if we think of them as following on temporally, in a time *after* time and *after* this life. So to think would be to make eternity and immortality temporal and time-conditioned, and this they precisely are not.

Indeed, we know very well that eternity has no before or after. In the classic definition of Boethius, taken over by Aquinas, it is 'the totally simultaneous and perfect possession of changeless life'. Eternity is not an endless duration in which God lives: eternity *is* God's life; eternity is God. Kierkegaard paradoxically said: 'God does not exist: He is eternal'. Aquinas was more accurate in expression, but not fundamentally different in thought, when he said that 'He who is' is the most proper of our names for God, because this best points to God's Eternal Now.

Thus, even at the natural level, immortality is a participation in the life of God; a participation that is possessed, though only inchoately, and apprehended, though only imperfectly, in this life and in temporal experience. This is why Wittgenstein was able to say that the idea of immortality became meaningful to him when he reflected that he was conscious of obligations which he could not fulfil in this life.[5] This is, of course, the heart of Kant's postulation of immortality. This latter was not, as critics have so unfairly represented it, a naïve assumption of an everlasting existence, after this one, in which we would be for ever getting better and better. It was rather the affirmation that our being cannot be bounded by time, because our experience of moral obligation is of a call to be perfect, a call which is both inescapable, and, in terms of time, impossible. For Kant, therefore, immortality is our participation now in the eternal life of God, mediated to us through morality. It is fascinating to note that a thinker so remote from Kant as Jean Paul Sartre spoke of moral obligation as 'l'impossible necessaire', 'the necessary impossible'.[6]

The dialectic of the proof for immortality is, indeed, the same as the dialectic of the proof for God. *Only immortality is enough* to explain our present being, with its longings, aspirations, obligations, its sense of limit, finitude and failure; just as *only God is enough* to explain our existence and our experience of ourselves and of the world. Indeed, I doubt whether there can be any meaningful proof of immortality which is not, at the same time, at least incipiently, a demonstration of the existence of God and of our relatedness to him. St Thomas Aquinas' proof that God is our Supreme Good is at the same time a proof, from the experience of human aspiration and need, that God exists and that man is immortal. We are immortal because only God is enough.

The Last End

The same considerations apply to the language of the Last End or *Summum Bonum* in morals, and to the language of heavenly happiness as the reward of good actions in this life. God is not the 'Last End' in the sense of something to be enjoyed 'after' this life; nor is heaven a 'reward' merely consequent on or extraneous to the choices of this life. 'Last' in this language is not chronological, but ontological. 'Last End' signifies the ultimate meaning and direction or intention of every particular choice; the total significance of any given action. It is perhaps less misleading, though still analogical, to think of it as ultimate 'in depth' than as final in time. Similarly, 'heavenly reward' is not so much the consequence as the deepest meaning and value of each particular good act as being, at least implicitly, an act of love for God.

Misunderstanding of these terms has caused many of the most tiresome and the most stubborn misconceptions about Catholic moral teaching – and not only among critics. This is represented – perhaps, alas, sometimes lived – as a form of spiritual self-interest, if not insurance policy; a camouflaged utilitarianism as calculating as that of any Benthamite; an egoism totally alien to morality. Kant is responsible for much of this misconception. But it is all a great confusion. Heaven is willed or rejected *now*, and is continually re-willed or re-rejected now, by the basic orientation of one's life and the individual deliberate choices that shape or modify or displace that basic orientation. Heaven is not 'another place' or a 'final event'; it is God known and loved. It is absurd to say that heaven is gained without any relationship to the choice we have made and make of our lives before God. Every deliberate and free action is a choice for God in, or an exclusion of God from, a particular situation; it is an option for heaven or an option for the willed absence or exclusion of God, and this is what is meant by hell. There is no virtue that is not also implicitly an act of love of God, in and through the love of the good thing chosen; and therefore no virtue that is not also a choice of and indeed an instalment of the life of heaven. *In this sense*, though only in this sense, virtue is its own reward, its own heaven. There is no vice that is not a preference of a creature to God, an idolatrous substitution of a creature in the place of God, implicitly an act of rejection of God; and therefore no vice that is not also a choice of, and indeed an instalment of, the life of hell. *In this sense*, though only in this sense, vice is its own punishment, sin is its own hell.

This is the meaning of the classical definition of sin, coming down from St Augustine: *frui utendis, uti fruendis*: that is to say, to treat means as if they were the End, to treat the Absolute as if it were relative. That would implicitly mean making a creature our Absolute End, by loving it in such a way that God is excluded from our choice. This would be implicitly to treat God as an object which can be subordinated to others, ignored, abstracted from or postponed. It is in this sense that God is our Last End; no choice may exclude Him; every act must be, at least implicitly, directed towards Him. The Last End is present in the means; is willed or refused in the choosing of the means. This is the reason for the primacy of charity in moral theology, a doctrine already affirmed in St Thomas Aquinas' doctrine of the need for at least implicit charity for any act of virtue. For each fully deliberate choice is a 'Yes' or a 'No' to God; a 'Yes, Lord, I love You'; or a 'No, Lord, I do not love You, or at least not that much, or not now, or not yet'.

Rightly understood, this doctrine of Aquinas is not *fundamentally* different from the doctrine of Kant, so frequently regarded as its polar opposite. For Aquinas' 'Final End' or 'Happiness' or 'Supreme Good' is, as I have argued, implied *in* the virtuous or dutiful choice. A good thing is good, in the last analysis, because it participates in the goodness of God. To choose it for its own sake, for its goodness' sake, is to choose it for God's sake. Kant's formula, 'Duty for duty's sake', and Aquinas' formula, 'Duty for God's sake', do not exclude one another. God alone can be the ultimate foundation for any 'sake'. In this sense, Aquinas would have agreed with Nietzsche: 'Your virtue will have you do naught with "for" and "for the sake of" and "because"'.[7] For Aquinas also, virtue is its own reward; for virtue fundamentally is an orientation of will and act towards God. It is what Simone Weil would call a form of implicit love of God.

Eternity is Now
This rather long philosophical excursus has, I think, been necessary as an introduction to my main purpose, which is to show that the Christian life is not an evasion of the temporal. The relationship of the 'other world' and 'this world', of eternity and time, is only an aspect of the fundamental relationship between God and the world, between God and us. And we know that, even at the natural level, this relationship has only one tense, the present. The historian, Ranke, said: 'Every generation is equidistant from eternity'. We can similarly say, every instant is equidistant from creation, from eternity, from God. *Now* is the moment of our creation by God. *Now* is the moment of our encounter with God. *Now* is the moment of God's judgement of us. The *'kairos'* as well as the *'crisis'* of the creature is *now*. This explains the Christian insistence on the necessity and the possibility of a death-bed repentance. Any moment is a moment for turning to God, any moment can decide an eternity. God's call is now as His mercy is now, no less at the last moment than at any moment of life. We pray: 'Holy Mary, Mother of God, pray for us sinners now and at the hour of our death'. There are three 'nows' that matter: the 'now of time, the 'now' of eternity, the 'now' of death. The three, for all of us, will some day be one. That will be our moment of truth, our particular day of judgement, but also God's moment of mercy.

Christianity and Time
Turning now to the teaching of Christian revelation about the relationship between God and time, we find that it includes but wondrously transcends the

findings of philosophy. Time has now become the setting of sacred or salvation history. It is not for chronological convenience only that we date our era from the Birth of Christ and speak of 'the year of our Lord', as our forbears spoke of 'the year of grace'. Time from the birth of Christ onward is inescapably Incarnation time, the time of the meeting of divine and human, the time of the *sessio ad dexteram Patris,* the sitting in glory at the right hand of the Father, of the Risen Lord, the King of Ages. The Fathers of the Church loved to remind us that it is our human nature that in Christ sits in glory at the Father's right hand. St Hilary said that, since the Lord Jesus ascended into heaven, 'what we are is in God'.[8] In Christ, true Man as well as very God, the last epoch of history has been inaugurated, and human history has, as it were, entered into the very history of God. This is one fundamental reason why the recurrent myths and heresies of a New Age of the Holy Spirit, superseding the Age of Christ, are false. They are a rejection of the Incarnation, a refusal of time and of history.

It must not be forgotten that it was the Bible that brought into human experience the sense of time as rectilinear and irreversible. Christianity gave unique and absolute value to one unrepeatable instant, the instant of the Incarnation of God. This, and the events in Christ's life which followed it until the Ascension, are absolute beginnings in human history. There was, of course, history before; but it was felt to be tied to the cyclical wheel of nature, doomed like nature and nature's gods to eternal recurrence. Even Virgil's famous eclogue, written in celebration of the birth of the Emperor Augustus, and beginning with the line, '*Magnus ab integro saeculorum nascitur ordo'* greeted the beginning of a new series of eras, not of *the* New Era of time.

Christianity has always held that, because of Christ, we Christians live, not just in a new, but in *the* new and final period of human history, a period which can be superseded only by eternity, because eternity, in Christ, has entered history, and history, in Christ, has entered eternity. We live in what St Paul called the End-time. The 'now' of creation, of which I spoke, has become the 'today' of the Covenant, the 'today' of the Church. Our life history has become, with our baptism, part of the New Creation, the beginning, already, of the 'new heavens and the new earth', in but beyond time. Our time becomes the time of Mass, the time of the Eucharist, in which our earthly pilgrimage is already sacramentally completed, time is transcended, and we are made one with the Risen Body which has already passed out of this world to the Father.

Let us look at these aspects of Christian time more closely. We said earlier that our relationship with God has only one tense, the present. In full

Christian truth, we should say that our relationship with God has only one dimension; and that dimension is Christ. Now all that matters is to be 'in Christ Jesus'. It does not matter when one was born or even whether one is still alive in the flesh; so long as one is in Christ Jesus. Christ transcends history, annuls death. St Paul wrote:

> The life and death of each of us has influence on others; if we live, we live for the Lord, and if we die, we die for the Lord; so that alive or dead, we belong to the Lord. This explains why Christ both died and came to life; it was so that he might be Lord both of the dead and of the living.[9]

As Raniero Cantalamessa has put it, death and life are 'merely two different ways of being with Christ'.[10]

Christ's Coming

The Christian does not say: 'God's in His heaven, all's right with the world'. He or she says 'Our Father, who art in heaven ..... Thy Kingdom come, Thy Will be done on earth, as it is in heaven'. God's in His heaven; therefore all's *wrong* with the world; because His Will is not being done in it; and all's wrong with me until I begin in earnest doing His Will and striving to make it done on earth as it is done in heaven.

Christians, above all, say: 'Christ our Lord, is in heaven; but He has left us on earth, with a mission to accomplish, with a New Commandment to live by, with a world to consecrate. And he will come again to judge us on our discharge of that mandate'. After the Ascension, as the Apostles were gazing up to heaven after our Lord, two angels said to them: 'Why are you standing here looking up to heaven? Jesus will come again'.[11] As though to say: 'Why are you standing here gazing helplessly to heaven? There is work to do for Jesus on earth until He comes again'. Jesus Himself said: 'When the Son of Man comes, will he find any faith on earth?'[12] That depends on us, or rather on our co-operation with Christ's grace. We have to keep faith with Christ, to spread faith in him, to move the mountains and remake the earth by that faith.

Camus is in the tradition of Nietzsche and Marx when he says:

> Historical Christianity puts off until after history the conquest of evil and of murder; but these are suffered here in history and must be fought here.

This is the old semantic confusion. Christian eschatology is 'after history' – but in the sense of being also the divine depths of present history. The Last Things are 'last' in the sense of being also the ultimate meaning and value of present things. It is *in this world* and *in this life* that we find and prepare for our other world and our after life. There is no eternity for us except that which we begin to live already in time. It is because the Christian believes in eternity that he or she is urged on by the love of God in time and can have no rest from redeeming time. Exactly contrary to what Nietzsche claims, the Christian feels the urge to involve himself or herself in these times, so as, by God's grace, to redeem them. The more evil the times, the greater the urgency. It is Christianity which stresses the eternal value of each passing 'now', for now is the sacrament of the present moment of encounter with Christ. It is a distinctively Christian thought that we shall not pass this way again. Camus wants a faith which 'gives all to the present'. But that is Christian faith. Karl Marx had the celebrated phrase:

> The philosophers have only *interpreted* the world in various ways, the point, however, is to *change* it.[13]

Christianity had been teaching this and Christians had been struggling to do it, long before Marx. The Constitution on the Church in the Modern World says:

> The Church teaches that our eschatological hope does not detract from the importance of earthly tasks, but rather provides new motives for fulfilling them.[14]

The Last Things Are Now
The essence of the Christian life is the living of what we call the theological or the 'theologal' virtues, faith, hope and charity. Each of these is a 'now' already inserted in eternity, in the very bosom of the Blessed Trinity. These virtues are the work of God's grace in human lives; but, though exemplified in what is human, their terminus is God. They are the earthly beginning of a journey whose 'itinerary' is towards God and whose 'journey's end' is life with God. Faith is to know God and Jesus Christ, whom He has sent; and, Christ tells us, this already is eternal life.[15] Faith is the firm possession of things to be hoped for, the conviction of the present reality of things that are not seen.[16] Faith is not an alternative for works (even for Luther, though that is not my present concern). Faith, though it is God's gift, is also struggle. Faith is the victory that overcomes the world. But the world is too much

with us, in us, and of us, for the overcoming ever to be complete, or the struggle to cease, while breath remains. We struggle, indeed, with the guarantee of victory; for as Abbot Vonier put it, 'Christ has won our battles for us, long before we were born'.[17] But we must fight to win, for the battles are our battles too; and it is not shadow-boxing; blows that beat only the air have no value either for time or for eternity![18]

Hope has the same characteristic of being the state of mind and will of one who lives here on earth with thoughts and desires fixed on heaven. Like Christian life itself, hope is poised between 'the already' and the 'not yet'; Christ is *already* here, but he is *not yet* seen face to face in all his glory, for 'hope that is seen is not hope', but confident waiting;[19] grace is *already* here and is an instalment of glory, but glory is *not yet* come. St Paul exhorts Christians to:

> Let your thoughts be on heavenly things, not on the things that are here on earth because …. The life you have is hidden with Christ in God.

Nevertheless, living by Christ's life means living in such a way as to shape earthly society into a state of readiness to receive Christ when he comes again in glory. So:

> When Christ is revealed, and he is your life, then you too will be revealed in all your glory with him.[20]

Finally, charity, the greatest of these three, is also a 'here' and a 'now' inserted into eternity. It is loving God now; and also seeing Him and loving Him in each neighbour we chance to encounter, here and now. St John says:

> If any one says, I love God, and hates his brother, that person is a liar. For he that does not love his brother whom he sees, how can he love God whom he does not see?[21]

What does this mean except that, if we do not see and serve God in our neighbour, who is His image, then we will not see or serve God at all. No prayer, no act of piety, no religious benefaction, will avail us anything without efficacious love of our fellow-men; for the Christian, God is one who 'took hold' of our flesh, and in our flesh He is encountered and served.[22] When Christ comes in judgment, it will be to question us on our treatment of our fellow men and women, His brothers and sisters. What we did for them He holds as done for him. What we refused to them, He holds as refused to Him.[23] Philip Larkin was quoted as saying: 'The only morality that interests me is one that has to do with people'. It might seem to be the only morality that interests our Lord too!

The 'Today' of the Sacraments

The Christ who sits at the right hand of the Father is also the Christ who comes. He is God who is and who was and who is to come.[24] He joins us at every point of the Emmaus Road of our lives, always 'making as though he would go further'[25] and drawing us ever with Him, beyond ourselves, to the Father.

He comes, above all, in the sacraments. He comes, not to take us out of this world, but to keep us from evil in this world;[26] to give us strength to overcome the evil in ourselves and in the world. He comes to make us, now and here, part of the New Creation which is already begun, already potent, in this world of ours. At our baptism, as at Christ's, the Spirit of God is hovering over the waters for a new scattering of darkness, a new ordering of chaos, a new destruction of the forces of evil and of death. The Church never ceases, in her prayer, to praise God for this New Creation and to dedicate herself to its advancement through the world of men and women and through the world of nature.

There is nothing in Nietzsche or in Marx to equal the 'this-worldliness' of the Psalms, and especially of the Church's use of them. Psalm 28 was initially a great cosmic hymn:

> The Lord's voice resounding on the waters,
> the Lord on the immensity of the waters;
> the voice of the Lord, full of power,
> the voice of the Lord, full of splendour.
>
> The Lord's voice shattering the cedars
> ....
> The Lord's voice flashes flames of fire.

But the Church, in her liturgy, applies this Psalm to baptism; Christ's first, then ours. She hears in it the voice which said in the Beginning, 'Let there be light'; and the voice which said above the Jordan water: 'This is my Beloved Son'. Baptism, as much as creation, is the work of the God of glory who thunders and 'flashes flames of fire'. Baptism is a cosmic event as well as a personal and spiritual one. It shares in the New Creation of the world. It makes us, in our very flesh, a beginning of God's new creation. It commits us to work to the end that this new creation, for which the world of matter itself groans and travails, be brought to its consummation in the glory of the Second Coming.

This commitment is renewed and fortified by the Holy Eucharist. The Mass is no escape from the world, no substitute for work. It is rather the consecration of the whole world of work to God. The Mass is sacred *action*. It is the prayer of a people on the march. It is our Exodus, our Pasch; our passing through this world, out of this world, but by our use of this world, with Christ to the Father. The Jews ate their Pasch in haste, with loins girt up for a journey. The Blessed Eucharist is always Viaticum, food for a journey which brooks no dallying and no postponement. It was fitting that the processional elements in our Mass were restored by the Vatican Council. They have profound significance. The Mass is also mission. *'Ite missa est'* 'Go, the Mass is ended', can also mean, 'Go, live your Mass; go pray your work; go consecrate the world'. The Vatican Council's Constitution on The Church in the Modern World says:

> Our Lord left us a guarantee of our hope and food for our journey in the Sacrament of Faith, in which elements taken from nature, grown by the work of men and women, are changed into His glorious Body and Blood, in a banquet of fraternal communion which is a foretaste of the heavenly Banquet.[27]

In the Eucharist, heaven and earth meet, the eternal and the temporal fuse. In it, our worldly toil is already in principle finished, our earthly journey already completed. For he whom we offer, he whom we receive, is already, in our flesh and for our sakes, in the Peace of the Father in the unity of the Holy Spirit. Our work goes on, but with the conviction that it has eternal value; our struggle and suffering go on, but with the assurance that they are the birth-pangs of the New Creation; our upward journey resumes, but with the certainty that it cannot fail now because our Christ has reached the summit and we, like mountain climbers to their Sherpa guide, are tied to him by faith and baptism. Our Lord says: 'He that eats my flesh and drinks my blood, has everlasting life'; (not, 'will have' it, but *'has it'*, now.) 'And I will raise him up on the last day'.[28] Already, through our communion with Christ's Risen Body, the Resurrection is at work in our mortal body.

The writer of the Letter to the Hebrews, recalls the 'Today' of the Convenant, from Psalm 94, and applies it to Christ's celestial Sacrifice:

> Every day, so long as this 'today' lasts, keep encouraging one another, so that none of you is hardened by the lure of sin.[29]

God, in the psalm, warned sinners that they would never enter God's rest. The Letter goes on to warn us that we too could fail to enter the rest where Christ has already entered before us:

> We must do everything we can to reach this place of rest, or some of you might copy this example of unbelief.[30]

The message of the Eucharist is not rest, but haste, not repose, but struggle and toil. In the Eucharist we touch and receive the Body which is at rest; but what it shows the Father for our sake is not its rest, but its wounds. St Ignatius Loyola asked us to pray that we may learn 'to fight and not to heed the wounds, to labour and to look for no reward except that of knowing that we do God's holy will'.

Nietzsche spoke contemptuously, blasphemously, of 'redeeming blood-drops'. But the Eucharist makes present for us the Blood which makes us responsible for the life and death of our brothers and sisters. For it is the Blood shed 'for us and for all so that sins may be forgiven'. It sends us out to bring in the others. Péguy said: 'What will He say to us if we come to Him without the others?'

Nietzsche cried, on the last page of *Thus Spake Zarathustra*: 'Do I strive after *happiness*? I strive for my *work*.' But this is the message of Christianity. St Thérèse of Lisieux understood it well. She wanted nothing of an eternity of rest. She said

> If my desires are granted, my heaven shall be spent on earth until the end of the world. Yes, I wish to spend my heaven in doing good on earth ... I shall not be able to take any rest until the end of the world and so long as there are souls to save. But when the Angel shall say, 'Time is no more', then I shall rest, then I can rejoice; for then the number of the elect shall be complete and they shall all have entered into their joy and their rest.[31]

Zarathustra's last words are:

> 'This is *my* dawn, *my* day beginneth. Come up, then, come up, thou Great Noon.' Thus spake Zarathustra, and issued forth from his cave,

glowing and strong as the sun at dawn coming forth from the dark mountains.[32]

Poor Nietzsche! His most majestic rhetoric, his most moving poetry, were anticipated long before by the voice of the Church, extolling the nobility of the baptised body, speaking the meaning and glory of this earth, renewed in Christ.

This voice is nowhere better heard than in the Church's use of the psalms. Father Louis Bouyer has written:

> Whenever people cease to pray the psalms, the atmosphere of prayer in which the New Testament was composed seems to be lost, and with it the genuine understanding of all the New Testament brought us which is most radically new.[33]

For example, Psalm 18 was originally a great hymn of the Universe.

> There He has placed a tent for the sun;
> it comes forth like a bridegroom coming from his tent,
> rejoices like a champion to run its course.
>
> At the end of the sky is the rising of the sun;
> to the furthest end of the sky is its course.
> There is nothing concealed from its burning heat.

The Church, with her extraordinary Christo-cosmic realism, sees the sun as a symbol of Christ, coming forth eagerly, joyously from Mary's womb, impatient to run his course through human history until his Ascension; and still from heaven irradiating everything temporal with the eternal fire of his love.

Christianity indeed holds that this world, isolated from God, is nothing. But it holds, with St Thérèse, that what pleases God most is to bend down to this nothing of ours and transform it into fire. The words are re-echoed by Teilhard de Chardin when, in his *Mass on the World*, offered in prayer and desire at a time when he was unable to celebrate Mass, he cried out:

> I shall go up this morning in thought to the high places of the world; and, child of the Earth that I am, as well as child of Heaven, and in virtue of my priesthood, and which you have given to me, I shall, on

all that is to be born this day and on all that and to die this day, invoke your Fire.[34]

Whether consciously or not, Teilhard was giving the Christian answer to Zarathustra.

Contempt for the World?

Nevertheless, Christian vocabulary does give some prima face plausibility to the charge that it despises the world and worldly tasks. Many Christian spiritual classics speak of human 'nothingness' and ask us to pray for and strive towards an attitude of contempt for one's self and for this world. Indeed there are many hallowed phrases of Christian spirituality which seem to dismiss 'this world', 'the body', 'the flesh' as worthless, if not outrightly sinful. One thinks of St Augustine's classic phrase, '*amor Dei usque ad contemptum sui*', 'love of God to the point of despising self', as the opposite to '*amor sui usque ad contemptum Dei*' 'love of self to the point of despising God'. One thinks of the '*contemptus mundi*', or '*fuga mundi*', 'contempt for the world' and 'flight from the world', of much of the monastic tradition. One thinks of the Christian insistence on 'mortification' (literally the 'putting to death') of the self. How can such phrases be reconciled with any respect for one's body or any proper self-esteem, or with any this-worldly mission or indeed with any authentic humanism?

I begin with the phrase '*contemptus mundi*', 'contempt for the world'; I wish to examine its meaning more closely. It is undeniably a recurring theme of Scripture and of Christian tradition that we must despise this world and indeed 'hate' it, avoid contamination by it, 'die' to it, in order to gain the world to come. The calls to 'contempt for the world', or 'flight from the world', have been recurring notes of Christian spirituality for much of Christian history. 'Worldliness' has been a term of reproof for Christians and 'other-worldliness' a term of praise, indeed a sign of saintliness. Is it only now that Christians are discovering – or pretending to discover – 'this world', the world of men and women, of science and technology, of work, of service, of concern for the earth and for human progress, of work for peace, justice and the integrity of creation? Is this discovery not an opportunistic attempt to climb aboard the liberal or humanist band-wagon rather than be run over by it? Many critics of Christianity would immediately answer 'Yes' to the second question. But a significant number of Christians would answer 'Yes', with varying nuances, to the first. It is a plain fact that many writings, which until lately ranked among the classics of Christian spirituality, have been found unreadable and pronounced intolerable by many committed Christians and Catholics, and especially the young, in recent decades. One outstanding example is *The Imitation of Christ*,[35] which formerly was commonly called, simply *The Imitation*. I shall try to show that this is a hasty judgment, based largely on what in the last chapter I called semantic confusions.

The Imitation

It is true that today's Catholic, anxious, with the modern Church and with the Vatican Council, for dialogue with and engagement in the contemporary world, if he or she opens *The Imitation* at all, will bark the shin at the very title of the first chapter: 'Of the Imitation of Christ, and the Contempt of all the Vanities of the World'. Reading on, he or she will find that the whole visible world seems to be treated with this same contempt.

> Vanity of vanities and all is vanity but to love God and serve Him alone ... This is the highest wisdom, by despising the world, to make progress towards the kingdom of heaven ... Study, therefore, to wean your heart from love of visible things and to direct yourself to the things unseen ...[36]

There is no need to multiply citations. I readily acknowledge that this language stirs, in the older among us, memories of many sermons, retreats, meditations, spiritual readings, of the past.

But let us try to look beyond words to their meaning. There is a inadequacy, an analogousness, in all human language about the spiritual; and analogy misread is misinterpretation. We have seen this already in this chapter in respect of the 'Beyond' which is also the 'Within', the Eternal which is also the Now, the 'world to come' which is also the spiritual wholeness and depth of this present world. But this linguistic ambivalence is reinforced by a shift which time and cultural change have brought to a key dichotomy in the New Testament, that of 'flesh' and 'spirit'. By 'flesh', the Bible and St Paul meant, not 'body' as opposed to 'soul', but the whole man considered in his separateness and distance from God, man as mortal while God is the Immortal; man as fickle, while God is Faithful; man as sin-prone, while God is the All-Holy. Especially, the word 'flesh' meant man as unredeemed, unregenerated, un-recreated in Christ. By 'spirit', St Paul meant, not the soul as the 'spiritual part' of man, but the whole person as made new in Christ. In the risen Christ, the New Man, man's body too becomes spirit; and bodily union between man and woman in the sacrament of marriage becomes the symbol of that which is for us the very source of Spirit, namely the union of God with human nature in Christ and the loving union of Christ with His Church.[37]

There has undeniably been from time to time a strain in Christianity which has literally despised and feared the body, and particularly sexuality, as a source of temptation and sin, the enemy of the spiritual. Some trace this to alleged Platonic influence on some of the early Church Fathers. But the Church has also been mindful of St Paul's teaching that the body is the temple of the Holy Spirit, that God dwells in the body, and that Christ has redeemed it, and sanctifies it. The whole sacramental system emphasises that the body is consecrated in baptism, anointed in confirmation and destined to share, as body, in the bodily resurrection of Jesus Christ.

But, in this present life, we are not yet fully 'in Christ', nor shall we ever be while anything mortal is left in us. This mortal life is therefore marked by a struggle between that which is 'christened', '**Christ**-ened', in us and that which is not yet '**Christ**-ened'. There is that in our soul and body which resists '**Christ**-ening' and this is 'flesh'. There is that in our body and soul which is, by Christ's saving acts and our acceptance of them, '**Christ**ened', and this is 'spirit'. The warfare between them marks the lifetime of a Christian man or woman. This tension, however, is not a soul-body dualism. It is not a contempt of the body, but a call for transformation of the body. It is not a *contemptus mundi,* but a *consecratio mundi*, a consecration of the world by the Holy Spirit. 'The World' in St John's Gospel means alternately the world which rejects Christ and must be rejected by disciples of Christ, and the world which God so loved as to send His only Son into it.[38]

When the classical spiritual writers speak of mortification of the body and contempt of the world it is always St Paul's 'flesh' as against St Paul's 'spirit' that is meant. For these writers, the 'world' and the 'body' mean creatures and the self considered apart from God and Christ, perhaps substituted for God and Christ, loved in the place of God and Christ. This is St Augustine's dichotomy: love of self to the point of despising God, love of God carried to the point of despising one's self. But this does not exclude the possibility and indeed the duty of loving God in oneself and in created things and loving oneself and created things for God, who, as Genesis tells us, looked on all that He had made and found it 'very good'. I referred above to St Augustine's classical definition of sin as *'uti fruendis et frui utendis'*. This, in St Augustine's terse language, means to treat as ends in themselves beings which are only means to the end;

that is to give to creatures the kind of love reserved for God alone and to give to God the kind of love appropriate only for creatures. If this be so, if sin is to enjoy created things as if they were God, and to use God as if He were a creature, then it will be virtue and sanctity to enjoy God in creatures and to love creatures and use creatures for God's glory. The language is, perhaps unconsciously, echoed in some sense by Kant when he speaks of using human beings as means only, rather than as ends in themselves. But St Augustine's point is that only God is an absolute End in Himself, and to treat creatures as ends in themselves is to substitute them for God and commit a kind of idol worship.

To return to the author of the *Imitation*. What I have suggested above, is, I submit, the heart of his thought. Already in his first chapter, the repeated contrast is between 'a long life' and 'a good life' – and these are two possibilities for this present life. The true vanity is 'to attend *only* to the present life and not to look forward to the things that are to come'. We could show the same for the rest of the book.

Indeed for the author of the *Imitation*, the same creatures which, apart from God, are vanity and illusion, are, seen in His light, sacraments of His presence and summons to prayer.

> If only your heart were right, then every created thing would be to you a mirror of life and a book of holy teaching.[39]

Detachment from creatures is, he writes, a way to interior freedom, a condition of attaining to

> the liberty of the sons of God; who stand above things present and contemplate the eternal; who with the left eye regard things passing, and with the right, those of heaven; whom things temporal draw not away to adhere to them; but they rather draw these things to subserve well the end for which they are ordained by God and appointed by that sovereign Artist, who has left nothing disordered in His whole creation.[40]

However paradoxical this may seem, I contend that the spirituality of the *Imitation* is not different in principle from the spirituality of *Le Milieu Divin*. Teilhard de Chardin, whom no one would accuse of being a hater or despiser of the world, writes:

One has need of everything, and one has need of nothing. Everything is needed, because the world will never be large enough to provide our taste for action with the means of grasping God. And yet nothing is needed, for, as the only reality which can satisfy us lies beyond the transparencies in which it is mirrored, everything that fades away and dies between us will only serve to give reality back to us with greater purity. Everything means both everything and nothing to me; everything is God to me and everything is dust to me: that is what man can say with equal truth in accord with how the divine ray falls.[41]

The Christian … is at once the most attached and the most detached of men. Convinced, in a way in which the 'worldly' cannot be, of the unfathomable importance and value concealed beneath the humblest worldly successes, the Christian is at the same time as convinced as the hermit of the worthlessness of any success which is envisaged only as a benefit to himself (or even a general one) without reference to God. It is God and God alone whom he pursues through the reality of created things. For him, interest lies truly *in* things, but in absolute dependence upon God's presence in them. The light of heaven becomes perceptible and attainable to him in the crystalline transparency of beings.[42]

Indeed the *contemptus mundi* of the *Imitation* is not far removed from the committed Christian's discontent with the world as it is and his or her passionate eagerness to build a world closer to God's plan of charity and justice, a world of love, community and brotherhood and sisterhood and care for the planet. In a chapter on 'The Different Motions of Nature and Grace', Thomas à Kempis uses the language of nature and grace rather than that of the world and God. In this chapter, he provides what could well stand as a programme for contemporary Christian lay involvement. The most 'radical' Christian might find the style archaic, at least in this translation, but could hardly better the content:

Nature labours for its own interest, and considers what gain it may derive from another. But grace considers not what may be advantageous and profitable to self, but rather what may be beneficial to many.

Nature loves ease and bodily repose. But grace cannot be idle, and willingly embraces labour.

Nature has regard to temporal things, rejoices at earthly gains, is troubled at losses, and is irritated at every slight injurious word. But grace attends to things eternal, and cleaves not to temporal things; neither is disturbed at the loss of things, nor exasperated with hard words, for it places its treasure and its joy in heaven, where nothing perishes.

Nature is covetous, and likes rather to take than to give, and loves to have things exclusive and private. But grace is kind and open-hearted, shuns private interest, is contented with little, and judges it more blessed to give than to receive.

Nature does all for her own gain and interest; she can do nothing *gratis*; but hopes to gain something equal or better for her good deeds, or else praise or favour; and covets to have her actions and gifts and sayings highly estimated. But grace seeks nothing temporal, nor requires any other recompense but God alone for its reward; nor desires anything more of the necessaries of this life than may serve her to obtain things eternal.

Nature rejoices in a multitude of friends and kindred, glories in noble place and descent, smiles on those that are in power, flatters the rich, and applauds such as are like itself. But grace loves even enemies, and is not puffed up with having a great many friends, nor has any value for rank or birth, unless when joined with greater virtue; rather favours the poor than the rich; sympathizing more with the innocent than with the powerful; rejoices with him that loves the truth, and not with the deceitful; even exhorts the good to be zealous for better gifts, and by the exercise of virtues to become like to the Son of God.[43]

Incongruous though the comparison seems at first sight, the 'nature' with which in *The Imitation* 'grace' is contrasted, the 'world' which St Augustine and *The Imitation* ask us to despise, would include what many secular peace activists or 'left-wing radicals' would rightly condemn as the 'military-industrial complex', or as untrammelled free-market capitalism, corporate greed and sleaze and 'aggressive accounting' scandals, such as those recently associated in media with names like Enron and WorldCom or, in Ireland, with Ansbacher-Cayman! Despising the world as it is – as St Augustine and *The Imitation* urge us to do – becomes motivation to change the world into the shape God wills it to have. Despising the selfish self is a precondition to cultivating the unselfish self, the self which loves others as much as it loves its own self and is ready to treat others and ensure that others are treated as it would wish itself to be treated. 'Flight' from the world as it is towards God leads to return to the world as needing to be changed into the shape God meant it to have. Far from being a renunciation of action in the world, it is a call to action.

This investigation of the *Imitation* has, I hope, been worth undertaking. It highlights a semantic problem very relevant to the themes we are discussing throughout this book. It also enables us to take note of the unfortunate consequences of the misunderstandings which turn many contemporary Catholics away from spiritual classics like the *Imitation*. It is unfortunate, because this book has been the daily food of so many saints. St Thérèse of Lisieux remarks that in the later years of her young life, no reading was of any help to her except the Gospels and the *Imitation*. Raniero Cantalamessa is one of those who deplore the present disaffection with the *Imitation*. He writes:

> A telling symptom of [the] decline in taste and esteem for the inner life is the fate that has overtaken *The Imitation of Christ,* which is a kind of introductory handbook to it. From being the book best loved by Christians after the Bible, it has become, in thirty years or so, the least read … The affirmation under Council auspices of the notion of a Church 'for the world' has resulted in the old ideal of a flight *from* the world being replaced by the ideal of a flight *to* the world.[44]

This is unfortunate especially because the *Imitation* propounds some of the most fundamental and inescapable principles of all Christian spirituality, indeed of Christian faith. It is unfortunate, and also paradoxical, in an age so much concerned with the existential depths of Christian living. For the *Imitation* is profoundly existential. Its impatient refusal of *divertissement* rivals Pascal. Its searing quest for authenticity resembles Kierkegaard. Its refusal of anonymous conformism, its determination to live steadfastly in face of death, anticipates Jaspers or Heidegger. Above all its biblical and eucharistic orientation brings it close to the Second Vatican Council and to contemporary theology. In brief, the *Imitation* is overdue for rehabilitation. It can help us to escape from distortions of the Second Vatican Council's call for Christian involvement in worldly tasks, noble and necessary and indeed essential as these are. It anticipates the Council's call to Christians to recentre their lives on Christ, who alone is the Holy One and through whom all life and all holiness come to us from God the Father through the working of the Holy Spirit.[45] The *Imitation* is fully in line with the call addressed by

Pope John Paul to the whole Church at the approach of the new millennium to recentre everything on Christ, and his insistence, as the new millennium dawned, that we shall be saved, not by a formula, but by a Person, the Person of Christ, and that we make a fresh start with Christ, contemplating his Face, and striving towards holiness, as we enter the 2000s.[46]

Attachment-Detachment

Attachment and detachment, concern and 'contempt', involvement and indifference, the magnetic poles of Christian spirituality, are stressed equally and with remarkable similarity by Thomas à Kempis and Teilhard de Chardin. No writer on the subject of Church and world should neglect or minimise the message of either. The joint affirmation of the Kingdom of God and the Kingdom of the world, is inseparable from Christian faith; the tension between Church and world is an essential part of Christian life. St Ignatius describes it in the *Spiritual Exercises*, as the choice between two standards, the standard of Jesus Christ and the standard of Lucifer, the latter rallying behind it all whose works in the world are evil. Jesus Christ said to his followers 'seek first the Kingdom of God and his righteousness'; but he added: 'and all those other things will be given you as well'.[47] 'These other things' include, in St Paul's words:

> everything that is true, everything that is noble, everything that is good and pure, everything that we love and honour, and everything that can be thought virtuous or worthy of praise.[48]

Elsewhere St Paul writes:

> As his fellow-workers, we urge you not to let your acceptance of his grace come to nothing. As he said, 'At the time of my favour I have answered you; on the day of salvation I have helped you'; well, now is the real time of favour, now the day of salvation is here. We avoid putting obstacles in anyone's way, so that no blame may attach to our work of service; but in everything we prove ourselves authentic servants of God; by resolute perseverance in times of hardships, difficulties and distress; when we are flogged or sent to prison or mobbed; labouring, sleepless, starving; in purity, in knowledge, in patience, in kindness; in the Holy Spirit, in a love free of affection; in the word of truth and in the power of God; by using the weapons of uprightness for attack and for defence: in times of honour or disgrace,

blame or praise; taken for impostors and yet we are genuine;
unknown and yet we are acknowledged; dying, and yet here we are,
alive; scourged but not executed; in pain yet always full of joy; poor
and yet making many people rich; having nothing, and yet owning
everything.[49]

What I mean, brothers, is that the time has become limited, and
from now on, those who have wives should live as though they had
none; and those who mourn as though they were not mourning;
those who enjoy life as though they did not enjoy it; those who have
been buying property as though they had no possessions; and those
who are involved with the world as though they were people not
engrossed in it. Because this world as we know it is passing away.[50]

The early Church was penetrated with this bi-polar passion. The Epistle to
Diognetus, written within some fifty years following the New Testament
period, says:

Christians are not distinguished from the rest of mankind either in
locality or in speech or in customs. For they dwell not somewhere in
cities of their own, neither do they use some different language, nor
practise an extraordinary kind of life ..... But while they dwell in cities
of Greeks and barbarians as the lot of each is cast, and follow the
native customs in dress and food and other arrangements of life, yet
the constitution of their own citizenship, which they set forth, is
marvellous, and confessedly contradicts expectation. They dwell in
their own countries, but only as sojourners; they bear their share in all
things as citizens, and they endure all hardships as strangers. Every
foreign country is a fatherland to them and every fatherland is foreign
..... Their existence is on earth, but their citizenship is in heaven. They
obey the established laws, and they surpass the laws in their own lives
..... In a word, what the soul is in a body, this the Christians are in the
world ..... The soul is enclosed in the body, and yet itself holds the
body together; so Christians are kept in the world as in a prison-
house, and yet they themselves hold the world together ..... So great
is the office for which God has appointed them, and which it is not
lawful for them to decline.

Bishop John Robinson, who quoted this passage[51] spoke, almost as Teilhard
de Chardin spoke, of the Christian's extraordinary combination of

'detachment and concern', where Teilhard had spoken of 'passionate indifference'. It is important to discuss further the question of whether this attitude is conducive to or compatible with genuine commitment to the betterment of the world and of our fellow-human beings. Humanists and socialists would probably insist that 'detachment' is incompatible with concern; and some Christian activists might agree. At first glance, they would seem to have cause. Christians might seem committed to a sort of systematic insincerity or bad faith or 'ulterior motives'. Do they simply *use* this world as an opportunity for gaining merit for the next world? Do they merely *use* their fellow-humans as occasions of 'making acts' of charity directed, not at brother and sister humans, but at God and, ultimately at self-interest? Camus thought so; and suggested that Christian charity is merely a kind of sublimated self-interest and is incompatible with authentic human concern.[52]

It is a first principle of dialogue that we do not identify an opponent's position with caricatures or deformations of it. We Christians have sinned often in this respect in the past. I believe that, in this instance, Camus has substituted a pathology of Christian charity for the genuine thing. It is possible to 'hand out' charity as a merit-gaining reflex, without any love. Indeed, the many unhappy associations which have attached to the word 'charity' warn us that this has often happened; how else could the awful phrase have originated, 'as cold as charity'? But when this has happened, it has had nothing to do with the charity of Christ. For this means loving the other as another myself. It means loving the other as made in the image of God; and the image of God is precisely what is most uniquely personal in the other. Christian charity means loving the other as Christ has loved me; and that is with a uniquely personal caring, indeed with a love unto death like Christ's love for us. The love of the saints for the poor has always been of this sort. The Christian's concern for this world is by no means hypocritical, or self-interested. It is in the true sense disinterested and unselfish. In our own day, it is exemplified in Mother Teresa of Calcutta and in Jean Vanier and in thousands of unknown others.

The humanistic value of the Christian outlook is particularly shown in its power to preserve us from a temptation which sometimes besets social reformers, which is disillusionment leading to cynicism or despair, on the one hand, or to elimination of the socially 'unfit', on the other. So many social ideals nobly launched have failed to change the human, all too human, in humankind. So many secular utopias have been thought to justify horrendous sacrifices of human lives or to end in apparatchiks' self-serving corruption, or, in ruthless forms of predatory capitalism. One need only think of marxist-leninism of the Soviet or Maoist variety; or of the multiple miseries inflicted on the innocent poor by the waging of 'hi-tech' war which only the wealthiest nations can afford and for which in the end it is the poor who pay, often with their lives.

Christian faith and hope protect against such desertion. The Christian knows that social reform is a duty; for the Kingdom of God, which he or she works for, is a kingdom of love, and therefore of justice, equality, truth, freedom and peace. But the Christian knows also that social reform is never enough; for 'man does not live by bread alone'; 'we have not here a lasting city, but seek one that is to come'. Nothing is so constant a theme in Christian experience as that of beginning all over again. Clemenceau called the Church 'L'eternelle recommenceuse', 'She who is always beginning again'. We can never despair of any human being; for God never ceases to wait for each 'prodigal' son or daughter. But it is doubtful if we can ultimately continue to believe in human beings, as history and self-knowledge reveal them, or to love human beings, as experience of ourselves and sometimes of others shows them, unless we believe in God who made them and, who, in spite of everything, loves them and commands us to love them. Gabriel Marcel terminates his reflections on the triumphs and torments of personal relationships by saying: 'We must hope in God for the sake of us'.

The Christian's hope in human beings is unshakeable; just because it is a hope in God for humanity. The Christian knows the desperate urgency of working for humanity in God's name: it is 'now' that is the acceptable time; it is 'today' we must hasten, because it will not long be today.[53] But the Christian also knows that it will take all of human history to reap the harvest of God and to make the world ready for the Kingdom of God, and it is not for us to set a planning date for the process, or to decide, as some commissars and gauleiters and 'free-booting' capitalists have done, that some groups are weeds to be liquidated before the harvesting.

Contemplation and Action

The Church will always, of course, put God first. 'God first served', 'Dieu premier servi', is her unchanging motto. The liturgy, will always be the Church's first and last and specifying task. For the liturgy, leitourgia, etymologically, means the ergon of the laos, the work of the people, the specifying task of the people of God. It is the service of God, 'Divine Service', which is the defining work of the People of God. Priesthood, at the service of the people of God, is primarily at the service of God on behalf of the people; it is of necessity 'cultic', that is its *raison d'être*. But this does not mean that priestly work is confined to sanctuary or sacristy. The Kingdom of the God of worship is a Kingdom of love, justice and peace; worship of Him must lead to work for a society that reflects these values.

For all Christians it is not a question of prayer *or* work, contemplation *versus* work; both are essential; the two should be inseparable. Many leading Christians, and indeed the Church herself in the Vatican Council, have warned us of the great danger in our time of neglecting contemplation for the sake of action. Furthermore, they have been concerned lest our modern and thrilling rediscovery of liturgical and community prayer might lead to a lessened appreciation of personal and meditative or contemplative prayer. I shall quote in this regard Saint Teresia Benedicta, Edith Stein, then Father Hans Urs von Balthasar and the Liturgy Constitution of the Second Vatican Council.

Edith Stein was a distinguished intellectual in the pre-World War II German university world, and a philosopher of note; Husserl called her his favourite pupil. Of Jewish background, but a professed atheist, she became a Catholic in 1922 and an enclosed Carmelite nun in 1934. She described religious life as a life totally turned towards God:

> The motive, principle and aim of the religious life is to forget oneself entirely in an utterly loving surrender to God, allowing one's own life to end and leaving room for God's life.
>
> The more completely this is realized, ever the more richly is the soul endowed with divine life. But divine life is love, overflowing, unforced, self-giving love; love which humbles itself compassionately for each creature in need; a warm, nourishing love which protects, instructs and forms us; love which mourns with those who mourn, rejoices with the joyful, and puts itself at the service of every creature so that each creature becomes what the Father wishes it to be – in a word: the love of the divine heart ...[54]

Hans Urs von Balthasar speaks of what can happen when contemplation is neglected:

> Either the sacramental principle is pushed to extremes and has a quasi-magical power attributed to it, or else mundane activities are held exaggeratedly sacred, and a kind of theology of the things of

earth set up, which ascribes to business, technology, material well-being, the State and secular culture, an over-riding place among the factors which build up and further the Kingdom of God – this view is currently held nowadays precisely where contemplation is undervalued. ... A liturgical movement unaccompanied by a contemplative movement is a kind of romanticism, an escape from time, and inevitably calls up, by opposition, the counter-romanticism of a false conception of the sacred character of secular activity.[55]

And the Liturgy Constitution of the Second Vatican Council says:

The spiritual life, however, is not limited solely to participation in the liturgy. The Christian is indeed called to pray with others, but he or she must also enter into the quiet room to pray to the Father in secret; furthermore according to the teaching of the apostle, he or she must pray without ceasing.[56]

Let me again quote the *Imitation of Christ* and Father Teilhard de Chardin. The author of the *Imitation* writes:

If, likewise, in all events, thou depend not upon things as they appear outwardly, nor regard with a carnal eye things seen and heard, but if instantly, on every occasion, thou enter, like Moses, into the tabernacle to consult the Lord, thou shalt sometimes hear the divine answer, and shalt return instructed about many things present and future. [57]

Teilhard writes, in *Le Milieu Divin*:

Were it not for these moments of more efficient or explicit commerce with God, the tide of the divine omnipresence and of our perception of it would weaken until all that was best in our human endeavour, without being entirely lost to the world, would be for us emptied of God.[58]

Christian experience teaches us that (purity of vision for the divine in things) is preserved by recollection, mental prayer, purity of conscience, purity of intention, and the sacraments.[59]

We must, in an age of activism, rediscover the importance of silence and the power of silent prayer. We read in the Book of Revelation that, when the Lamb had broken the seals of the Bible to reveal its meaning, 'there was silence in heaven for the space of half an hour'.[60] That is the soul of meditation, silent pondering in the mind and in the heart of the word of God. Indeed, in a world of noise, of rush and rat-race, our churches, monasteries, retreat-houses, hermitages, poustinias, prayer and meditation groups, become more and more a necessity for the Christian people, if not, indeed, for all who seek to retain their humanity and even their sanity, in our 'admass' culture.

This is not escapism. The late Archbishop Michael Ramsey, in his book, *Sacred and Secular*, quotes Pope Gregory the Great:

> Holy men go forth as lightnings when they come forth from the retirement of contemplation to the public life of employment. They are sent and they go, when from the secrecy of inward meditation they spread forth into the wide space of active life. But after the outward works which they perform, they always return to the bosom of contemplation, there to revive the flame of their zeal and to glow as it were from the touch of heavenly brightness. For they would freeze too speedily amid their outward works, good though they be, did they not constantly return with anxious earnestness to the fire of contemplation.[61]

It was the contemplation of Pope Gregory which sent Augustine out to the wide spaces of geography and history which were to be marked by the conversion of England.

Contemplation, too, is always at the service of charity. Love of God cannot be separated from love of neighbour. Every Christian mystic would subscribe to the declaration of St John of the Cross that, if he were rapt in contemplative union with God, and were told of a poor man at the door, he would leave his trance to give bread to the beggar. This sentiment is echoed later by St Vincent de Paul, who said:

> If at a time set aside for prayer, medicine or help has to be brought to some poor man, go and do whatever has to be done with an easy mind, offering it up to God as a prayer … When you leave prayer to help some poor man remember this – that the work has been done for God.[62]

Mother Teresa of Calcutta taught her Missionaries of Charity that:

> The Holy Hour before the Eucharist should lead us to the holy hour with the poor. Our Eucharist lacks something if it does not lead us to love and serve the poorest of the poor. ...
>
> We begin the day by trying to see Christ through the Bread [of the Eucharist] and during the day we continue to see him hidden beneath the torn bodies of the poor.

Many of those who work most untiringly for the poor and marginalised, and who campaign most courageously against injustice and oppression in the world today are men and women of prayer. I name only a few, like the late Abbé Pierre, who founded the Emmaus Communities for the homeless; Marthe Robin, the contemplative, who founded the worldwide caring movement, the Foyers de Charité; Jean Vanier who set up the L'Arche communities where volunteers (including himself) live in complete equality and sharing with people with learning difficulties; Sister Helen Prejean, who campaigns against the death penalty; Father Shay Cullen, who campaigns against sex slavery in the Philippines; Sisters Drs Ursula Sharpe and Carol Breslin and others, MMM, and Sister Dr Miriam Duggan OSF, whose work with Aids victims in various African countries deserves to be better known. For such persons it is never a question of God *or* world but of world *because of* God. The same is true of many Irish Protestant missionaries who also work with the world's poorest in all the continents. Cardinal Daniélou once remarked that 'if Christians have ever neglected earthly tasks, this certainly was not because they loved God too much'. Similarly Cardinal de Lubac wrote:

> If Christians have failed time, it is not because they were too preoccupied with eternity.

Yet the 'either/or' myth dies hard. An Irish newspaper heading of July 2002, à propos of the impact of bad weather on farms and a Government Minister's measures to help farmers, reads; 'Minister moves to help farmers, while others turn to prayer'. It did not seem to occur to the sub-editor that it is possible, and indeed necessary, to do both!

Contemplation actually issues in work. There is no need to recall the place of labour, manual labour and intellectual labour, in the whole monastic tradition of the west. *Laborare et orare* was a 'monkish' motto which must be given much of the credit for making agriculture scientific and keeping Europe civilised. Aldous Huxley wrote:

> The Benedictine Order owed its existence to the apparent folly of a young man who, instead of doing the proper, sensible thing, which was to go through the Roman Schools and become an administrator under the Gothic emperors, went away and, for three years, lived alone in a hole in the mountains. When he had become 'a man of much orison', he emerged, founded monasteries and composed a rule to fit the needs of a self-perpetuating order of hard-working contemplatives. In the succeeding centuries, the order civilised north-western Europe, introduced or re-established the best agricultural practice of the time, provided the only educational facilities then available, and preserved and disseminated the treasures of ancient literature. For generations Benedictinism was the principal antidote to barbarism. Europe owes an incalculable debt to the young man who, because he was more interested in knowing God than in getting on, or even 'doing good' in the world, left Rome for that burrow in the hillside above Subiaco.

Contemplation issues too in beauty: the love of nature's beauty and the creation of beauty in art. There is no need to recall how the Church, in her desire to 'pray on beauty', as St Pius X put it, has been a constant inspirer and patron of painting and sculpture, architecture and the arts. The religious renewal of our own time is being accompanied by an overdue, but impressive, revival of religious art, particularly in the areas of sacred art, architecture and sacred music; and I am happy to say that this has, in the decades following the Vatican Council, been one of the signs of religious vitality in many parts of Ireland. Much work is still being done that is of poor quality, but the good shines more brightly in contrast.

Pope Pius X's call for people to 'pray on beauty' has lost none of its relevance. Contemplation has gone hand in hand too with love of the soil, with love of nature's beauty. *Stabilitas loci,* stability of place, is part of the making of the monk as well as of the fine herds and careful husbandry of the monastic farm and the superb craftsmanship of the monastic workshops. All good monks will re-echo Abbot Stephen Harding's statement, that he liked 'the rule and the place'. Monastic settlements were often, to begin with, places of 'horror and vast solitude'; but they were later turned into places of beauty, with names like Beaulieu, Bonne-fontaine, Clairvaux, Clarté-Dieu, la Bonté-Dieu, L'Abondance-Dieu, la

Grace-Dieu, Fleury, Vallambrosa, Fountains Abbey, Mellifont (or fount of honey).

Science, Politics, Charity

The chief duty of human beings on the earth is not toil for its own sake but the humanising of the earth in the interests of its divinising, its 'minding' by men and women, in order that they may give it back in adoration, praise and prayer, and above all in the Eucharist, to God who gave it and was 'mindful' of man, making human beings sharers in His own 'minding' of the earth which He created. As Psalm 113 puts it:

> The heavens belong to the Lord
> but the earth He has given to men.

Supremely, the duty of men and women is to win the world for Christ, in order He may give it back to His Father and God may be all in all.

To complete the creation by charity and justice – this is already prescribed in the Book of Wisdom as the task of human beings:

> God of our ancestors, Lord of mercy,
> who by your word have made the universe,
> and in your wisdom have fitted human beings
> to rule the creatures that you have made,
> to govern the world in holiness and saving justice
> and in honesty of soul to dispense fair judgement,
> grant me Wisdom, consort of your throne,
> and do not reject me from the number of your children.[63]

There is no complete answer to human problems except universal charity, for charity is the whole fulfilment of God's law, of love, of justice, equality, development, peace and care for the planet. The Church's insistence on the law and morality of charity and justice will always be the supreme *salus populi* of the world. This alone can save science from enslaving or destroying people. None other than Bertrand Russell once wrote that the greatest threat to modern man lies in 'power without love'; 'power without wisdom', where wisdom means 'a right conception of the ends of life'. Unbeliever though he notoriously was, he even suggested that the answer may lie in Christian tradition:

Christianity emphasises the importance of the individual soul and is not prepared to sanction the sacrifice of an innocent man for the sake of some ulterior good to the majority.[64]

Elsewhere, Russell wrote: 'What the world needs is Christian love or compassion'.[65]

It is a long time since Bergson declared that the frighteningly powerful *mécanique* of modern man needed a *mystique* to civilise it. The over-developed body of modern science was calling out, he said, for a 'supplement of soul'. To adapt words from the Epistle to Diognetus, we can say that Christians must be the soul of this modern world of industry, science and technology; of computers, microchips and the internet; of bio-chemistry, biogenetics and DNA.

Science, however, in itself, like everything human, is ambivalent. It can be put to good use or to bad according to the moral goodness or evil of those who possess it. Science can bring bombs to Vietnam and Afghanistan and Iraq or bring wheat to the Sahel; just as it can deliver medicine to Africans threatened with Aids – or withhold necessary drugs from them by the action or inaction of drug companies anxious to maximise profits. The same research which could feed the world's starving millions, eliminate malaria or ultimately conquer cancer and Aids, can also prepare nameless horrors of bacteriological warfare. Few have stated this better than President John Fitzgerald Kennedy, who declared that contemporary man has both hands armed with unprecedented power by the might of modern science. One hand wields the power to eliminate starvation, conquer disease, abolish illiteracy, distribute prosperity and equality of opportunity across the continents. The other hand wields the power to press buttons that will unleash nuclear megadeath or biochemical destruction of living species over most of the planet Earth. The power for good, the power for evil, come impartially from the cold ethical neutrality of the same science. Whether the good hand or the evil hand will be used depends on man's moral and spiritual choices and decisions. We seem to be approaching a time when the very survival of mankind may depend on human decisions. It is not by science alone that man comes of age, but by charity, by love, and, the Christian will add, by divine grace.

But though we see so clearly and rightly the primacy of charity, we are perhaps not so quick to admit that charity is not enough. Charity needs to be efficacious, to be institutionalised. Charity needs structures, needs science and technology, needs politics and needs legislation for social justice.

There is some truth in the poet, John Elsom's, bitter remark: 'The man who says that all human problems could be solved by love, is bluntly a fool'. It is supremely true that man lives not by bread *alone*; but it is not implied that he does not live *also* by bread. Maritain said that the great moral and political problem is to ensure that all men and women may eat their bread in justice and liberty. Giorgio la Pira, who was a member of the Secular Third Order of the Franciscans and an outstanding Christian layman, when he was Mayor of Florence, saw in politics the effective modern means of fulfilling the Christian works of mercy and living in the spirit of the Beatitudes. Social welfare does feed the hungry and clothe the naked. The National Health Service does visit and nurse the sick and the old and the handicapped. Housing legislation does harbour the homeless. Among la Pira's political ideals was that in every human community every family should have its house and God should have His. Berdyaev said:

> Bread for myself is a material problem: bread for other people is a spiritual problem.

Just as there is not a dichotomy, God *or* man, the next world *or* this one; so there is not a dichotomy, charity *or* state welfare. Charity can and must work also through state welfare and politics, both that the charity may be effective and that the welfare may be love. When we have come to the end of politics we are back at the primacy of charity. It is not just the public purse but the private heart that needs to be opened. St John says:

> If anyone is well off in worldly possessions
> and sees his brother in need
> but closes his heart to him,
> how can the love of God be remaining in him?
> Children,
> Our love must be not just words or mere talk,
> but something active and genuine.[66]

Social Justice

The social teaching of the Church, the social action of Christians, political action by Christians, were never so necessary as at the present time. The Council's Constitution on the Church in the Modern World is in part a rallying call for the social apostolate based on the social teaching of the Church. It is also a call to Christians to see in politics a way of working for the Kingdom of God in the light of the Gospel of Christ and, in this spirit, to consider involving themselves actively in political life. This, however, is not a call for a professedly Christian political party, but for political engagement, regardless of party, in furtherance of Gospel values. One of the great needs in both parts of Ireland is for young men and women of intelligence, moral integrity and commitment to social justice to become involved in political life.

The sources of the Church's social teaching are biblical. Never was the voice of justice so piercing as in the Hebrew prophets. Christ's Gospel teaches us that the terms of the last judgement are such that the social worker and the politician can hope to hear from Christ the Judge himself: 'I was hungry and you gave me to eat … I was homeless and you housed me …' A journalist has written that the campaign for debt remission on the occasion of the advent of the year 2000 had its origin, not in politics, and certainly not in economics, but in the Old Testament Book of Leviticus and its teaching about the Year of Jubilee. The liturgical community must be a community of charity as well as a community of prayer. Julian the Apostate wrote about Christians in 362:

> Why do we not observe that it is their benevolence to strangers, their care for the graves of the dead, and the pretended holiness of their lives that have done most to increase atheism.

('Atheism' was his name for Christianity!)

A report (The Ilychev Report) from a commission set up in Soviet Russia in the 1970s to evaluate the progress, or lack of progress, in the marxist-leninist campaigns against religion in Soviet Russia in 1970s, called on communists to take note of and try to emulate the charitable works of Christians. Already St Paul adjured his Ephesian converts:

> Anyone who was a thief must stop stealing; instead he should exert himself at some honest job with his own hands so that he may have something to share with those in need.[67]

The whole Church, as the Vatican Council's Constitution on the Church makes plain, must be a communion of charity, and only then will it be a light to the nations. From the Pope, whom St Ignatius of Antioch described as him 'who presides over charity', through bishop and priest to every lay man and women, we must speak, live and serve charity.

This means serving justice, which provides the structures of charity, and peace, which is the work of justice. In all this, the Constitution on the Church in the Modern World keeps repeating, the main responsibility rests with the laity. Their first task is to be holy, to fill themselves with the mind of Christ, the spirit of the Beatitudes, the flame of charity. But also they will need to acquire the relevant professional competence. Not all that they do as Christians in the world will be or needs to be mandated by the hierarchy or will be entitled to claim the Church's authority. It is part of the lay person's baptismal call to holiness and to Christian witness and action in the world.

The Church, both clergy and laity, will act in these domains with ardour but with genuine humility. Catholics must recognise, the Vatican Council declares:

> the great distance that separates the message the Church preaches from the human weakness of those to whom it is entrusted.

The Council document goes on:

> They are mistaken who, knowing that we have here no abiding city but seek one that is to come (cfr. Hebrews 13:14), think that they may therefore shirk their earthly responsibilities.... Nor on the contrary are they any less wide of the mark who think that religion consists in acts of worship alone and in the discharge of certain moral obligations, and who imagine they can plunge themselves into earthly affairs in such a way as to imply that these are altogether divorced from the religious life. This split between the faith which many profess and their daily lives deserves to be counted among the more serious errors of our age.
>
> Let there be no false opposition between professional and social activities on the one hand and Christian life on the other. The Christian who neglects temporal duties neglects his duties towards his neighbour and even towards God, and jeopardises his eternal salvation. Christians should rather rejoice that they can follow the example of Christ, who worked as an artisan. In the exercise of all their earthly activities, Christians can thereby gather their human, domestic, professional and social and technical enterprises into one vital synthesis with religious values, under whose supreme direction all things are harmonised into God's glory.[68]

Echoing this teaching, the Irish Catholic Bishops, in their Pastoral Letter on Justice in 1977, declared:

> One of the urgent needs in the Church today is to remove the partitions separating religion from life and tending to keep religion confined to Sundays and to churches. We must bring the faith into everyday life. We must take religion out into the streets, the factories, the offices and the farms. That is the only way to make our love of God and our prayer genuine ... This Letter is meant as a call to us to ask ourselves whether our concept of religion gives proper place to justice and charity, as well as to Mass and the sacraments and prayer. If it does not, then it could not claim to be the religion of the Bible or of Jesus Christ.[69]

Pope John Paul II, in his Apostolic Letter for the new millennium, warned against settling for 'a life of mediocrity, marked by a minimalist ethic and a shallow religiosity'. He called for 'pastoral initiatives adapted to the circumstances of each community', initiatives and pastoral plans which will

> enable the proclamation of Christ to reach people, mould communities and have a deep and incisive influence in bringing Gospel values to bear in society and culture.[70]

We shall return to some of these themes in the following chapter, 'The Christian and Work'.

Chapter IV

THE CHRISTIAN
AND WORK

Work is the primary way in which humans can exercise their God-given mandate to 'mind' the earth and mould it to the purposes of God, its Creator. A newspaper report once quoted a worker in London as saying, in reference to a priest's intervention in some local agitation concerning coloured immigrants, that 'it was both dirty and under-handed ... to try and bring religion into this matter'. This shows a very great misunderstanding of the nature of religion, particularly the Christian religion. Every matter is of concern for faith in Christ and faith concerns every matter. There is no situation to which one's following of Christ is not relevant. If there is something which is really 'dirty and under-handed', it is a Christian who holds that religion concerns prayer and the sacraments, but has nothing to do with work and labour relations, politics and technology and journalism, business and accountancy and banking, world peace and justice and global sustainable development.

The Popes and Labour

That Christian living belongs in the middle of weekday work and life and not at its Sunday edges only has been the constant teaching of the Church and the insistent message of the modern Popes. From Leo XIII to John Paul II they have been calling on Christian people and all people of good will to address the great global issues of peace, justice and the integrity of creation. In particular they have been analysing, in the light of Sacred Scripture, the nature and purpose and meaning of human work, and have condemned abuses of work and exploitation of workers and of the poor, whether by capitalism or by communism.

In 1891, Pope Leo, in *Rerum Novarum*, in words that would make headlines even today, denounced a capitalist system which placed upon the shoulders of the toiling masses 'a yoke little better than that of slavery itself'. It was when capitalist and imperialist philosophy and practice had reached new heights of power and success and self-righteousness that Leo vindicated the cause of 'working-men, surrendered, isolated and helpless, to the hard-heartedness of employers and the greed of unchecked competition'. Industrial barons and most politicians and economic experts were all pitted against him when he spelled out, in the face of triumphant capitalism, the right of workers to organise themselves, for their own protection, in labour unions.[1]

Pope Pius XI, forty years later, showed equal boldness and insight in criticising a capitalism of the cartel and the stock-market, which had grown more sophisticated and more callous in the interval. He called it 'the international imperialism of money'. In *Quadragesimo Anno*, written in 1931, to mark forty years since *Rerum Novarum*, Pius XI wrote:

> This accumulation of power, the characteristic note of the modern economic order, is a natural result of limitless free competition, which permits the survival of those only who are strongest, and this often means those who fight most relentlessly, who pay least heed to the dictates of conscience … the whole economic regime has become hard, cruel and relentless in a ghastly measure.[2]

In the same document, the Pope challenged a philosophy of production according to which

> bodily labour, which even after original sin was decreed by Providence for the good of man's body and soul, is in many instances changed into an instrument of perversion; for from the factory dead matter goes out improved, whereas men there are corrupted and degraded.[3]

Pope Pius XII and Pope John maintained and indeed intensified this witness of the Church to the dignity of work and its place in God's plan. In striking words, Pope Pius XII, in a broadcast message on Christmas Eve, 1953, deplored the trend whereby, in contrast to immense scientific and technical progress, there is a drastic deterioration in moral and spiritual values. As a result, he said:

[Man] is being transformed into a giant of the physical world at the expense of his spirit which is reduced to that of a pygmy in the supernatural and eternal world.

None other than the US General Omar Bradley had remarked on Armistice Day, 1948, that: 'Ours is a world of nuclear giants and ethical pygmies'.

Pope John XXIII, in *Mater et Magistra*, published in 1961 to mark the seventieth anniversary of *Rerum Novarum*, insisted that 'human beings are the foundation, the cause and the end of every social institution'. He called on lay Christians to assume resolutely their responsibilities in this world of work, of science and of technology. He continued:

[The] laity must not suppose that they would be acting prudently to lessen their Christian commitment in this passing world. On the contrary, we insist that they must intensify it and increase it continually ... Let no one imagine that a life of activity in the world is incompatible with spiritual perfection. ... It is a gross error to suppose that a person cannot perfect himself except by putting aside all temporal activity, on the plea that such activity will inevitably lead him to compromise his personal dignity as a human being and as a Christian. ... That a person should develop and perfect himself or herself through daily work ... is perfectly in keeping with the plan of Divine Providence. The Church today is faced with an immense task; to humanise and to Christianise this modern civilisation of ours.'[4]

In the same encyclical, Pope John reminded all Christians that they

are called to share in Christ's own divine life ... even when they are engaged in the affairs of the world. Consequently, their work becomes a continuation of Christ's work, filled with redemptive power. ... Thus is man's work exalted and ennobled ... It becomes a means whereby the Christian way of life can leaven this civilisation in which we live and work – leaven it with the ferment of the Gospel.[5]

In the same year, 1961, one year before the opening of the Second Vatican Council, Pope John XXIII, himself of small-farming stock in Bergamo, turned his attention also to the problems and rights of those who work on the land. In the encyclical, *Mater et Magistra*, he addressed the problem of the 'flight from the land' and asked:

> What can be done to reduce the disproportion in productive efficiency between agriculture on the one hand, and industry and public services on the other; and to ensure that agricultural living standards approximate as closely as possible to those enjoyed by city dwellers who draw their resources either from industry or from the public services in which they are engaged?[6]

Part of the answer, he argued, must come from the

> the suitable development of essential public services in country areas: roads, transport, means of communication, housing, health services, elementary, technical and professional education ...[7]

He went on:

> While it is true that farm produce is mainly intended for the satisfaction of man's primary needs, and the price should therefore be within the means of all consumers, this cannot be used as an argument for keeping a section of the population – farm workers – in a permanent state of economic and social inferiority, depriving them of the wherewithal for a decent standard of living. This would be diametrically opposed to the common good.[8]

Written in 1961, the words are of striking relevance to Ireland, North and South, in the Year 2004; but they have taken on a new urgency with the passing of the decades.

Pope Paul VI added his own characteristic note of passionate intensity to the teaching of his predecessors. He spoke, at Easter 1967, in his encyclical, *Populorum Progressio*, of the scandal of the increasing world gap between rich and poor. He called for 'a transition from less human to more human conditions':

> Less human conditions are the lack of material necessities for those who are without the minimum essential for life; the moral deficiencies of those who are mutilated by selfishness; oppressive

social structures, whether due to abuses of ownership or to the abuses of power.

He expressed his hope for

> a ... humanism which would promote a new kind of development, giving primacy to human dignity and human rights.[9]

Quoting Pope John, in *Mater et Magistra*, Pope Paul said:

> Every effort must be made to ensure that the company is indeed a true community of persons, concerned about the needs, the activities and the standing of each of its members.[10]

Speaking of the global situation and the pressing need for a more just world order, he stated:

> The present situation must be faced with courage and the injustices linked with it must be fought against and overcome. Development demand bold transformations, innovations that go deep. Urgent reforms must be undertaken without delay.[11]

In the same encyclical Pope Paul insisted that increased production is not an end in itself but must be put at the service of men and women. All programmes and plans for economic expansion

> should reduce inequalities, fight discriminations, free man from various types of servitude and enable him to be the instrument of his own material betterment, of his moral progress and of his spiritual growth. To speak of development is, in effect, to show as much concern for social progress as for economic growth. It is not enough to increase over-all wealth for it to be distributed equitably. It is not enough to promote technology to render the world a more human place in which to live ...[12]

It was this tradition of Catholic social teaching which inspired Canon John Hayes, Parish Priest of Bansha, in County Tipperary, in the archdiocese of Cashel, who died in 1957. He founded Muintir na Tíre, a movement dedicated to the betterment of life in rural Ireland and to cooperative self-help among farmers. The same tradition inspired Christus Rex, a movement for the study and diffusion of Catholic social teaching through the holding of annual conferences and the publication of a quarterly journal. This movement was active from 1943 until 1967. Its name is perpetuated and its activity, in a greatly reduced form, is continued by the Christus Rex Trust, which aims to promote periodic lectures on the various themes of this great and developing body of social teaching.

Vatican II and Trade Unions

The voice of the Popes has been amplified by the solemn teaching of the Church in Council. The Vatican Council's Constitution on the Church in the Modern World, *Gaudium et Spes*, declares that:

> In economic enterprises it is persons who work together, that is, free and independent human beings created in the image of God. Therefore the active participation of everyone in the running of an enterprise should be promoted ... Among the basic rights of the human person must be counted the right of freely founding labour unions. These unions should be truly able to represent the workers and to contribute to the proper arrangement of economic life. Another such right is that of taking part freely in the activity of these unions without risk of reprisal.[13]

Needless to say, the demands of justice are reciprocal. The rights of labour are correlative to the duties of labour. This applies not only to the duties of the individual worker in respect of conscientious work and honest workmanship. It applies also to the duties of labour groups and of organised labour generally.

Increased power implies increased responsibility. In modern society organised labour, and, frequently, unofficial worker groups, do wield enormous power. If workers were to use this power without a strong sense of moral and social responsibility, they would be committing a similar wrong and showing a similar mentality as the capitalist at his most unscrupulous. The fundamental evil of capitalism was power without morality; and anyone or any association, be it employers' organisation or labour union, which uses power without justice and without compassion is committing a basic social sin.

The social teaching of Popes Leo XIII and Pius XI and Pius XII was naturally concerned with the problems concerning industrial work in the 'dark Satanic mills' of Victorian capitalism in the nineteenth and the early twentieth century. In my own ministry as priest and bishop in Belfast I was able to hear from older people first-hand accounts of conditions in Belfast mills in the early 1900s. From older people who remembered those times I heard stories of long hours spent in clammy, steam-filled workplaces, where girls – sometimes still only children – stood barefoot in water as they spun and weaved long hours daily for paltry wages. In the early decades of the twentieth century, Sister Vincent Wallace, a Daughter of Charity who was for forty years Principal of a large primary school in the Lower Falls Road area, fought a long and ultimately successful battle to have girls released from work for a half-day's schooling; this was a great step forward for child workers in Belfast, a city which was then one of the success stories of the Industrial Revolution. On such workers was the prosperity of a few in nineteenth-century and early twentieth-century Belfast built.

Pope John Paul II on Work

Pope John Paul II was the first Pope to address comprehensively the question of work itself, its nature, meaning and purpose, its role in personal development, its place in God's plan for the planet Earth. In his encyclical, *Laborem Exercens*, issued in 1981, and marking the ninetieth anniversary of *Rerum Novarum*, he described a new revolution in the world of work and production no less important than the Industrial Revolution which Leo XIII had addressed ninety years earlier. This document marked a dramatic event in the Pope's own life; the text was complete and ready for publication on 15 May, the date on which *Rerum Novarum* was published ninety years earlier, but publication was held up by the bullet in St Peter's Square which might have ended the Pope's life. The actual publication date of *Laborem Exercens*, was 15 September 1981.

Another personal touch in this encyclical is that manual work is explicitly included in its purview. There are echoes of Karol Wojtyla's own wartime experience as a manual labourer in the limestone quarry and later in the Solway chemical plant near Krakow in the years between 1940 and 1945. His personal memories of shovelling lumps of limestone into railway cars in the quarry and hauling buckets of lime at the plant are reflected in his reference to 'those who work in the mines and quarries, steel workers at their blast furnaces, those who work in builders' yards and construction-work, often in danger of injury or death'. Young Karol Wojtyla's reflections on work and his personal experiences of workers and their conditions and their grievances, and sometimes their justified anger, culminated, forty years later, in Pope John Paul II's *Laborem Exercens*.[14] Manual work too, he here writes, has the dignity that comes from the mandate given to Adam in Genesis; the work of manual labourers, no less than that of intellectuals, scientists and technologists, advances the 'subduing' of the earth and serves human development and the 'elevating of the cultural and moral level' of the human family. The dignity of work comes from the inherent dignity of the human being, created in God's image; the whole greatness of work, he wrote in one of his poems, 'dwells inside a man'.

Pope John Paul II was a poet of some distinction in his own native Polish. Some of his poems were about work, and in these his esteem for work and for manual workers is evident. One poem, 'In memory of a fellow-worker', published in a collection entitled *The Quarry*, tells how:

> A stone smashed his temples
> and cut through his heart's chamber.
> They took his body, and walked in a silent line.
> Toil still lingered about him, a sense of wrong …

This 'sense of wrong' done to workers and echoes of the silence and unimportance to which some employers would seek to condemn them, are found in other poems. One, entitled 'The car factory worker' has these lines:

> They stole my voice; it's the cars that speak.
> My soul is open. I want to know
> with whom I am fighting, for whom I live.
> Thoughts stronger than words. No answers.
> Such questions mustn't be asked out loud.
> Just be back every day at six in the morning …

The Pope understands the anger of workers, but suggests that the anger can eventually be transcended by 'an explosion of love'.[15] Given his passion to resist wrong, it is no wonder that the steel workers of Gdansk had such fellow-feelings for this poet-Pope and that he became one of the greatest factors, if not the greatest, in the collapse of Soviet communism. Mikhail Gorbachev himself declared that 'nothing that happened in Eastern Europe would have happened without the Polish Pope'.

This Pope was well qualified to address the new aspects of work which have emerged in the last quarter of the twentieth century, such as information technology, globalisation, multinational corporations, consumerism. These offer new economic opportunities, but they also pose new dangers such as the growing gap between the rich Northern hemisphere and the poor South, unsustainable development with depletion of earth's non-renewable resources, and pollution of the planet; the exploitation of producers and workers in poorer countries by unfair trade practices maintained by rich nations and by low wages paid by the rich corporations to workers in poor countries. He warns of the danger of repeating the errors of nineteenth-century capitalism; of seeing workers as mere 'tools' of production, a mere 'workforce', a source of 'manpower', while capital remains the absolute owner of production and employers' and shareholders' profit remains its overriding aim and end. The Pope reminds us that 'the principle of the priority of labour over capital' is fundamental in Catholic social teaching, because the human being has primacy over things; the worker is a human person, and his *being* human is more important than his *having* assets. Human dignity has absolute precedence over material assets; the accumulation of profits to the detriment of workers' human dignity and human rights can never be justified.[16]

An important theme of *Laborem Exercens* is that of the 'indirect employer', namely the State and its corpus of labour laws, and the international community and its laws of trade.[17] These, he urges, must enshrine the principles of the primacy of the person, the human rights of workers and the rights of employers and their respective responsibilities and their interdependence; they should be such as to lessen, rather than increase, the disparity of wealth and income between rich and poor within nations and between the wealthy nations and the poor nations of the world. They should conduce to the progressive elimination of the great human and social evils of hunger, poverty and unemployment. These scourges are not due solely to natural causes, but are often the result of greed and abuse of power by the wealthy, and of violations of the human rights of the weak by the strong. The ideology of neo-capitalism or liberal capitalism remains tainted by the same errors as those of the old nineteenth-century free market capitalism, The Pope declares:

> The position of 'rigid' capitalism continues to remain unacceptable, namely the position that defends the exclusive right to private ownership of the means of production as an untouchable 'dogma' of economic life. The principle of respect for work demands that this right should undergo constructive revision both in theory and in practice.[18]

The encyclical, *Centesimus Annus*, written, as the name indicates, to mark the centenary of *Rerum Novarum* (1 May 1991), returns to the analysis and criticism of both Marxist communism and liberal capitalism. The Pope writes from a background of the experience of both in his native Poland. He asks whether, after the failure of communism, capitalism should become the goal of countries trying to rebuild their economy and society, and the model for Third World countries seeking to develop their economies and improve living standards. In response to the question, he admits the positive features of capitalism, such as the role it accords to business and to the rights and responsibilities of property; the space it provides for 'free human creativity in the economic sector' or what is usually called entrepreneurship; its fostering of freedom of trade and the market; and in general its respect for human freedom. But he points equally to the defects of capitalism and its failure to address adequately the problems of marginalisation and exploitation which still exist in capitalist economies themselves as well as in the underdeveloped world. He denounces 'a radical capitalistic ideology' with its blind and misplaced trust in 'the free development of market forces'. He calls for 'a strong judicial framework' which would keep capitalism subservient to ethical norms and to authentic human developments. He emphasises again the principle that private ownership is morally justified only by its effectiveness in creating 'opportunities for work and human growth for all'.[19] This would surely be a good message for the world leaders to have pondered upon as they gathered for the World Summit on Sustainable Development in 2002.

Catholic social teaching, therefore, constantly repeats the message that there is no such thing as an 'absolute and untouchable' right to ownership or to property. 'The right to property is subordinated to the right to common use of the goods of creation.'[20] As the Irish Catholic Bishops said in their joint pastoral letter, *The Work of Justice*, published in 1977:

> There is no such thing in justice and no such thing in Catholic teaching as an absolute right to do what I like with my money, my capital, my property, or my land. The proper description of Catholic teaching about property or wealth is 'private ownership with social function'.[21]

In 1983, the Irish Catholic Bishops said:

> Those who have money cannot let themselves be guided solely by the profit motive. ... money cannot 'follow its own laws' of maximum

return. The use of money is subject to the law of God … Profits must not be given priority over persons.[22]

The words are still acutely relevant to the Ireland and the world of 2004.

Capital and labour, however, need not be set in opposition to one another. Because of the primacy of the person, both capital and labour should cooperate for the good of each and for the common good of the community. The 'indirect employer' mentioned above, as well as the 'direct employer' should respect the rights of each of the partners in production, namely capital and labour, but should foster cooperation between them. The model of 'social partnership', which has developed in the Republic of Ireland over recent decades, can be one effective way of promoting that cooperation and is generally felt to have delivered appreciable benefits. It should be capable of, and it needs, further adaptation to new situations as they emerge. It should never overlook the needs and the rights of the disadvantaged groups, who do not sit at the negotiating table, just as they do not sit at the Cabinet table, but who are directly affected by the decisions taken around those tables. These groups are largely without voice and without political influence; but this is all the stronger reason why they should not be overlooked. Nor indeed should the 'social partners' ignore the needs and rights of poorer nations whose people, in a globalised world economy, are also affected by those decisions.

Attention is paid in *Laborem Exercens* to the family aspects of work and the right to a family wage. The encyclical stresses also the need for both direct and indirect employers, labour laws, and so on, to provide for adequate 'quality time' for workers, in terms of time spent with family and children, time for necessary rest and holiday time. In our age of traffic congestion, time and stress of getting to and from work, the pressures of competition and the ceaseless drive of employers to increase profits, this emphasis is very timely. It is time that both governments and employers should address the impact of such factors on marriage and family life and on the upbringing of children; they should take steps to make work more 'family-friendly'. The encyclical lays particular stress on the importance of making work more 'woman-friendly'. I allow the encyclical to speak for itself:

In many societies women work in nearly every sector of life. But it is fitting that they should be able to fulfil their tasks in accordance with their own nature, without being discriminated against and without being excluded from jobs for which they are capable, but also without lack of respect for their family aspirations and for their specific role in contributing, together with men, to the good of society. The true advancement of women requires that labour should be structured in such a way that women do not have to pay for their advancement by abandoning what is specific to them and at the expense of the family, in which women as mothers have an irreplaceable role.[23]

The family, based on monogamous marriage, is our greatest social asset; it is a prime duty of government to protect it.

Structures of Sin

Pope John Paul II has added a new theme to the study of social justice, one which is of increasing relevance to the state and future of the planet and of world peace. It is the concept of social sin. Pope John Paul II first spoke of the social aspect of sin in his Exhortation on *Reconciliation and Penance*, following the Synod of Bishops devoted to this theme in 1984. Here he stressed the social dimensions of personal sins, their repercussions on the holiness of the Church, their effects on the moral environment of the family, the community and society. This social dimension is particularly strong in the case of sins against human life, born or unborn, sins against the dignity, the rights and the rightful freedoms of other persons. Finally, there are sins against other human groups, whether races or tribes or social classes or communities, nations or continents, where individual or group decisions or actions inflict injustice, poverty, discrimination, or even unjust war, on others. Such decisions constitute 'situations of sin', 'social sins'; but these result from an accumulation of personal sins, for each of which some individual person or group bear individual and personal responsibility.[24]

This concept is developed more fully in Pope John Paul's encyclical, *Sollicitudo Rei Socialis*, or *Social Concern*, published in 1987. This encyclical was published to mark the twentieth anniversary of *Populorum Progressio*, that 'distinguished' document, as the present Pope calls it, of Pope Paul VI. Here Pope John Paul speaks of 'structures of sin', and declares that these spring from individual and group choices and decisions, which are themselves often rooted in 'the all-consuming desire for profit' and 'the thirst for power', seeking to impose one person's, one group's or one nation's will on others 'at any price'.[25] Although social in consequence, such choices and decisions are 'always linked to concrete acts of individuals who introduce these structures, consolidate them and make them difficult to remove'.[26]

In *Centesimus Annus*, published in 1991, Pope John Paul returns to this theme. He stresses the global dimension of such decisions; for they create a 'human environment' and can give rise to 'specific structures of sin which impede the full realisation of those who are in any way oppressed by them'. Attention, therefore, needs to be given to what the Pope calls a 'social ecology' of work.[27] I return to this question in my concluding chapter on 'The Minding of Planet Earth'.

Throughout this encyclical, Pope John Paul's chief concern is to ensure that work be seen as having for its purpose the human development of the worker, his or her personal, moral and spiritual growth, and the moral and cultural progress of society. Work is one of men's and women's chief means of fulfilling God's call to them in the beginning to develop the earth for God's glory. Work should be a means of spiritual growth. Man has a duty to work; man is privileged to be given through work a place in God's plan for creation and redemption. The Pope writes:

> Work is an obligation, a duty, on that part of man ... Man must work, both because of the Creator, who commands it, and because of his own humanity, which requires work in order to be maintained and developed. Man must work out of regard for others, especially his own family, but also for the society he belongs to, the country of which he is a child, and the whole human family of which he is a member, since he is the heir to the work of generations and at the same time a sharer in building the future of those who will come after him in the succession of history.[28]

Pope Paul VI had said in *Populorum Progressia*:

> Man, created in God's image, must cooperate with his Creator in the perfecting of creation and communicate to the earth the spiritual imprint he has himself received.[29]

In *Centesimus Annus*, Pope John Paul II says:

> The Church sees it as her particular duty to form a spirituality of work which will enable all people to come closer, through work, to God, the Creator and Redeemer, to participate in His salvific plan for man and for the world, and to deepen their friendship with Christ in their lives by accepting through faith, a living participation in Christ's

threefold mission as Priest, Prophet and King, as the Second Vatican Council so eloquently teaches.[30]

It is to the specific question of the spirituality of work that the remainder of my present chapter is addressed.

The Bible and Work

The duties as well as the rights of labour flow from the Christian theology of work; that is to say, from the statement, based on divine revelation and the reflection of the Church upon it, of what work is in the Christian vision. This Christian theology of work is a message of extraordinary power and richness, far eclipsing the Marxist theory of labour. Indeed, much of the power of Marx's theory is, I suggest, appropriated from the Bible and from Judaeo-Christian tradition. Not for nothing was Marx the grandson of a line of rabbis, nurtured on the messianic longings for redemption of a chosen people.

In some religious traditions, work is regarded as profane or as ignoble. In the Bible, on the contrary, work is seen as a sharing in the very activity, and indeed the nature, of God. In the story of creation in Genesis God is Himself revealed as a worker, and man's working week is to be planned on the model of God's own activity in the creation of the world, with a regular alternation of days of labour and Sabbath days of rest.

Greek religious thinking, and that of most pagan cultures, is marked by the conviction that the gods are suspicious and jealous of man's work. They suppose that the gods see man's mastery of the earth through work as a threat to their own power and control over man and over the earth. This thinking is typified in the myth of Prometheus, the hero who defied Zeus, scaling the heavens in the teeth of the gods' angry thunderbolts in order to steal fire from heaven and make it the possession of men on earth. For his impious act, the gods chain Prometheus as a prisoner in the nether world.

The fire is, of course, a symbol of man's work, culminating in the science and technology which make man master of earth and sky and space. Karl Marx took it for granted that the teaching of the Bible was identical with this myth. He assumed that the Christian God, like Zeus, kept Prometheus, namely man the worker, man the scientist, and man the technocrat, in chains. For him, Prometheus became the symbol of the Communist worker, rebel against God. He called Prometheus 'the noblest of saints and martyrs in the calendar of philosophy'.[31]

'Fill the Earth and Conquer it'

But the truth of biblical revelation is the diametrical opposite. It was the Bible which unchained Prometheus; and wherever Christian religion spread the promethean myth evaporated. In the Book of Genesis, we find God handing over stewardship of the earth to man, whom He created precisely for this purpose:

> God said, 'Let us make man in our own image, in the likeness of ourselves, and let them be masters of the fish of the sea and the birds of heaven ...'; and God blessed them, saying to them, 'Be masters of the fish of the sea, the birds of heaven and all living animals on the earth' ...[32]

Later on we read:

> The Lord God planted a garden in Eden and there He put the man He had fashioned ... The Lord God took the man and settled him in the garden to cultivate and take care of it.[33]

The two creation narratives in Genesis are complementary. God gives humans the mandate both to master the earth and to take care of it, to be both cultivators and stewards. I develop this point more fully in my concluding chapter.

Instead of resenting man's mastery of the earth and conquest of the skies, God commands them. Instead of chaining Prometheus, God liberates him. All man's work, whether it be with hoe and plough or the most modern bulldozer or giant crane, all man's achievement, from mulecart to supersonic jet, from currach to spaceship, are part of the commission God gave to man in the morning of his creation. Indeed work and industrial progress, scientific knowledge and technological power, are the result and the expression of man's being created in the image and likeness of God. It is ironic and tragic that these successes should sometimes turn man away from God, when instead they are gifts of His goodness and proof of His presence.

Atheistic Theories of Work

It is, of course, true that men can use the triumphs of their genius as pretext for blasphemy and atheism. The Bible itself knows of an atheist attitude to work and technology. The Pharaoh, anticipating Marx, taxed Jewish workers with using religion as a means of escape from work. Marx was to call religion an 'opium'. Pharaoh's charge was:

> They are lazy, and that is why their cry is, 'Let us go and offer sacrifice to our God'. Make these men work harder than ever, so that they do not have time to stop and listen to glib speeches ...
>
> You are lazy, and that is why you say, 'Let us go and offer sacrifice to the Lord ...'[34]

At the tower of Babel men built expressly to show their independence of God. They were punished with failure, not because of their architectural genius, but because of their impious and false philosophy. Babel can be seen as the prototype of modern marxist and secularist philosophies of work. Pronounced as 'babble', Babel symbolises the intellectual confusion and the failure in communications between cultures and religions which continue to bedevil human relations and to endanger world peace. It is true that the non-Judaic sources, from which the Babel narrative in Genesis probably derives, retain traces of the promethean myth; but this is alien to the rest of Genesis and the rest of the Judaeo-Christian Bible and even more alien to the New Testament.

Marxists declare that science and God are incompatible. In more recent years Soviet spokesmen claimed that space travel proves that God does not exist, since their astronauts had not encountered Him in space. Dr Edmund Leach, though not a Marxist, began his BBC Reith Lectures with the words:

> Men have become like gods. Isn't it about time that we understood our divinity. Science offers us total mastery over our environment and our destiny ...[35]

But the true God of the Bible *made* man to be like God and *called* him to 'total mastery over his environment and over his destiny', provided that this be exercised in full conformity with God's design. Why, then, need that very likeness and that very mastery be made pretexts for denying God, their Author?

Christ and Work

But it is the New Testament, above all, which reveals the full meaning of work in Christian life and in the history of salvation. The fact that Christ worked as a journeyman carpenter and was known as a man of working-class background was not merely a fact of His human history; it was also a manifestation of His Divine Sonship and a revelation of the nature of God. Jesus said: 'My Father goes on working and so do I'.[36] God's work of creation continues in His sustaining in being of the created world, and human work is a sharing in that creating and sustaining work of God. Work was also a corollary of the reality of the Incarnation; it was a necessary part of God's entering fully into human history and into solidarity with human beings, whom He has called to be His brothers and sisters. '[Christ's] state was divine', St Paul tells us, 'yet ... he emptied himself to assume the condition of a slave and became as men are. ...'[37]

But Christ became a worker also in order to sanctify work and to make work a means of salvation, liberation and sanctification for humanity. The Christian's life is a prolongation throughout history of the work of Christ. As God the Father, the Eternal Master-Worker, sent Christ, His Son, into the world to repeat and renew His work of creation and salvation, so Christ sends the Christian to re-live and re-enact the works and mysteries of the New Creation. The Christian is called to be Christ in the world, to do Christ's works in the world. He is sent to Christianise the world of work and to share, through Christianised work, in the redeeming of the world.

The Gospels and the Acts of the Apostles describe the saving work of Christ as taking place between His baptism in water in the Jordan and his baptism in blood upon the Cross. His baptism in the Jordan marked Him out as the Paschal Lamb of God who was to save His people and the world by shedding his blood on the Cross in atoning sacrifice and entering into the presence of God by His Resurrection and Ascension, so as to 'prepare a place for us'. Between the two baptisms, Our Lord's life is a constant straining urgency of upward hastening.

> I have a baptism I must still receive, and how impatient I am until it is accomplished.[38]

The whole story of the Gospels is an insistent, unresting, 'going up' of Jesus to Jerusalem, to the Passion, and through the Passion and Resurrection, to the Father. St Mark tells us:

> They were on the road going up to Jerusalem, and Jesus was walking ahead of them; and they were amazed, and those who followed were afraid.[39]

They were afraid of His determined look, of His hurrying pace. They were frightened of the fire that burned Him up. St Luke says:

> It is fire that I have come to spread on the earth, and what more do I wish than that it should be kindled.[40]

Baptism and Work

One of the ways in which Jesus determined to spread this fire on the earth was through our baptism. This, unlike St John's baptism with water only, was to be baptism 'with the Holy Spirit and with fire'.[41] This baptism of ours not only calls us to walk Christ's road with Him; it makes our life and work in the world a part of Christ's own work in the world. It gives us too, like Him, fire in the heart, passion to press on with Him, uplifting humanity and the earth to the Father, through our prayer and through our work.

Jesus' baptism in the Jordan consecrated Him for His redeeming work. It made Him the Anointed One: it marked Him as the Christ. It anointed Him with the Holy Spirit as Prophet, King and Priest of all mankind throughout all time: Prophet to proclaim God's Kingdom; King to make God's reign effective and triumphant in a world dominated by Satan, by sin, and by the works of death and darkness; Priest to offer for humanity the sacrifice of its noblest life and purest love in His own scourged Body and to enable men and women to offer themselves and their lives and loves and hopes, their toil, their achievements and their pain, through Him and with Him and in Him, to the Father.

Immediately after His Baptism, Jesus' redeeming work began: it shall not end until the last one of the redeemed is brought up by him to the welcome of the Father. We can see the urgency of that work in St Mark's description of what happened after Jesus' baptism: 'Immediately the Spirit drove him out into the wilderness' to face the temptations of the devil. 'Immediately' – the word is one of the distinguishing characteristics of St Mark's gospel, a gospel of urgency and haste.

We tend to look on the Temptations of Christ in the desert as a prelude to Christ's public ministry. Instead they give us insight into its very heart. Jesus in the desert was about His real work – which is freeing the world from the grip of sin and bringing all that is in the world into free and loving service of God, to serve whom is to be freed from slavery and to become oneself a King. The whole of Jesus' life, from this first encounter to the hour of final combat with Satan on the Cross, is one uninterrupted struggle to free man and his world from sin and let *God* be God in all the earth.

We Christians are called to share in Christ's mission. In our baptism Christ's life becomes our life, Christ's work becomes our work, Christ's fire becomes our fire. As Christ was anointed by the Holy Spirit in the Jordan and sent to challenge the devil and set free the world for God, so we are anointed by the Holy Spirit in our baptism and sent into the world of the third millennium to challenge the evils at work in it, to unthrone its false gods and let the true God be its God. At our baptism, we become other Christs. We become **Christ**-ened. We get the task from God of **Christ**-ening the world.

The whole of our lifetime will be needed to complete our baptism. The whole of human history will be needed to complete the baptism of the world. But we do not need to be afraid. Christ is ahead of us. His way is the direction of history. With Christ we shall never fail humanity or history, we shall never be irrelevant to our times. He is the hope of ages, the Lord of the millennia, the beginning of all things and their end, the Alpha and the world's Omega Point.

The Christian, therefore, sees work as something done not only for Christ, but also with Christ and indeed, in a real sense by Christ, working in him or her. Men's and women's work is part of Christ's mission in the world. The Christian sees work, not just as something to be endured or 'offered up', but as something to be freely and lovingly offered, in the assurance that it is both redeemed and redeeming, for oneself and for humanity. The Christian does not see work as a place outside religion and apart from prayer. For the Christian, as it has always been for the monk, labour is also prayer, work is also adoration. Through the toils and strains and pressures of man's work, Christ is at work, 'reconciling the world to Himself'. For every baptised person knows that 'as Christ is, so we are in the world'. Through their work the laity become with and through Christ, sharers in his redemption of the world. As the Vatican Council puts it in the Constitution on the Church:

> The laity consecrates the world itself to God, insofar as they are worshippers whose deeds themselves are holy.[42]

Prophets, Kings and Priests
Baptism first of all gives all Christians, lay as well as clerical, a share in Christ's Prophetic mission of spreading the Kingdom of God. As the Vatican Council has said, Christian lay persons must 'let the power of the Gospel shine forth in their daily social and family life'.

> Let them not hide this hope in the depths of their hearts but let them express it also in the programme of their secular lives ... This evangelisation, that is, this announcing of Christ by a testimony of life as well as by the spoken word, takes on a new efficacy from the fact that it is carried out in the ordinary surroundings of the secular world.[43]

Now, when we are faced with a new paganism not unlike like the old Greco-Roman one, only more sophisticated and more seductive, Christian lay men and women must assume again their baptismal mission of evangelising the world. This begins in the Church and in prayer, but is carried on also in the workplace, be it factory or farm or research laboratory, in office or home, in school or college, in public service or in business, or in media. It is done, not just by words, but by the quality of one's life and by the excellence of one's work. St Paul's words to the Philippians were never more relevant than they are today:

> You live in an age that is twisted out of its true pattern and among such people you shine out as beacons to the world, upholding the message of life.[44]

Christ's Kingship over Matter

Secondly, by baptism Christian lay persons become sharers in Christ's Kingly power over the material world. For the world of matter too is redeemed by Christ. Matter too will be transfigured by the glory of the Risen Christ and transformed into the new heavens and the new earth of Christ's final triumph. But now it is redeemed only in hope; and, as St Paul says, 'it groans and sighs' in longing for its full redemption.

Work should be a sharing in God's creation and in Christ's New Creation of the world. It should lead men to satisfaction and fulfilment, harmony and brotherhood. Its result should be: 'God saw that it was good'; but sin intervened and work became also toil and drudgery, and a sharing in Christ's Cross. Sadly also, when sin entered in, work became a frequent cause of discord and hate, envy, injustice, violence and death. It was so already with Cain; and Cain's dispute with Abel could be called the first labour dispute. But for the Christian the brand of Cain is effaced by the brand of Christ; and the Christian has the duty of putting the brand of Christ on work. The Christian knows that he or she shares in Christ's power to break the grip of evil on the world of work and make God's rule prevail there in justice and truth, solidarity and love between those whom Christ calls to be sharers in his work.

Trade union activity, improvement of working conditions and of labour relations, promotion of reciprocal justice in industry and of genuine community endeavour in production, these are not just secular activities; they are part of our sharing by baptism in Christ's Kingship over work. They carry on in the 2000s Christ's victorious struggle against Satan, entrenched now in power and selfishness, greed and spite and injustice, whether on one side or on the other in industrial relations and entrenched also in the abuse of power in globalised industry and trade. Baptism obliges Christians to be responsible trade unionists or enlightened and ethical industrialists, or honest accountants and bankers and morally responsible economists or investors or planners, and politicians of integrity and moral and social commitment. This is how Christ's New Creation is extended into the world of work, industry, business and politics. The urgent need for this in today's Ireland scarcely needs to be emphasised.

Work and Christ's Priesthood

The third privilege and duty of the Christian lay person is to share in the priestly role of Christ. Christ is Priest of humanity and Priest of the universe, reconciling both men and all creatures with God. Greek mythology spoke of Atlas as holding up the world on his shoulders. But Christ is the true Atlas, raising the world to God in his uplifted arms upon the Cross.

Renewing that sacrifice in the Mass, Christ makes it possible for us to offer him and ourselves with him and the world with ourselves, to the Father. Every Mass is offered in a sense on the altar of the world, the altar of shop floor and workbench, factory bay and building site and research laboratory. At every Mass the toil and sweat of the world's workers, what the Vatican Council calls 'the joys and the hopes, the griefs and the anxieties, of the men of this age', are offered to God at the Offertory, along with the pure, holy and immaculate Victim which is Christ, and through Him they give glory to the Father of all. Teilhard de Chardin's *Mass on the World* (*La Messe sur le Monde*) is a meditation coming from a time when, on a scientific expedition in the desert of Ardos, in the Asian Steppes, he was unable to celebrate Mass. This meditation seems to have been written on the feast of the Transfiguration of the Lord in the year 1923. He saw himself as placing on the eucharistic paten all the life and work and struggle and growth and progress on the planet and all the evolving processes within the matter of the planet and the cosmos; and pouring into the chalice all the pain and suffering and decay and evil on the planet and offering all this to God through Jesus Christ and in union with his sacrifice. He was confident that through this 'spiritual Mass', united with the actual Masses offered across the world, a great 'Diaphony' was taking place, whereby the warm glow of the divine presence was being cast across 'every fact and every element' of the world.[45]

We can even see in the bread and wine before the Consecration a synthesis and symbol of man's labour. Pope Paul remarked, in his very first encyclical, *Ecclesiam Suam*, published in 1964, that 'the bread which [science, technology and labour] produce becomes sacred for table and for altar'.[46] But, above all, in the Eucharist, all the work and struggle, all the ache and aspiration of the world, become sacred to God in the Flesh of His Son, which was 'given for the life of the world'.[47] Man's work is made worthy of the Eternal Master-Worker of creation through the aching arms of Christ, the Worker of redemption.

Bring Christ's Peace to Others
Work is a powerful means of applying Mass to the world. The Blood of Christ is made present at Mass 'for us and for all for the forgiveness of sins'. To borrow the words of Charles Péguy, it is the Christian's mission, received at Mass, to go and bring 'the others' to Christ. Mass in principle undoes the murderous divisiveness of the first labour dispute, which led Cain to murder Abel. 'Am I my brother's keeper?' asked Cain. Mass makes us our brother's and sister's keeper, responsible for building brotherhood and sisterhood among people, at peace with Christ and with each other. At the end of Mass, the People of God are sent out into the world of work with a message 'The Mass is ended: go in peace'. This means: 'The Mass of the altar is ended; the Mass of farm and factory and laboratory and office and family and home is begun. Go, People of God, People of the Mass, and bring Christ's peace and justice and solidarity into the world of work and into the world through work'.

In the Book of Revelation, we read:

> Blessed and holy is his lot who has a share in the first resurrection ...
> They will be priests of God, priests of Christ; all these thousand years
> they will reign with him.[48]

The reference is to all baptised Christians. The first resurrection is shared in by us at our baptism. The thousand years is all human history until the Second Coming of Christ. The message is that all the baptised are already sharers with Christ in his mission in the world, bearers of the hopes and destiny of mankind, co-responsible with Christ and with one another for the supernatural redemption and for the natural progress of the earth.

The Vatican Council says:

The expectation of a new earth must not weaken but rather stimulate our concern for cultivating this one. For here grows the body of a new human family, a body which even now is able to give some kind of foreshadowing of the new age. Earthly progress must be carefully distinguished from the growth of Christ's kingdom. Nevertheless, to the extent that the former can contribute to the better ordering of human society, it is of vital concern to the Kingdom of God.[49]

Divine Creation and Human Work

Christianity has always seen work as man's participation both in the creation of the world by God and in the New Creation of the world in Christ. For the biblical writers, the creation and the history of salvation are never separated. Creation is the beginning of God's love for humanity and His call to humanity. God, unlike the nature and fertility deities of the pagans, did not envy the earth to men and women or dispute its ownership with them. He made it freely, out of love. His freedom in creating it is the foundation of man's loving service in labouring it. 'The heavens belong to the Lord; but the earth He has given to men and women'.[50]

To look after the earth is for man a divine commission. Indeed this mastery of the cosmos increases man's resemblance to God:

> The Lord fashioned human beings from the earth .....
> and made them in his own image .....
> He clothed them in strength, like himself. ...[51]

Science and technology, in all their branches from astronomy to sub-atomic physics to biochemistry are implicitly blessed by this divine commission. The only condition is that man accept the earth as a gift and acknowledge in gratitude the Giver and the purpose of the gift. At Babel men sinned and were self-thwarted, not because they built, but because their motive was defiance of God, not love for Him. But since Pentecost, science and technology and industry can be, not only service to God, and not only a mastery of matter, but also a building up of human beings as living stones making up the Temple of God which is the Body of Christ.

For the Bible, too, work has the character, which the Marxists loved to give to it, of heroic struggle against oppressing elements, slavery, injustice and evil. In Genesis, creation is God's victory over chaos and the brute forces of darkness. God's commission to mankind to take over the earth, is His handing over to men and women of a sharing in the work He himself began at the creation. Our Christian motivation for work is proposed by the author of the First Letter of St Peter:

> Each one of you has received a special grace, so, like good stewards responsible for all these different graces of God, put yourselves at the service of others ... . If you are a helper, help as though every action was done at God's orders; so that in everything God may receive the glory, through Jesus Christ, since to him alone belong all glory and power for ever and ever.[52]

The New Creation

It is above all the certainty of Our Lord's victory, the sureness of the presence amongst us of His glorified Body, the firm expectation of the New Heavens and the New Earth, already begun in Christ, already begun in us through our baptism into his death and resurrection and through the Eucharist – this is what defines the manner of presence of the Church in the world and the nature and final purpose of the work of the Christian in the world.

Everything we do should spring from this faith and reveal this hope. St Paul uses the word for citizenship, '*politeusthe*', (from the same root as the word for politics) when he urges the Philippians:

> But you must always behave (*politeusthe*) in a way that is worthy of the gospel of Christ, so that whether I come to you and see for myself or whether I only hear all about you from a distance, I shall find that you are standing firm and united in spirit, battling, as a team with a single aim, for the faith of the gospel, undismayed by any of your opponents.[53]

It is the resurrection which gives us the heart to work. At the end of the great chapter on the resurrection in his First Letter to the Corinthians St Paul says:

> So, my dear brothers, keep firm and immovable, always abounding in energy for the Lord's work, being sure that in the Lord none of your labours is wasted.[54]

This resurrection, in which we participate by our baptism, is made really, truly and substantially present for us in the body of Christ, given for us on the Cross and given to us in our Eucharist. In the Eucharist the new creation is already a reality.

In our work, however menial and unimportant it might seem, whether it be so-called intellectual or so-called manual work, we are participating in Christ's New Creation of the world. It is a mistake to regard intellectual work as inherently superior to manual work; as if intelligence were not expressed in the skills of human hands as much as by the achievements of human intellect; as if 'body language' were not sometimes as expressive of one's thought and feelings, as one's locutions. It is also mistaken to contrast 'knowledge-based' work with manual work, as though the latter were not also based on knowledge. Both contribute equally to the progress of mankind and the purposes of God. It is of course important, to affirm in our time the spiritual aspect of what is called intellectual work. It too prepares for the New Creation of the world, whether in science, in all its branches, in technology, in all its domains, in information technology, in mass communications, in journalism, in business or in philosophy. New sciences and new technologies have revolutionised our understanding of the world and our communication of that understanding; they are an important and now essential part of our fulfilment of God's mandate to mankind in the beginning of creation to 'fill the earth and subdue it'. The exciting new world being opened for us today in the fields of science and technology lends itself no less to Christian involvement and is even more in need of a Christian presence than the older ways of rural living in our country formerly were.

Work and the New Creation
We sometimes speak as though redemption and the new creation were concerned with souls only and that the body is outside their scope. This is not so. Body and soul are redeemed together; the Church's sacraments of redemption touch bodies as well as souls, indeed touch the souls through the body. What is done to and with bodies has its place in the new creation which Christ inaugurates. In this regard it is interesting to recall remarks of C.G. Jung, the renowned depth psychologist. In his book, *Modern Man in Search of a Soul*, Jung recalled how, over thirty years, he had had patients, many hundreds of them, from all round the world, and he concluded:

> Among all my patients (over thirty-five years of age) there has not been one whose problem in the last resort was not that of finding a religious outlook on life. It is safe to say that every one of them fell ill because he had lost that which the living religions of every age have

given to their followers, and none of them has been really healed who did not regain his religious outlook.[55]

The splendour of the new creation, in which our work in this world participates, has seldom been more powerfully expressed than by St Thomas Aquinas, in the last chapter of the *Summa Contra Gentiles*. With a lyricism of language which is unusual for him and which in parts rivals Teilhard, Aquinas writes:

> When, therefore, the last judgement is completed, human nature will be entirely established in its goal. However, since everything bodily is somehow for the sake of human beings, at that time, also, the entire bodily creation will be changed to be in harmony with the state of the men and women who then will be. And because they will then be incorruptible, the state of generation and corruption will then be taken away from the whole bodily creation. And this is what the Apostle says: that 'the creature also itself shall be delivered from the servitude of corruption, into the liberty of the glory of the children of God'. (Romans 8: 21). Hence, one holds in accord with the faith that at the last the world will be purified by fire, not from corruptible bodies alone, but from that infection which the place incurred by serving as the dwelling of sinners. Since, then, the bodily creation will at the last be disposed in harmony with the state of man – since men and women, of course, will not only be freed from corruption but also clothed in glory, as what has been said makes clear – necessarily even the bodily creation will achieve a kind of resplendence in its own way.
>
> And, hence, the saying of the Apocalypse (21: 1) 'I saw a new heaven and a new earth'. And Isaiah (65: 17-18): 'Behold I create new heavens, and a new earth: and the former things shall not be in remembrance and they shall not come upon the heart. But you shall be glad and rejoice forever'. Amen.[56]

If Christians have such a conviction of the meaning and the ultimate aim and outcome of work, if they really *believe* it, no marxist and no humanist could outdo Christians in human energy, enthusiasm or dedication to the good of this world and the progress of humanity, for the glory of God, but at the same time for the love of our fellow-humans. Nietzsche's promethean Man was to be an 'arrow of longing for the farther shore'. How much more is that true of Christian man or woman? St Paul says:

Not that I have secured it already, nor yet reached my goal, but I am still pursuing it in the attempt to take hold of the prize for which Christ Jesus took hold of me. Brothers, I do not reckon myself as having taken hold of it; I can only say that forgetting all that lies behind me, and straining forward to what lies in front, I am racing towards the finishing point to win the prize of God's heavenly call in Christ Jesus.[57]

Nietzsche taunts Christians:

They must sing better songs ere I learn belief in their Saviour: his disciples must look like the saved.

But in the New Testament it is the followers of Jesus Christ who sing a new song; and the song they sing is a Hymn of the Universe at the same time as being a Hymn to Christ, its Head. We find it in St Paul, who may well have taken it from a chant in the earliest Christian liturgy:

He is the image of the unseen God,
the first-born of all creation,
for in him were created all things
in heaven and on earth:
everything visible and everything invisible,
thrones, ruling forces, sovereignties, powers –
all things were created through him and for him.
He exists before all things
and in him all things hold together,
and he is the Head of the Body,
that is, the Church.

He is the Beginning,
the first-born from the dead,
so that he should be supreme in every way;
because God wanted all fullness to be found in him
and through him to reconcile all things to him,
everything in heaven and everything on earth,
by making peace through his death on the cross.[58]

In the stresses and pressures of modern work, and even in the stress of getting to and from work, often indeed in the sheer drudgery of work and at times the apparent purposelessness of it all, it is hard to keep this vision of work and this sense of its meaning and value. It can help to pause in prayer and to situate our work, whatever it be, in its context in the place which God has assigned to each of us in His providential plan of creation and redemption and ultimate glorification of humanity and the cosmos. We can do this best in the morning Eucharist, before the day's work begins, or the midday Eucharist when we have a brief interlude in the working day. It can be done at morning prayer, indeed perhaps while waiting in traffic jams. It can be done in the traditional devotion of the Morning Offering. It can be done even in a simple but slow and reverent signing of ourselves with the Sign of the Cross. But these devotional acts must be made real through making sure that our work is well and honestly and professionally done, so that of itself it truly gives glory to God. Some students during my teaching years used to write 'AMDG' (*Ad Maiorem Dei Gloriam*; 'For the greater glory of God') at the top of their script, perhaps hoping that this pious note might compensate for inadequacies in their script! But the work will not give glory to God unless it is as honest and competent as the author can make it. Such work is sowing seeds of justice and love, which may seem small and unimportant, but which will bear fruit for eternity.[59]

Cardinal Newman expresses all this well in his prayer:

> My God you have created me to do you some definite service. You have given some work to me which you have not given to any other. I have my place in your plan. I may never know what it is in this life but I will be told it in the next. Therefore, I will trust you in all things. ...

A story is told of a workman employed on a building site where the foundations were being laid for a new cathedral. A crowd of curious onlookers was blocking the entrance as he tried to make his way through with a barrow-load of bricks. He called out: 'Please make way', and when someone asked, 'What are you doing?', he replied, 'I'm building a cathedral'. The end result ennobles the toil of construction. Christians can see in their work a much greater outcome to their toil: they are helping to build a cathedral of 'living stones', transformed human beings, where the resurrected and transfigured Jesus Christ is the 'main corner stone' and they, his followers, are being themselves 'built into a house where God lives, in the Spirit.'[60]

The Transfiguration

This is the vision which inspires the iconographic tradition of the Eastern Church. This tradition never attempted to depict the resurrection event itself; no 'fuller [or painter] on earth' could depict that. The nearest we come to it is in the series of icons of the Transfiguration, the best-known of which is the 'Transfiguration of Novgorod'. Christ stands on the pinnacle of the rocky mount of the Transfiguration, bathed in a numinous whiteness which is like pure light in bodily shape. Rays stream from Christ's body to illuminate the figures of the prostrate Apostles; this will empower them to speak with conviction and courage of what they have seen and heard 'on the holy mountain'. The rays bring light and life even to the barren rock and cause verdure in its many shades of green to burst forth from between the fissures of the rocks. Everything in the universe, all of nature, all of humanity, is touched by the light radiating from Christ, and is transformed, transfigured, by the touch.

Christian men and women can see their toil as a preparation for and a contribution to that sublime transformation. There is a teleology of human work: its glorious final end gives meaning to its present, often inglorious, reality. Its end is the final consummation of the work of redemption painfully wrought by Christ; and this is the final setting free of creation, as well as of humanity, from the contamination of sin. St Paul describes it in a splendid passage:

> I think that what we suffer in this life can never be compared to the glory, as yet unrevealed, which is waiting for us. The whole creation is eagerly waiting for God to reveal his sons. It was not for any fault on the part of creation that it was made unable to attain its purpose, it was made so by God; but creation still retains the hope of being freed, like us, from its slavery to decadence, to enjoy the same freedom and glory as the children of God. From the beginning till now the entire creation, as we know has been groaning in one great act of giving birth; and not only creation, but all of us who possess the first-fruits of the Spirit, we too groan inwardly as we wait for our bodies to be set free. For we must be content to hope that we shall be saved – our salvation is not in sight, we should not have to be hoping for it if it were – but, as I say, we must hope to be saved since we are not saved yet – it is something we must wait for with patience.[61]

It is this vision of a world reflecting the transfigured Christ that inspires Joseph Mary Plunkett's poem:

> I see his blood upon the rose
> And in the stars the glory of his eyes,
> His body gleams amid eternal snows,
> His tears fall from the skies.
>
> I see his face in every flower;
> The thunder and the singing of the birds
> Are but his voice – and carven by his power,
> Rocks are his written words.
>
> All pathways by his feet are worn,
> His strong heart stirs the ever-beating sea,
> His crown of thorns is twined with every thorn,
> His cross is every tree.[62]

This is the vision which enabled Gerald Manley Hopkins to give 'glory to God for dappled things', which he found in the most unlikely places throughout the whole of nature, both animate and inanimate, in

> landscape plotted and pieced – fold, fallow and plough;
> and all trades, their gear and tackle and trim;

all of which

> He fathers forth whose beauty is past change.

In Hopkins's vision, for him or her who has eyes to gaze in wonder,

> The world is charged with the grandeur of God ... .
> Because the Holy Ghost over the bent
> World broods with warm breast and with ah!
> Bright wings.

But we do need eyes to see; we need to take time to look, and to look contemplatively at the world; we need

A heart lost. All lost in wonder at the God Thou art.

And so

> I walk, I lift up, I lift up my ears, eyes,
> Down all that glory in the heavens to glean our Saviour;
> And eyes, heart ...
> These things, these things are here, but the beholder
> Wanting; which two when they once meet,
> The heart rears wings bold and bolder,
> And hurls for him, O half hurls for him off under his feet.[63]

The same radiance from Christ is found by Patrick Kavanagh in the most unlikely places:

> Green, blue, yellow and red –
> God is down in the swamps and marshes
> Sensational as April and almost incredible the flowering of our catharsis.
> A humble scene in a backward place
> Where no one important ever looked
> The raving flowers looked up in the face
> Of the One and the Endless, the Mind that has baulked
> The profoundest of mortals. A primrose, a violet,
> A violent wild iris – but mostly anonymous performers.
> Yet an important occasion as the Muse at her toilet
> Prepared to inform the local farmers
> That beautiful, beautiful, beautiful God
> Was breathing His love by a cut-away bog.[64]

Michael Casey, the sculptor, discovers this beauty in pieces of oak or yew buried for perhaps five thousand years in the boglands of Longford and Offaly, and, by his work as artist, draws out new beauty from it in his carvings and sculptures.

Still more beautiful is the heritage of 'human dignity, fraternity and freedom', which men and women by their work create and transmit. I have already quoted the Vatican Council as saying that this work is 'even now able to give some kind of foreshadowing of the new age' of which this age of human history is the prelude.[65] Pope John Paul II concludes his encyclical on work with the words:

Let the Christian who listens to the word of the living God, uniting work with prayer, know the place that his or her work has not only in earthly progress but also in the development of the Kingdom of God, to which we are called through the power of the Holy Spirit and through the word of the Gospel.[66]

The Second Vatican Council's Constitution on the Church in the Modern World, *Gaudium et Spes,* says:

Christians, on pilgrimage towards the heavenly city, should seek and savour the things that are above. This duty in no way decreases, but rather increases, the weight of their obligation to work with all people in building a more human world.[67]

Pope John Paul II comments on these words in the Post-Synodal Apostolic Exhortation in which he communicates the findings of the Synod of Bishops for Europe, held in the year 2000. He says:

Though it is impossible to create within history a perfect social order, we know that God blesses every sincere effort to build a better world, and that every seed of justice and love planted in the present will bear fruit for eternity.[68]

Gaudium et Spes ends with words from St Paul, and they form an appropriate ending for this chapter on the Christian and work:

Glory to be him whose power, working in us, can do infinitely more than we can ask or imagine; glory to be him from generation to generation in the Church and in Christ Jesus for ever and ever. Amen.[69]

Chapter V

THE MINDING OF PLANET EARTH (1)

In the title of this chapter, the word 'minding' is understood as meaning 'looking after', 'taking good care of'. The notion of taking good care of planet earth has taken on a new interest and become more topical in recent decades, but it is not a new concept. We find it in the first book of the Bible, the Book of Genesis, where we read that 'the Lord God created man and woman and told them to fill the earth and conquer it', or, as the second creation narrative puts it, God 'took the man and settled him in the garden of Eden to cultivate it and take care of it', (Genesis 1:28; 2:15). The picture is one of human beings as stewards of the Creator, entrusted by God with the task of taking good care of God's creation, the earth, and being accountable to God for the care they take of it. I return to this biblical picture in the closing pages of my final chapter.

The term 'ecology' was not part of common speech until the 1960s and 1970s. The term covers many issues, and people differ in the degree of emphasis that they lay on some issues rather than others. In part one of this chapter, I concentrate on the need to acknowledge the finite nature of the planet's resources and the dangers posed by over-consumption of these resources. In part two, I call attention to the unequal and unjust distribution of the planet's resources among the inhabitants of the planet and the moral imperative to work for a more equitable and more just access to these resources by those who are currently denied such access. In this second part I also discuss some of the injustices inherent in the present world order (or dis-order!) and I conclude with reflections on an authentically Christian vision of planet earth.

In part one of the chapter I quote extensively from official documents relating to ecology from Church sources, Catholic, Orthodox and Protestant, and from secular sources. There is undeniable agreement across the spectrum of the documents about the range of issues which an integral ecology must embrace. Inevitably, the secular studies omit the reference to God the Creator of the planet and of its inhabitants, and to God's design that the planet's resources be fairly shared between its human population. Nevertheless, they agree with the faith-based studies to this extent, that they recognise that the planet earth is the provider of the special kind of produce and the particular kind of environment without which humans cannot survive, and that all human beings have rights of just and fair access to that produce and to that environment.

The review of these documents shows that a considerable degree of convergence of teaching on ecology between the Churches has developed over the years. It seems clear also that there is a considerable degree of convergence between Church-based and secular statements on care of the earth. All stress the inter-relatedness of the problems of conservation of the planet, safeguarding of the environment, economic development, poverty in one part of the world confronting wealth and superfluity in the other, war and weapons of war, security, terrorism. All these documents copiously illustrate the relationship between ecology, development, poverty, human rights, justice and peace; indeed between the triad now commonly enumerated as justice, peace and the integrity of creation. Sadly, however, one has to conclude that the nations of the earth, particularly the wealthy nations, continue to ignore ecological warnings and consequently to flout irrefutable ecological evidence; and cannot find peace with God, the Creator, or with the earth or with one another.

The duty of responsible care of the earth is a constant in Christian teaching. The notion of human 'stewarding' of the earth is a feature of patristic and medieval theology. It was restated by the Second Vatican Council, not as an innovation, but as an ongoing, if sometimes neglected, truth of Christian tradition. This is not to claim that all Christians were faithful to the biblical injunction or complied with Church teaching; or even always understood biblical teaching in its fullness. There were abuses, and indeed grave ones; but the Bible and the Church are not to blame for these.

Earth: Our Fragile Home

The sense of planet earth as limited, fragile and precarious – needing to be treated with care – was imprinted upon human consciousness in a new way by the exploration of space and the first human landing on the moon. The view of earth as seen from the moon's surface brought this vividly home to us all. In some of the photographs of earth taken from outer space, the earth appears to me as like an egg without its shell, held together by its thin membrane; a mere pin-prick could pierce the membrane and the contents would fall apart. The impact is best described in the words of the first astronauts to see the earth from outer space.

The American astronaut, James Irwin, wrote:

> The earth reminded us of a Christmas tree ornament hanging in the blackness of space. As we got further and further away it diminished in size. Finally it shrank to the size of a marble, the most beautiful marble you can imagine. That beautiful, warm, living object looked so fragile, so delicate, that if you touched it with a finger it would crumble and fall apart. Seeing this has to change a man, has to make a man appreciate the creation of God and the love of God.
>
> Suddenly from behind the rim of the moon, in long slow-motion movements of immense majesty, there emerges a sparkling blue and white jewel, a light, delicate sky-blue sphere laced with slowly swirling veils of white, rising gradually like a small pearl in a thick sea of black mystery. It takes more than a moment to fully realise that this is Earth … home … My view of our planet was a glimpse of divinity.

Ulf Merbold of Germany wrote:

> For the first time in my life I saw the horizon as a curved line. It was accentuated by a thin seam of dark blue light – our atmosphere – I was terrified by its fragile appearance.

The moral imperative of ecology is well expressed in the words of Oleg Makarov, of the USSR, one of the astronauts of the Soyuz series of spacecraft:

> We hope that everyone will come to share our particular cosmic perception of the world and our desire to unite all the peoples of the Earth in the task of safeguarding our common and only, fragile and beautiful, home.[1]

Church and Ecology
John Passmore, great though his contribution to philosophy and the history of ideas was, and undoubtedly important and timely though his book was, shows a limited understanding of the Christian tradition, particularly in its Catholic

expression, in his book, *Man's Responsibility for Nature*. He argues against the claim that Christian teaching passes moral judgment on man's relationship to nature and concludes that what he calls 'Stoic-Christian traditions' are 'not favourable to the solution of [the] ecological problems' of the Western world, because they 'deny that man's relationship with nature is governed by any moral principles'.[2] Such views, are widely shared. They stem in part from the misconceptions I discussed in Chapters I and II, to the effect that the Catholic Church was historically the enemy of science. These views suffer also from the common fault of ignoring the philosophical and theological tradition of the medieval period. This notorious 'jump over the Middle Ages' has characterised much of modern culture; though there are encouraging signs more recently of a rediscovery of medieval philosophy, particularly that of Aquinas. I hope to show in this chapter that there are in Christian teaching clear and firm moral principles governing man's relationship with nature and that these principles are favourable to the solution of the ecological problems confronting humanity in the third millennium.

The Second Vatican Council declares that it is part of 'the design of God', that mankind should 'develop the earth so that it can bear fruit and become a dwelling worthy of the whole human family':

> Manifested at the beginning of time, the divine plan is that man should subdue the earth, bring creation to perfection and develop himself. When a person so acts, he simultaneously obeys the great Christian commandment that he place himself at the service of his brother men and women.[3]

This divine plan intends the earth to be seen as the home of the entire human species, with all races and tribes and peoples and nations entitled as of right to fair access to its basic resources, such as soil, air and water, and a fair share of its produce. The Council states:

> God intended the earth and all it contains for the use of all men and all peoples; so created goods should flow fairly to all, regulated by justice and accompanied by charity.[4]

When men and women carry out this divine mandate, the Council says, they are simultaneously helping creation to fulfil its purpose and promoting solidarity and justice within the human family. They are indeed helping to create the consciousness and the reality of 'family' among the diverse races and nations of human beings on the earth. At the same time human beings are also thereby creating conditions in which 'the human spirit can be more easily drawn to the worship and contemplation of the creator' who reveals Himself in creation before revealing Himself in His Incarnate Word.[5]

Ecology, in the Christian perspective, is closely connected with issues of peace and justice. The slogan, 'justice, peace and the integrity of creation', familiar to us from the World Council of Churches World Convocation held in Seoul in 1990, is well chosen.[6]

Catholic Teaching

Indeed the Catholic Church's social teaching has been addressing many of these problems since at least the end of the nineteenth century, when Pope Leo XIII issued his great encyclical, *Rerum Novarum*. This, as I pointed out in the chapter on 'The Christian and Work', has been followed by a series of papal encyclicals on social and global issues. Pope John XXIII, in his 1961 encyclical, *Mater et Magistra*, to which I have referred already, spoke of the discrepancy between the 'developed' and the 'undeveloped' world, between the rich nations and the poor, as one of the most difficult and dangerous problems of the century. He called for a solidarity which would bind rich and poor nations together 'as members of a common family' and which would make it

> impossible for wealthy nations to look with indifference upon the hunger, misery and poverty of other nations whose citizens are unable to enjoy even elementary human rights.

He warned that unless this happens,

> it will not be possible to preserve a lasting peace so long as these glaring economic and social inequalities persist.

He declared that 'we are all equally responsible for the undernourished peoples' and denounced 'as nothing less than an outrage to justice and humanity to destroy or to squander goods that other people need for their very lives'.[7]

Noteworthy is Pope John XXIII's *Pacem in Terris*. Issued in 1963, this encyclical was one of the first modern studies from Church or State to address such topics as interdependency between states, subsidiarity, the interconnectedness of economic development, poverty and peace, the urgency of international cooperation to avert disputes which could bring danger of war. Memorably, Pope John XXIII declared:

> In an age which boasts of its atomic power, it no longer makes sense to maintain that war is a fit instrument with which to repair the violation of justice.[8]

The theme of development and the ethical issues surrounding it was treated by Pope Paul VI in his 1967 encyclical *Populorum Progressio*. In this challenging document the Pope recalled the teaching of the first pages of the Bible:

> 'Fill the earth and subdue it'; the Bible, from the first page on, teaches us that the whole of creation is for man, that it is his responsibility to develop it by intelligent effort ...

All human rights, 'including those of property and of free commerce', should be subordinated, he states, to the principle that the earth is designed by God to serve the needs of the entire human family and its produce should be shared in accordance with the demands of justice and of charity. Development is indeed the new name for peace, he says, but development must serve human rights for all and not simply maximise profits for the few.[9]

The teaching of *Populorum Progressio* was carried further by Pope John Paul II in a commemorative encyclical issued twenty years later, in 1987, with the title *Sollicitudo Rei Socialis*. Here Pope John Paul stresses the moral criteria for authentic development. Among these, he gives first place to the obligation to respect the God-given order of nature:

> One cannot use with impunity the different categories of beings ... – animals, plants, the natural elements – as one wishes, according to one's own economic needs. Secondly, one must realise that natural resources are limited, some are non-renewable: to use them as if they were inexhaustible and as if mankind had absolute dominion over them is to deprive others of due access to them. Thirdly, one must avoid types of development which result in pollution of the environment, with serious consequences for the health of the population.

The Pope goes on, in the same encyclical, to lay further stress on the moral limitations on man's 'domination' over nature:

The dominion granted to man by the Creator is not an absolute power ... The limitation imposed from the beginning by the Creator himself and expressed symbolically by the prohibition not to 'eat of the fruit of the tree' (Genesis 2: 16-17) shows clearly enough that, when it comes to the natural world, we are subject not only to biological laws but also to moral ones which cannot be violated with impunity.

A true concept of development cannot ignore the use of the elements of nature, the renewability of resources and the consequences of haphazard industrialisation – three considerations which alert our consciences to the moral dimension of development.[10]

Pope John Paul II returned to the ecological question in his encyclical, *Centesimus Annus*, issued in 1991 to mark the centenary of *Rerum Novarum*. Here he stressed the strict moral conditions attached by God to man's mandate to 'conquer' the earth and 'subdue it'. The Pope wrote:

Man thinks that he can make arbitrary use of the earth, subjecting it without restraint to his will, as though it did not have its own requisites and a prior God-given purpose, which man can indeed develop but must not betray. Instead of carrying out his role as a cooperator with God in the work of creation, man sets himself up in place of God and thus ends up provoking a rebellion on the part of nature, which is more tyrannized than governed by him.

The Pope concluded:

The decisions which create a human environment can give rise to specific structures of sin which impede the full realisation of those who are in any way oppressed by them.[11]

The Second Vatican Council requested the setting up of organisms for study and action on the themes of peace and justice. Pope Paul VI duly set up, in January 1967, the Pontifical Council, Justice and Peace and this was followed by national or regional Councils for Justice and Peace, set up by Episcopal Conferences throughout the world. These, and particularly the Pontifical Council in Rome, have done much to conscientise people to the problems of justice, peace and the integrity of creation.

In the whole area of care for the earth, the question of women's equality and of women's rights is of crucial importance. Traditional agriculture was, and in many countries still is, a partnership between men and women; yet the role of women often remained, and still remains, a strictly subordinate one. Even in so-called 'developed' societies, women's labour is sometimes underpaid and even exploited. The involvement of women as virtual 'sex slaves' in what is called the 'sex trade' is a gross violation of human rights. Domestic violence is directed predominantly against women and is a blight on so-called 'advanced' societies as much as on 'underdeveloped' countries. The question of women's rights is a necessary part of the ecology agenda.

The Second Vatican Council declared:

> When they have not yet won it, women claim for themselves equality with men before the law and in fact.

It must still be regretted that fundamental personal rights are not yet universally honoured. Such is the case of a woman who is denied the right and freedom to choose a husband, to embrace a state of life, or to acquire an education or cultural benefits equal to those recognised for men.[12]

The other Churches have also been active in the domain of ecology; indeed much work has been done by the Churches jointly in a truly ecumenical spirit. A joint organism called SODEPAX was set up, bringing together the Pontifical Council and the World Council of Churches for the purpose of ecumenical collaboration in the areas of 'society, development and peace'. All this has been in parallel with United Nations' initiatives in the successive Development Decades from 1960 onwards and many other UN projects related to development, environment, poverty and world peace.

The Pontifical Council in Rome has published many excellent documents in these related fields. One of the earliest of these was published in 1970 with the title, *The Angry Seventies*. Its author was Barbara Ward (or Lady Jackson), who was a member of the Pontifical Council; it was commissioned and published by the Council itself. This was a challenging document, one of the early 'alarm calls' alerting society to the gravity and urgency of the ecological dangers threatening us. Its tone is reflected in the author's concluding paragraph:

As we read the portents – the cold statistics, the burning realities – it is hard to believe that a great deal of time is left in which to reverse the world's drift via indifference to destruction.

Yet the paragraph ends on a note of hope in what can be done, in the name of Christ and by his power, by Christ's followers, who believe in a Kingdom of justice, love and peace.[13]

Three years later, in 1973, Barbara Ward followed this up with another study, entitled *A New Creation: Reflections on the Environmental Issue*. This too was commissioned by the Pontifical Council for Justice and Peace, and published by that Council.

The Pontifical Council has issued an impressive number of texts related to the themes of this chapter. I instance the 1986 document, *At the Service of the Human Community, an Ethical Approach to the International Debt Question*; the 1994 text, *The International Arms Trade, An Ethical Reflection*; and the 1997 text, *Towards a Better Distribution of Land, the Challenge of Agrarian Reform*.

The Pontifical Academy of Sciences brought together groups of leading scientists, specialists in the relevant domain, to study the dangers of nuclear war. Three important statements resulted, namely: *Declaration on the Consequences of the Employment of Nuclear Weapons* (1981); *Declaration on the Prevention of Nuclear War* (1982); and *Nuclear Winter: A Warning* (1984).[14]

Finally, the Synod of Bishops chose the theme 'Justice in the World' for its 1971 session and published its conclusions in a text with this title. Indeed, Barbara Ward's 1973 publication was one of a series of texts commissioned and published by the Pontifical Council by way of commentary and reflection on the conclusions of the 1971 Synod.

World Council of Churches
In illustration of the teaching of other Churches I refer to documents from both World Council of Churches and Orthodox Church sources. The World Council of Churches, following a seven-year consultation process, held a World Convocation in Seoul in 1990. The Convocation published a text with the title *Ten Affirmations on Justice, Peace and the Integrity of Creation*.[15] I shall try to summarise this document, quoting salient passages, in the hope of giving a flavour of the 'affirmations' to which the Council committed its member Churches. I follow the enumeration used in the document itself.

Introduction

In this world marked by injustice, violence and the degradation of the environment we wish to affirm God's covenant which is open to all and holds the promise of life in wholeness and right relationships. Responding to God's covenant we profess our faith in the Triune God who is the very source of communion ...

Affirmation I: We affirm that all exercise of power is accountable to God ...
'Those who wield power – economic, political, military, social, scientific, cultural, legal, religious – must be stewards of God's justice and peace ...'

Affirmation II: We affirm God's option for the poor
'The poor are the exploited and the oppressed. Their poverty is not accidental. It is very often a result of deliberate policies which result in the constantly increasing accumulation of wealth and power in the hands of a few. ...'

'While we support the need for diaconal services and urgent response to emergencies, we recognise in our time that the needs of 'the least' can only be met by fundamentally transforming the world economy through structural change. ...'

Affirmation III: We affirm the equal value of all races and peoples.
'In Jesus Christ, all people of whatever race, caste or ethnic descent are reconciled to God and to each other. Racism as an ideology and discrimination as a practice are a betrayal of the rich diversity of God's design for the world and violate the dignity of human personality. All forms of racism – whether individual, or collective or systematic – must be named sin and their theological justification heresy ...'

Affirmation IV: We affirm that male and female are created in the image of God ...
Christ affirmed the personhood of women and empowered them to a life of dignity and fullness ...

We *affirm* the creative power given to women to stand for life wherever there is death. ...

We *will resist* structures of patriarchy which perpetuate violence against women in their homes and in a society which has exploited their labour and sexuality. ...

Affirmation V: We affirm that truth is at the foundation of a community of free people ...
Today, new technologies offer possibilities of wider communication and education for all ... we *affirm* that access to truth and education, information and means of communications are basic human rights. ...

Affirmation VI: We affirm the peace of Jesus Christ.
'The only possible basis for lasting peace is justice (Isaiah 32: 17) ...'
'We *will resist* doctrines and systems of security based on the use of, and determined by, all weapons of mass destruction, and military invasions, interventions and occupations. We will resist doctrines of national security which are aimed at the control and suppression of the people in order to protect the privileges of the few ...'

Affirmation VII: We affirm the creation as beloved of God.
'As Creator, God is the source and sustainer of the whole cosmos. God loves the creation. Its mysterious ways, its life, its dynamism – all reflect the glory of its Creator. God's work of redemption in Jesus Christ reconciles all things and calls us to the healing work of the Spirit in all creation. ...'
'Today all life in the world, both of present and future generations, is endangered because humanity has failed to love the living earth; and the rich and powerful in particular have plundered it as if it were created for selfish purposes. The magnitude of the devastation may well be irreversible and forces us to urgent action. ...'

Affirmation VIII: We affirm that the earth is the Lord's.
'The land and the waters provide life to people – indeed to all that lives – now and for the future. Millions are deprived of land and suffer from the contamination of water. ... We *will resist* any policy that treats land merely as a marketable commodity; that allows speculation at the expense of the poor; that dumps poisonous wastes into the land and the waters; that promotes the exploitation, unequal distribution or contamination of land and its products. ...'

Affirmation IX: We affirm the dignity and commitment of the younger generation. ...
Poverty, injustice and the debt crisis, war and militarism, hit children hard through the dislocation of families, forcing them into work at an

early age just to survive, inflicting malnutrition upon them and even threatening their survival. ...

'We *affirm* the dignity of children which derives from their particular vulnerability and need for nurturing love. ... We *will resist* any policy or authority which violates the rights of the younger generation and which abuses and exploits them. ...'

Affirmation X: We affirm that human rights are given by God.
There is an inseparable relationship between justice and human rights. Human rights have their source in God's justice which relates to an enslaved, marginalised, suffering people in concrete acts of deliverance from oppression (Exodus 3: 7b) ... The right for peoples to work out their own models of development and to live free of fear and free of manipulation is a fundamental human right which should be respected, and so should the rights of women and children to a life free of violence in home and in society. ...

We *affirm* that human rights are God-given and that their promotion and protection are essential for freedom, justice and peace. To protect and defend human rights, an independent judicial system is necessary.

The Orthodox Church
In June 2002 the Ecumenical Patriarch Bartholomew convened specialists to a symposium on religion, science and the environment, conducted, unusually, aboard ship in the Mediterranean and the Adriatic. As a conclusion to the symposium, the ship called at Venice and here the Patriarch and Pope John Paul II, the latter from Rome via television, simultaneously signed a joint declaration on human stewardship of the environment. They asked Catholic and Orthodox believers to work together with one another and with others of good will 'to heal and care for God's creation'. They expressed agreement on the ethical principles to be applied in the ecological domain and deplored

> the degradation of some basic natural resources such as water, air and land, brought about by an economic and technological progress which does not take into account its limits.

They ended, however, on a note of hope:

It is not too late. God's world has incredible healing powers. Within a generation, we could steer the earth towards our children's future. Let that generation start now, with God's hope and blessing.

From the documents emanating from the Catholic Church, the Orthodox Church and from the Protestant Churches which I have summarised, it can be seen that a very considerable convergence of teaching between the Churches has developed over the years.

Caring for the Earth: John Paul II

Pope Paul VI designated 1 January as a date to be observed as World Day of Peace, and asked that New Year's Day be so designated and so observed annually. He issued a special Message on the theme related to peace for this date each year. Pope John Paul II has followed this precedent. The result has been a series of papal texts constituting a powerful corpus of teaching on peace and its manifold preconditions and implications. Pope John Paul II made care for the earth the theme of his message for the World Day of Peace on New Year's Day 1990. The message is entitled: *Peace with God the Creator, Peace with all of Creation*.[16] The Pope began his message with the words:

> In our day there is a growing awareness that world peace is threatened, not only by the arms race, regional conflicts and continued injustices among peoples and nations, but also by a lack of due respect for nature, by the plundering of natural resources and by a progressive decline in the quality of life.[17]

The Pope spoke of an 'ecological crisis' and insisted that it is a moral problem. The very word 'ecology' has moral implications. The term derives from the Greek word for 'house' or 'home'. It reminds us that planet earth is our home, a home which we share with all the rest of the human family. We are morally responsible for the effect our behaviour has on the other members of the human family who share with us the same planetary home. That home has resources adequate to meet the basic needs of all, but the resources are not unlimited and are not indestructible. If one section of humanity grabs an unfairly large share of the world's resources, others will be left with less than their just share. If we irresponsibly waste or destroy or pollute a common resource of humanity – such as air, water, soil, and the conditions which make these elements life-bearing – then we inflict harm and injustice upon other human beings now living and upon future generations as well; in other words, we commit sin.

The Pope states that 'depletion of the ozone layer and the related "greenhouse effect" have now reached crisis proportions' and he calls the 'destruction of the environment' one troubling aspect of a 'profound moral crisis'. He supports the view that 'the right to a safe environment' should be 'included in an updated Charter of Human Rights'. He declares that the ecological problem cannot be addressed without international solidarity. He asks that modern society 'take a serious look at its own life-style' and pleads that 'simplicity, moderation and discipline, as well as a spirit of sacrifice, must become a part of everyday life'. For this to take place, 'an education in ecological responsibility is urgent: responsibility for oneself, for others, and for the earth'.[19]

Science, Technology and Industry

During most of the modern era, science was seen as the great instrument for human progress through the conquest of nature and the control of natural processes which it makes possible. The applications of science in industry and technology were generally seen as being without question the avenue to endlessly increasing material prosperity and to limitless improvement of the quality of life. It is true that science and technology are among mankind's greatest achievements. They have made possible hitherto unimaginable progress in the areas of knowledge, health, life expectancy, agriculture and food production, literacy, communications, information technology. It would be very foolish indeed if ecologists were ever to give the appearance of being opposed to science and technology or to industrial development. This would condemn the movement to being dismissed as one made up of luddite eccentrics. Indeed, it would be self-contradictory: it is science itself which has alerted us to the existence of an ecological crisis and which offers us possibilities for the overcoming of the crisis.

What is needed is rather that those involved in science and technology, together with the leaders of industry and political leaders, should take very seriously their responsibility for the human habitat, for the welfare of the earth and its atmosphere, for the whole environment. They must have a sense of what has been well called 'ecological accountability'. Pope John Paul declares that respect for life, and above all for the dignity and rights of the human person, is the ultimate guiding norm for any ecologically sound economic, industrial or scientific progress.

Science, technology and industry, however, if developed indiscriminately and divorced from ethical norms and from a sense of moral responsibility, can endanger the whole future of the planet. Pope John Paul says:

> We cannot interfere in one area of the ecosystem without paying due attention both to the consequences of such interference in other areas and to the wellbeing of future generations.[20]

The Brandt Report

The ecological crisis facing modern society has also been the subject of many State-sponsored and international studies and reports in recent decades. One of the better known of these is the report of the Independent Commission on International Development issues, which met under the chairmanship of Willi Brandt. Brandt was Federal Chancellor of West Germany from 1969 to 1974; hence the report is usually termed *The Brandt Report*. A commission, representative of countries in both the Northern and the Southern Hemispheres, to consider development issues and their impact on North/South relations was proposed by Robert S. McNamara when he was President of the World Bank. The actual commission was set up in 1977; it was truly international and genuinely independent. It held ten full meetings before issuing its report in December 1979.[21]

Willi Brandt, in his introduction, stresses the need for a new international world order, if mankind is to avert chaos. He wrote:

> We see a world in which poverty and hunger still prevail in many huge regions; in which resources are squandered without consideration of their renewal; in which more armaments are made and sold than ever before; and where a destructive capacity has been accumulated to blow up our planet several times over.[22]

He goes on:

> Whether these matters are discussed in Boston or Moscow, in Rio or Bombay, everywhere there are people who see their whole planet involved, at a breathtaking pace, in the same problems of energy shortage, urbanisation with environmental pollution, and highly sophisticated technology which threatens to ignore human values and which people may not be able to handle adequately.[23]

Brandt points to several instances of waste of non-renewable resources:

> The oil stock of our planet has been built up in a long process over millions of years, and is being blown 'up the chimney' within only a few generations. Exhaustion of these resources is foreseeable but their replacement by alternative fuels is not. Pollution and exploitation are all-embracing, whether of the atmosphere or soil, or of seas which are being over-fished with little regard to replenishment. Are we to leave our successors a scorched planet of advancing deserts, impoverished landscapes and ailing environments?
>
> The grave consequences of increasing soil erosion and desertification should also concern all of us. Unchecked deforestation at its present rate would halve the stock of usable wood by the end of this century (and deprive more than one billion poor people of their essential fuel for cooking). The 'absorptive capacity' of trees, which checks carbon dioxide pollution, would be reduced to a dangerous level. It is not just a risk to the environment, it is a plundering of our planet, without regard for the generations to come.[24]

The Report stressed that all ecological problems must be addressed together, and can be resolved only in a moral context. The Report states:

> The new generations of the world need not only economic solutions, they need ideas to inspire them, hopes to encourage them, and first steps to implement them. They need a belief in man, in human dignity, in basic human rights; a belief in the values of justice, freedom, peace, mutual respect, in love and generosity, in reason rather than force.[25]

A change of heart is needed, and indeed a change of philosophy and a new moral vision. The Report sees little hope for change until the industrialised countries move away from:

> a guiding philosophy which is predominately materialistic and based on the belief in the automatic growth of the gross national product and what they regard as living standards.

One of the messages of the Brandt Report is that war and poverty in the world are closely related to one another:

History has taught us that wars produce hunger, but we are less aware that mass poverty can lead to war or end in chaos. While hunger rules peace can not prevail. He who wants to ban war must also ban mass poverty.[26]

The Thorsson Report

There was much discussion in the 1970s and 1980s about economic development and its impact on world poverty, on income imbalance between rich and poor in the world and on planetary resources, and about the relations between development and disarmament. A report on *Development and International Economic Cooperation*, sub-titled *Study on the Relationship between Disarmament and Development*, was commissioned by the United Nations and was submitted to the General Assembly in October 1981. It is referred to as The Thorsson Report, from the name of the chairman of the study group that prepared the report. I call attention to some of its conclusions as an indication of the kind of consensus that was developing in these decades in the matter of ecological concern, its causes and its remedies.

The Report defines development as 'the complex of social and economic changes which can tend to improvement in the quality of life for all' (par. 33). It alerts the UN to the need to question 'long-held presumptions on the inexhaustibility of the world's resources'.[27] The Report returns repeatedly to the great and growing risks to world order and peace which are posed by the glaring disparities in the world between rich and poor states and people; declaring that these disparities are the root cause of insecurity and that true national security for the rich and the powerful consists in concerted measures to reduce these disparities by working towards a 'new international economic order'. The report insists that 'competitive accumulation of weapons' does not bring security, but only increases insecurity. It calls for a new understanding of 'national security', which will stress forms of security other than military forms. It affirms:

> The issue of greater equality between the peoples of various nations has been widely proclaimed as the principal moral imperative of our time.[28]

The Thorsson Report points out that 'the combined explosive yield [of nuclear warheads currently deployed] is about one million times greater than the bomb dropped on the city of Hiroshima in August 1945', adding that a 'general nuclear exchange' would immediately cause 250 million deaths, with tens of millions to follow in the ensuing days and weeks. It admits that these data have little meaning except as 'a categorical imperative that nuclear war must never happen'. In a sentence which recalls Pope John XXIII, the Report states:

> It is clear, in other words, that there is no conceivable national interest or complex of interests in the pursuit of which the large scale use of nuclear weapons could be construed as a rational act.[29]

The Report lists worrying signs of depletion of non-renewable resources such as arable soil, water, energy, oil; and speaks of the effect on the environment of 'greenhouse gases' and other emissions; but these issues are dealt with more comprehensively in other reports, to which I shall turn later.

World Charter for Nature
First I refer to the 'World Charter for Nature' which was presented to the United Nation's Organisation on 28 October 1982. The Charter stressed the importance of maintaining 'essential ecological processes and life support systems and ... the diversity of life forms'. Notably, it pointed out that 'competition for scarce resources creates conflicts, whereas the conservation of nature and natural resources contributes to justice and the maintenance of peace'.

The recommendations made in the Charter, however, are couched in such general and vague terms as to be of limited practical help. It must be admitted that the Charter has had little effect. Its predictions about future conflicts were, nevertheless, well founded. Many specialists believe that armed conflicts are likely in future to centre on access to oil and water, as they have centred in the past on occupation of soil and 'lebensraum'.

Global 2000 Report
The most thorough and exhaustive study of the ecological problems confronting humanity as we enter the third millennium is The Global 2000 Report to the President, sub-titled Entering the Twenty-First Century, published in the United States in 1980. It appeared in three closely printed volumes, aggregating some eight hundred pages.[30]

President Jimmy Carter called for the study in 1977, saying that he wanted it completed in one year as a aid to longer-term planning by his administration. The study in fact took three years to complete. Its merit lies in its identifying the main areas of threat to planet earth and its environment as the study views them, and its drawing up of carefully researched projections of the outcomes to be expected by the year 2000 if present trends continued. The Report cannot be ignored by any person or group interested in or having a responsibility for the well-being of the planet and its inhabitants. The authors are fully justified in stating that:

> The Study represents the [US] Government's first attempt to produce an inter-related set of population, resource, and environmental projections, and it has brought forth the most consistent set of global projections yet achieved by US agencies.[31]

The conclusions of the Global 2000 Report are, in its authors' own words, disturbing; they indicate the potential for 'global problems of alarming proportions' as we enter the third millennium. The Report begins by a review of the present position and projections for future outcomes in respect of planetary resources. As we enter the twenty-first century, the Report concludes:

> The environment will have lost important life-supporting capabilities. By 2000, 40 per cent of the forest still remaining in the lesser developed countries in 1978 will have been razed. The atmospheric concentration of carbon dioxide will be nearly one-third higher than preindustrial levels. Soil erosion will have removed ... several inches of soil from crop lands all over the world. Desertification ... may have claimed a significant fraction of the world's rangeland and cropland. Over little more than two decades, 15-20 per cent of the earth's total species of plants and animals will have become extinct – a loss of at least 500,000 species. ...
>
> The world will be more vulnerable both to natural disaster and to disruptions from human causes. ...
>
> Few if any of the problems addressed in the Global 2000 Study are amenable to quick technological or policy fixes; rather, they are inextricably mixed with the world's most perplexing social and economic problems.[32]

Cutting down the forests, including the primeval rain forests, can sometimes be seen as the advance of civilisation, through the clearance of new land for cultivation or for grazing. The destruction of the culture and way of life and even of the life itself of the tribal peoples who dwell there is ignored, if not regarded as a necessary consequence of 'progress'. Ignored too is the destruction of the natural habitat of countless animal, bird, insect, vegetable and plant species, which go back millions of years, but which, once destroyed, are for all future time irreplaceable. The consequences for the environment include desertification, soil erosion, flooding, famine, starvation and death for hundreds of thousands; but, in the boardrooms of the great business corporations these seem to feature only if and in so far as they may impinge upon the digits in their profit and loss account. Floods, famine and disease are usually seen as natural disasters, but they very often have a substantial man-made component.

The facts on agriculture are particularly worrying. The Report states:

> Perhaps the most serious environmental development will be an accelerating deterioration and loss of the resources essential for agriculture. This overall development includes soil erosion; loss of nutrients and compaction of soils; ... crop damage due to increasing air and water pollution ... and more frequent and most severe regional water shortages. ...
>
> Deterioration of soils is occurring rapidly in less developed countries. ... Principal direct causes are over- grazing, destructive cropping practices, and use of woody plants for fuel. ...
>
> Present rates of soil loss in many industrial nations cannot be sustained without serious implications for crop production.[33]

A disturbing feature is that steps taken to improve soil productivity and to reclaim arable land can have the contrary effect. For example, irrigation damages water quality by adding salt to the water, which then returns to streams and rivers. Pesticides, designed to increase crop yields, become pollutants which damage water and which also have adverse effects on soil quality and productivity. Through an accumulation of human activities soil deterioration and soil erosion are increasing yearly: six million hectares of soil are lost each year to desertification.[34] Present rates of soil loss in many industrial countries are, the Report states, unsustainable. Good agricultural land is obviously also lost to urban growth and to motorway development, inseparable though these are from industrial and economic growth.

A particular cause of concern, and even alarm, is the extinction of species and the loss of plant and animal genetic resources. The Global Report says:

> An estimate ... suggests that between half a million and 2 million species – 15-20 per cent of all species on earth – could be extinguished by 2000, mainly because of loss of wild habitat but also in part because of pollution. Extinction of species on this scale is without precedent in human history.[35]

Another estimate suggested that, if the present rate of destruction of species continues unchecked, one quarter of all life forms now existing on earth could become extinct for ever before the year 2010. Bio-diversity has direct relevance for the future of the human species; as the Global 2000 Report states:

> four-fifths of the world's food supplies are derived from less than two dozen plant and animal species.[36]

One of the main causes of extinction of species, as I have said, is destruction of tropical forests. Forests, especially in less developed countries, are being razed continuously; 40 per cent of these forests were projected to disappear in two decades. A further result will be that the carbon dioxide in the atmosphere will have increased by at least one-third in these less developed countries.[37]

Energy supplies and access thereto are also a potential source of tensions and a likely cause for future conflict. Increasing demands on oil reserves, expanding use of fuel wood (which the Global Report calls the 'poor man's oil'), and growing consumption of animal and crop waste for fuel, with a consequent loss of these materials for soil productivity – all of these factors point to energy conservation as one of the great problems of the third millennium. The Report insists that a 'world transition' away from dependence on oil must take place, but 'there is still much uncertainty as to how this transition will occur'.[38]

Indeed the 'transition' seems more remote than ever, as oil dependency is growing inexorably, rather than diminishing. It is extraordinary that, despite all the warnings, the countries of the 'developed' world and the developing countries with the highest economic growth rate, like China and India, seem to be recklessly increasing oil consumption, as if oil supplies were unlimited; whereas reliable indications point to their possible virtual exhaustion, perhaps within five or six decades. Meanwhile, all this oil-burning is almost certainly contributing to climate change to a dangerous degree. One wonders what more might be needed to create a sense of urgency about the ecological future of humankind.

When nuclear fission became possible, it seemed for a time that nuclear energy would solve all the world's energy problems. The euphoria was short-lived. The Global Report is candid about the difficulties: 'these include concerns relating to reactor safety, nuclear waste disposal and international security'.[39]

Water is essential to life, whether plant, animal or human. Access to fresh water supplies is likely to be one of the great international problems of the future. Disputes over access to shared rivers are likely to be a cause of increased tensions and carry the potential for armed conflicts in the future.[40] Proposals for diversion of major rivers, particularly in Eastern Russia, also carry danger of far-reaching climatic change.

Atmospheric change is an existing danger to which the Global 2000 Report alerts us. Increasing concentration of carbon dioxide in the earth's atmosphere, linked to the combustion of fossil fuels, is one of the causes of earth-warming, leading to climate change, melting of polar ice, raising of sea levels, loss of shoreline flatlands and catastrophic flooding. I have mentioned the 'hole in the ozone layer' as one of the consequences of such emissions. Another is 'acid rain', with its harmful effects on land and water, and indirectly on crops and fish stocks. Fish stocks are already threatened by over-fishing and fish is a main staple of diet for many.[41]

Some of these problems could be said to stem from the change in so-called 'developed countries' from subsistence agriculture to industrial agriculture, or to put it another way, from farming as a way of life to farming as a source of profit. This may be unavoidable and some of its consequences are undoubtedly beneficial; but there is a price to pay. Another way of characterising the change to which I refer could be to say that many modern people seem to have lost or are losing the sense of limits. They seem to assume that prosperity is unlimited; that food and other material goods are unlimited; indeed that earth's resources are unlimited; that there are no limits to the progress of science, and especially that there are no moral limits to mankind's using or abusing or wasting the earth's resources as it pleases. The French writer, Stanislas Fumet, wrote a book in the 1940s with the title *L'impatience des limites (Impatience with Limits)*[42]. Fumet was remarkably prescient; the title could stand for a widespread modern mentality. We have to learn once more that there are material limits to earth's resources, and moral limits to our use of them, imposed by respect for the rights of others and by reverence for God, the Creator, who made human beings stewards, and not plunderers, of the earth. The fact of death should be enough to remind us that everything human and earthly is limited.

If I may speak personally, I thank God to have been brought up in a rural environment at a time when wilful waste, whether of food or of water or of materials, was held to be morally wrong; when saving, whether of money or of goods, was seen as morally virtuous; when re-use (what we now call re-cycling) of used garments and materials was normative; and when farmers respected the quality of the soil and its need for recurrent fallow periods of 'rest' to allow its self-renewing powers to operate. It was an ecologically-friendly culture before the term came into use. It was a frugal culture, but, in my recollection, a happy one. It would be absurd to ask for a return to that culture, but its values, rightfully adapted to the changed conditions of today, are as relevant, and indeed as necessary, today as ever they were.

Barbara Ward points to places where much of that way of life survives in our own time – namely in religious communities, where men or women live what she calls 'the ungreedy life', based on 'giving' more than on 'receiving'. These communities, she suggests, are 'the joyous people of the twentieth-century', offering to the modern world models of an alternative life-style, suited to 'the times of justice which lie ahead'.[43]

The Global 2000 Report called for decisive action if 'progressive degradation and impoverishment of the Earth's resources in the years to come' are to be avoided. The Pope speaks of the 'urgent moral need for a new solidarity especially in relations between the developing nations and those that are highly industrialised' if the ecological crisis is to be effectively tackled. The Brandt Report endorsed the necessity of 'interdependence' as a 'precondition of human survival'.[44]

Dr Herbert Braun of Switzerland, in an article on what he calls 'The Non-Military Threat Spectrum', in the *SIPRI Yearbook 2003*,[45] makes equally gloomy predictions about such factors as natural disasters, technological risks like Chernobyl, the 'destabilisation of the ecological system', the ageing of the population, particularly in 'developed' societies, demography and health, the 'interconnectedness of risks'. He sees all these risks as inexorably increasing, to a point where 'in the not too distant future the load on the system will exceed the limits of the capacity to repair it'. He is speaking primarily from the perspective of Switzerland, but his argument applies more widely to the richer countries of the world generally. In the light of all these studies, concerns about the planet and the environment can no longer be dismissed as 'scare-mongering' by a few over-excited 'eco-fanatics'. The facts are undeniable, the problems are urgent, and delay in addressing them reduces the options for effective action. It is truly depressing that these successive reports, warnings and calls for urgent action have been so largely ignored, nationally and internationally.

Indeed, study of these reports reminds one very strongly of the problems besetting the Roman Empire in its declining years. The Empire was the 'developed world' of its time, faced with and vastly outnumbered by what it called the 'barbarians' (the 'less developed countries' of the time) beyond its frontiers and relying mainly on its military strength and on the historic fear its Legions aroused to keep the 'barbarians' at bay. The posture of some of the dominant world powers of today recalls the words of Horace: *'Oderint dum metuant'*; 'Let them hate, so long as they are afraid'. Horace spoke in a different context, but his words could well have been used to describe the attitude of the Roman Empire to its subjugated non-Roman peoples and towards the 'barbarians' beyond the frontiers of the Empire. They could well describe the attitudes of some in the rich and powerful 'North' towards the poor and weak 'South' today.

Population Growth and Poverty
In many international reports on care of the earth the question of population is given much prominence and in some overpopulation is claimed to the be the chief cause of poverty. The question is controversial as well as complex. It would take at least another long chapter to do the question any sort of justice, so I do not pretend to do justice to it here. I venture only a few remarks. There is certainly a connection between population and poverty; but it is by no means clear whether poverty fosters population growth or whether population growth causes poverty or in what proportion they are causally interrelated. Babies are wanted and welcomed in poor countries for many reasons, but also as being economically advantageous; in rich countries they can be seen by some as economically costly. What does seem to be clear is that reduction in poverty would itself result in lower birth rates. That certainly seems to be the case all over the 'developed' world. This part of the world suffers in part from the opposite phenomenon of population decline; in several countries birth rates are now well below replacement level. In most 'developed' countries, a serious problem is emerging, that of ageing, when a

large expansion of the older or dependent generation is accompanied by a serious contraction of the younger and economically active generation on whom the elder citizens depend. The problems of pensions, the care of the old, the shortage of workers, are increasing incrementally in the Western World, including Ireland, and can have serious consequences for the whole economy, even as early as the middle of the century. Under-population, rather than over-population, is the problem of the future for the richer countries.

Some of the population-curbing policies, including the development aid policies, proposed by the richer states to the poorer states can seem to the latter as politically motivated policies, designed to curb their populations lest they become a threat to the demographically outnumbered rich. They can be perceived as a 'cheaper' way for the rich of dealing with world poverty than development aid or debt remission, a way that does not disturb their citizens' wallets or their lifestyles. By some, indeed, these policies are seen as a threat to the culture and values of the poor. Population-curbing policies imposed by the rich on the poor as a condition of development aid or of debt reduction are likely to increase tension and insecurity rather than reduce them.

Individual Responsibility
The problems enumerated in the Global 2000 Report and in other similar reports are not other people's or other countries' problems. They are our problems too; we too are responsible. We too contribute to global warming, with its potentially disastrous consequences for human health and the human habitat. The use of certain fertilizers and of propellants used in aerosol cans and refrigerants is a factor. Other examples of damage done by humans to the environment abound. Among them are the indiscriminate and unlawful use of hormones in animals intended for human consumption and of chemicals in food production and additives in food processing; the overuse of some types of weedkillers and defoliants; the consequent release of pollutants into waterways and of untreated sewage or oil spillage and industrial waste into our rivers and seas; the still imperfectly known and inadequately controlled development of genetically modified organisms. Other examples are over-fishing and the threatened extinction of fish stocks and fish species and the threatened extermination of many existing animal species, for sport or for the fashion industry or for profit. Unrestricted burning of bituminous coal and of fossil fuels, especially in or near cities, can no longer be justified. Industrial, medical and domestic waste is another threat to the environment. Illegal dumping of such waste is a socially

reprehensible and morally wrongful practice; while such dumping 'over the border' from the Republic of Ireland into Northern Ireland for illegal, and indeed sinful, profit is quite disgraceful. Nuclear waste and nuclear leaks obviously pose grave threats to human health, notably along our own East Coast, due, there is ample reason to fear, to the proximity of Sellafield. Chernobyl, of course, stands as a grim warning to the world of how not to develop nuclear power.

The problems and the need for a sense of individual responsibility for them, are brought nearer home when we think of the lethal pollution of some of Ireland's inland lakes and rivers through industrial or agricultural waste, such as chemical effluent from factories or silage seepage and animal slurry from farms. It is frightening to think that pollution can destroy fish and plant life in lakes and rivers, not just for now, but irreversibly and for ever. Our increasing dependence on motor transport, with the continuing growth in air traffic and consequent increase in oil consumption, are obvious examples. All this is due not to natural causes beyond human control, but to a series of individual decisions and choices, and for each single one of these choices and decisions one human being or one group or one corporate body is morally responsible. We need to begin to include ecological accountability in our personal moral audit in our examination of conscience and our confession of sins.

When we speak of cosmic catastrophe and global crisis we can give the impression either that the problems are of other people's making and solving, not ours, or that the problems are too vast and impersonal for us to do anything about. Pope John Paul insists on the moral responsibility of all of us and each of us for the environment. He says:

> Today the ecological crisis has assumed such proportions as to be the responsibility of everyone ... There is an order in the universe which must be respected, and ... the human person, endowed with the responsibility of choosing freely, has a grave responsibility to preserve this order for the well being of future generations. I wish to repeat that *the ecological crisis is a moral issue*.[46]

In 1981, speaking to the United Nations University in Hiroshima, Pope John Paul, in unforgettable words, declared:

> From now on, it is only through a deliberate policy that humanity can survive.

Greed

Crimes against the environment, such as those mentioned above, are often expressions of greed, the desire for greater and quicker profit. They are often crimes committed by richer and more powerful nations, corporations and individuals against the poor. Sometimes this is done without conscious advertence to the effects of certain actions on the poor. More often it is done consciously but with indifference to the consequences for others. There is a bitter truth in a remark made by Nuala O'Faolain to the effect that great powers nowadays rarely need wars to impose their will on poor countries, since 'economics is war conducted by other means'.

The Gospel of Christ has a very different message. It is not building bigger barns – or mansions – and storing up treasure for oneself that lead to happiness in heaven or even on earth. Barbara Ward puts it in a striking paragraph:

> Greed, avarice, rapacity and careless waste destroy men and destroy society. To suppose that the unfettered pursuit of unlimited wealth would not, in Emerson's words, 'go on to madness' contradicts every beatitude pronounced by Christ. If the strong, the rich, the rapacious and the careless 'inherit the earth', then there is no meaning in the Christian Gospel. But if today the pressures of material reality in the shape of possibly less abundant resources and a certainly growing deterioration in the natural environment begin to compel men and women to reconsider the goal of unlimited consumption and to stop seeking felicity in the latest car, the latest drink, the latest jet and the latest cosmetic, the Christian can say that the physical world is beginning to reaffirm the unchanging wisdom of the moral order. We do not choke or swill or waste our way to beatitude.[47]

The share of the world's wealth which poorer countries actually have can be illustrated by a few figures. The wealth of the world's ten richest billionaires is one-and-a-half times greater than the aggregate annual national income of forty-nine of the world's least developed countries. A few years ago it was calculated that a worker in a toy factory in Indonesia producing toys for Disney earned seventeen pence per hour while Disney's Chief Executive was reputed to earn £6,700 per hour. Over the past forty years, the income of the wealthiest countries in the world has doubled in relation to the income of the poorest. In 1960, the wealthiest 20 per cent earned thirty times more than the poorest 20 per cent; in 1997, they earned sixty times more.

The gap between rich and poor at world level is enormous, and it is widening by the year. The Thorsson Report told us that 'approximately one half of the world's people live in food deficit countries'.[48] Clare Short, formerly British Secretary of State for International Development, reminded us lately that almost three billion people worldwide have to survive on less than $2 per day. She tells us that 2.8 billion of our fellow human beings live on less than the amount by which we subsidise each European cow.[49] Meanwhile Bob Geldof states that we in the 'developed' world spend more on pet food than we do on combating the scourge of AIDS, which chiefly affects the very poorest countries of the world. A respected journalist has recently stated that business corporations spend more on working out how to make children buy food and toys than the British state spends on how to teach them to read and write.[50] The poor countries of the world are becoming poorer at the same time as the wealthy nations become richer. We are witnessing, as the Pope points out, 'the emergence of new inequalities which are accompanying the globalisation process', the very process whereby the wealth of the so-called developed world is being increased.

We must remember that Ireland now belongs to the wealthy part of our world. One estimate of a decade ago calculated that the amount of cash in circulation in the Republic of Ireland was in the order of £3 billion Irish punts – and this did not include credit card spending. Another estimate suggested that over the previous Christmas season some £70 million Irish punts were spent on children's toys, an average of nearly £100 per child.

We have all been reminded recently in Ireland of the scandal whereby children at their First Holy Communion are lavishly and expensively dressed and each child is reputed to collect on average €800 in cash on the occasion. Pending the finding of ways whereby these well-meant but unfortunate practices might be brought to an end, could the children meanwhile be persuaded to give at least half of the amount to the poor children of the Southern Hemisphere? This would surely be a more fitting way to mark the solemn occasion when a child receives Jesus in Holy Communion for the first time.

Material development, as Paul VI pointed out long ago, is often accompanied by moral underdevelopment. How otherwise can we remain indifferent to a situation where more than fourteen million children die every year from under-nourishment or sheer starvation and where close to a billion people exist at a level of absolute want? How otherwise can we tolerate without protest a situation where the terms of trade of our vaunted free global market economy are stacked against the poorer nations, whose import prices and whose export prices are both fixed by the wealthier nations, and fixed to the advantage of the wealthier nations? Not only do the rich nations grow richer while the poor nations grow poorer, but in certain respects the rich nations grow richer through exploitation of the poverty of the poor nations; in effect, through making the poor nations poorer. The rich control and exploit the trade of the poor. The rich often increase their profits by exploiting the low wages and sometimes the female labour and the child labour of the poor. Moral underdevelopment on the part of the so-called 'developed world' is a mild term to use for much of the exploitation. Pope John Paul's term 'structures of sin' is appropriate. In a globalised economy, where corporations relocate to wherever they can find workers willing to work for the lowest wages, investors with a conscience will – or should – be careful where they invest and shoppers where and what they purchase.

THE MINDING OF
PLANET EARTH (2)

World Poverty and Human Rights

I have referred to the connection between care for the earth and human rights, and between both of these and world poverty. The fiftieth anniversary of the UN's Universal Declaration of Human Rights occurred in 1998. On 1 January of that year, Pope John Paul II issued his usual Message on peace to mark the World Day of Peace. The Pope's message quoted the Preamble to the Declaration, which states:

> Recognition of the inherent dignity and equality and the inalienable rights of all members of the human family is the foundation of freedom and justice and peace in the world.

He quoted a further paragraph, as follows:

> Nothing in this Declaration may be interpreted as implying for any State, group or person any right to engage in any activity or to perform any act aimed at the destruction of any of the rights and freedoms set forth herein. (Art. 30)

The Pope noted, however, the 'tragic fact' that the Declaration 'is still being blatantly violated'. I wish to point to two ways in particular in which the spirit, if not the very letter, of the Declaration is being violated. I refer to world debt and to the arms trade. Both of these aggravate, and in part create, poverty in the underdeveloped world and further widen the gap between rich and poor in the world. This in turn contrasts glaringly with the noble ideals proclaimed in the Universal Declaration, for these ideals imply a right on the part of poorer nations to have access to a fair and just share in the world's wealth and in the benefits of the global market.

Debt and World Poverty

The governments of many of the least-developed countries (LDCs in UN parlance) borrowed heavily in the past in order to finance public services like health care and education and infrastructure projects, in the hope of thereby emerging from their systemic poverty trap. The loans were advanced by individual states or by international financial institutions such as the World Bank and the International Monetary Fund. The former are referred to as 'bilateral', the latter as 'multilateral' loans. This practice left these countries with heavy burdens of debt and of interest payments. The paradoxical situation arose that poor countries were soon annually paying their rich creditors more than they were receiving from them in development aid. The end result was that borrowing countries became more deeply sunk in poverty than they had been before.

Pope John Paul II was perhaps the first to call international attention explicitly to the problem of debt as a cause of deepening poverty in the world. He was speaking about it already in the 1980s. In 1986, the Pontifical Council, Justice and Peace, issued a powerful call for action on this problem, in the document entitled: *At the Service of Human Community: an Ethical Approach to the International Debt Question*. The Commission warned of 'dangerous and costly international insecurity' and of 'a potential build-up of serious conflict situations' unless this problem was tackled and the whole issue of world poverty addressed as a matter of urgency.[51]

In 1994, in his Apostolic Letter in preparation for the Jubilee of the year 2000, *Tertio Millennio Adveniente*, the Pope made the debt problem an integral part of the Church's programme for the Jubilee. He linked this problem directly with the biblical concept of Jubilee, as described in the Book of Leviticus. He wrote:

> In the spirit of the Book of Leviticus (25:8-12), Christians would have to raise their voice on behalf of all the poor of the world, proposing the Jubilee as an appropriate time to give thought, among other things, to reducing substantially, if not cancelling outright, the international debt which seriously threatens the future of many nations.[52]

Conferences of Bishops and individual bishops and their agencies for development and international aid across the world took up the challenge and began to put pressure on their governments to advance this cause. Support came from many non-governmental agencies and from well-known individuals, like the rock star Bono. The Pope's plea was not in vain. The worldwide Jubilee movement helped to change political attitudes in several countries. The United States Conference of Catholic Bishops, with its office of International Justice and Peace, was particularly effective. President Clinton announced in 1999 that the United States would cancel 100 per cent of the debts owed to it by highly indebted poor countries (HIPCs). Some other countries followed suit.

Trócaire, the development aid agency of the Irish Catholic Bishops' Conference, has strongly urged that the current criterion for debt remission be altered in such a way as to ensure that remission would have a direct impact on poverty eradication in the debtor country. Trócaire argues for a 'human development approach', whereby the financial resources needed for basic health and education and for the basic infrastructures essential for economic development would be subtracted from the debtor countries' revenue base *before* debt remission calculations are made. This, Trócaire argues, is essential if debt remission is to achieve its aim of reducing and eventually eradicating poverty. Trócaire estimates that full debt cancellation in twenty-six highly indebted poor countries would make possible a 7 per cent growth rate in these countries, sufficient to halve the numbers living in absolute poverty. At present, most of the remaining debt owed by poor countries is owed to international creditors such as the World Bank and the IMF.

In spite of significant progress, debt remains an albatross around the neck of many countries, particularly in Africa. The results for debtor countries can be catastrophic. Interest payments can usually be met only by further borrowing. The currency of the debtor country might even have to be devalued, with the consequence that prices, and especially food prices, rise and people go hungry. In order to raise money to meet interest payments, the debtor countries have been known to sequester more land to form ranches for pasture to raise animals for export to the creditor nations, often so as to supply the huge and powerful fast-food industry in the industrialised nations. Land essential for food for the indigenous population is thereby reduced and their supply of food restricted. Thus we have the cruel and shameful paradox that food has been exported from countries which are already suffering drastic food shortages and even hunger and malnutrition at home. Such tragedies have a quite special resonance here in Ireland since our own Great Hunger of the Famine. Financial institutions, banks and multinational corporations have an important role and responsibility in this process; they cannot morally 'demand contract fulfilment by any and all means, especially if the debtor is in a situation of extreme need.'[53]

Admittedly, in many poor countries, borrowed money or international aid money has been misappropriated by corruption or diverted by despotic regimes to finance the lavish lifestyles of despots and their retainers or for the purchase of weapons for the repression of their citizens or for the prosecution of inter-state or inter-tribal wars. But a new beginning in these countries is possible only when education is improved, employment increased and poverty reduced; and these developments in turn become possible only when the debt burden is lifted and development aid guaranteed; with, in both cases, direct linkage with poverty reduction established. The Pontifical Council for Justice and Peace asks politicians to try to explain to the electorate 'the positive effects of a more equitable international sharing of resources'.[54]

Overseas Development Aid

A study prepared for the UN in 1961 calculated that just 1 per cent of Net National Income (NNI) from the countries of the developed world would be sufficient to double personal living standards within the next quarter century. This sum was adopted as a target for Overseas Development Aid (ODA) for the First Development Decade (1961-1970). The calculation had at least the merit of showing that the aim of eradicating absolute poverty in the world is an attainable goal and the cost to developed countries would not be excessive. In 1964 and 1968 a different criterion for determining the ODA target was selected. Instead of Net National Income as the base, Gross Domestic Product (GDP) was chosen as base of calculation; and the target of 1 per cent of NNI was substituted by its equivalent of 0.7 per cent of GDP as the overseas allocation from each developed country. It was a modest target; but sadly, no country came near to meeting the target.

The UN kept trying; but the wealthier nations did not seem to see the eradication of world poverty as a priority. Some preferred to see the solution to the problem of poverty in the further opening up of markets, the freeing up of trade, the further extension of globalisation. They failed to see – or at least to admit – that these measures, unless they are guided and controlled by moral principles of global justice, favour the rich more than the poor and increase the gap between rich and poor, both nationally and internationally.

The UN, however, decided to mark the new millennium by announcing a series of Millennium Development Goals (MDGs). These were listed in September 2000 as follows: eradicating extreme poverty, achieving universal primary education, promoting equality between women and men, reducing child mortality, improving maternal health, combating disease (including

AIDS, TB, malaria), ensuring environmental sustainability, establishing a global partnership for development. Obviously, Overseas Development Assistance is essential to the attainment of these goals. The last millennium goal was stated to include a commitment to delivering 'more generous development assistance for countries committed to poverty reduction'. The proportion of people living in extreme poverty was to be halved by 2015. At a Conference in Monterey (Mexico) in 2002, the wealthier nations renewed their commitment to the MDGs and committed themselves specifically to increase ODA contributions annually up to 2006. The increased contributions were to come mainly from the EU and the US. The EU leaders, at a summit meeting in Barcelona in 2002, renewed this commitment. From now on, the eradication of poverty is – officially – a first and foremost priority both within nations and worldwide. Sadly, there is a great gap between words and actions, resolutions and implementation.

It is depressing to note that James Wolfensohn, president of the World Bank, at the opening of a conference in Shanghai in May 2004 on reducing world poverty, declared that the interest of the developed world in global poverty is now 'near a low point'. Addressing the conference itself, he pointed to the increase in poverty in sub-Saharan Africa, where the number of people in extreme poverty has doubled in recent years. He declared:

> It is nonsensical that the international community is spending only $50-$60 billion a year on overseas development, compared with $900 billion in military expenditure and more than $300 billion on agricultural subsidies.

Despite the Monterey commitments on aid and trade, he said, world development aid has not increased and trade negotiations are stalled.

The Millennium Development Goals are admirable; if and when implemented they will go far towards achieving the target of halving world poverty by 2015. Unfortunately, the UN, like many of us, is better at drafting and adopting fine resolutions that it is at implementing them. Only five countries (Denmark, The Netherlands, Sweden, Norway and Luxembourg) have so far met the UN target of 0.7 per cent in Overseas Development Assistance. It would be nice to have been able to add Ireland to that list. In fact, we reached only 0.16 per cent in 1990 and 0.41 per cent in 2002. The Taoiseach has formally committed the government to attaining the 0.7 target by the year 2007. Trócaire is pressing for a phased plan to achieve this target and for a multi-annual budgeting agreement on overseas aid, so as to ensure the quality of the development programme in the less developed countries for which the programme is designed.

Trócaire is gravely concerned also at the way in which the wealthier nations seem to be 'tying' aid to countries in which they have national political self-interest. It deplores the fact that, while half of the population of sub-Saharan Africa lives in absolute poverty, not one of its countries is among the top ten recipients of aid from the EU. Indeed, a Trócaire briefing paper of July 2003 points out:

> The low priority given to [sub-Saharan] Africa is especially evident. ... The last ten years has seen a marked shift away from these countries towards the Mediterranean and Eastern Europe.

The same paper points out, however, that Ireland allocates 85 per cent of its aid to low-income countries, second only to Greece with 97 per cent.[55] Nor should we forget the extraordinary generosity of Irish people in contributing to appeals from Trócaire and many other overseas aid agencies, who are constantly supporting development projects in less developed countries, as well as bringing emergency aid in crisis situations across the poorer regions of the world. It should be noted also that, wherever there is famine or earthquake or flood or man-made disaster across the world, invariably there are Irish priests or nuns or lay missionaries or aid workers on or near the scene and engaged in relief operations.

Ireland's priority countries for development assistance are Ethiopia, Lesotho, Mozambique, Tanzania, Uganda and Zambia. It is gratifying to note that considerable progress in reducing poverty has been registered in most of these countries. Rwanda is presently receiving particular attention from Trócaire.

Trócaire has urged the Irish government during its EU Presidency in 2004 to 'turn development financing promises into action'; to 'improve the poverty focus of EU aid', and 'improve its efficiency'; to 'commit to trade justice'; to work for 'reform of the international financial institutions and for increased debt relief'; and to 'build a political culture of sustainable development', especially on the occasion of EU enlargement. One could group these aims together as a programme for an EU which is not simply bigger but more just and which is a factor for justice in the world of the third millennium.

As always, the demands of justice correspond in the end with the enlightened self-interest of those concerned. Justice for the undeveloped world is in the long-term interest of the EU itself. Unless there is both commitment and action in tackling the injustice of world poverty, the future could be grim indeed. Dr Jan Pronk, in a lecture on the Millennium and Development Goals and related matters, delivered in December 2003 at the Institute of Social Studies at the Hague, said:

> Poor people do not resort to violence for the very reason that they are poor. But poor people who experience exclusion, who see no perspective whatsoever and who feel treated as less than human beings, may become convinced that there will never be a place for them or for their children in the world system resulting from globalisation. People who feel that the system is turning against them may turn their backs to the system and develop an aversion to that system and its values. Clearly, it is not their system anyway and its values – freedom, justice, solidarity, welfare, modernity – were clearly never meant to be extended to them. Aversion can turn into hatred, and hatred into violence. It is not so difficult to recruit people willing to use violence against a system from a large crowd that is excluded from that system. Nor is it difficult to recruit people within the global system who consider themselves legitimised to act on their behalf.
>
> Poverty is not a root cause of terrorism. But it can lead to violent action against a system that is believed to be a root cause of poverty.[56]

These are wise and timely words. They apply to situations within developed countries as well as to rich North/poor South relations. They have particular resonance in present-day Muslim-Western world relations.

The Arms Trade

A major source of poverty and hardship in the world and a prime cause of the widening gap between rich and poor nations, is the incidence across the world of wars, civil or tribal conflicts, and of terrorism. This in turn is made possible by the arms trade. We know to our cost in Ireland the havoc and the misery which are inflicted as a result of the traffic in weapons. This has equipped death-dealing paramilitary organisations and now equips criminal elements, with or without links to paramilitaries. The weapons illegally imported into Ireland are only a small fraction of those legally sold abroad, and more often sold by the wealthy nations to the poorer ones. It would seem that few 'products' are easier to purchase and legally trans-ship (or illegally smuggle) in the world market than weapons of war. Once more, some figures give an indication of the material extent and the moral enormity of the problem.[57]

The sixty years since the end of World War II might be seen in history as a period of comparative world peace; yet, many millions of people have been killed in war over that period, and it is calculated that there are at present at least fifteen million refugees who have been driven from their homes by wars. Violent crime and terrorism have assumed frightening proportions in many countries today; they are by-products of the arms industry, which is so vigorously promoted and so jealously defended by some of the world's leading nations. The Pontifical Council for Justice and Peace in 1994 declared: 'Never before has our earth known so many armed conflicts, fed by a proliferation of arms, which is often taken for granted'.[58]

The connection between military budgets and ecology and poverty can be illustrated by a few stunning examples taken from the 1979 Brandt Report: (the figures are those of 1979):

1 'The military expenditure of only half a day would suffice to finance the whole malaria eradication programme of the World Health Organisation, and less would be needed to conquer river-blindness, which is still the scourge of millions.
2 A modern tank costs about one million dollars; that amount could improve storage facilities for 100,000 tons of rice and thus save 4,000 tons or more annually: one person can live on just over a pound of rice a day. The same sum of money could provide 1,000 classrooms for 30,000 children.
3 For the price of one jet fighter (twenty million dollars) one could set up about 40,000 village pharmacies.
4 One-half of one per cent of one year's world military expenditure would pay for all the farm equipment needed to increase food production and approach self-sufficiency in food-deficit, low-income countries in a short space of time.'[59]

The Report remarks:

More arms do not make mankind safer, only poorer.[60]

In his introduction to the Report, Willi Brandt had said:

He who wants to ban war must also ban mass poverty.[61]

Even the 'security' imperative invoked to justify huge military expenditures is open to serious question. 'Security' is dangerously narrowly conceived if understood merely as military security. The Brandt Report called for:

> a new, more comprehensive understanding of 'security' which would be less restricted to the purely military aspects. ... Much of the insecurity in the world is connected with the divisions between rich and poor countries'
> 'The concept of security cannot be limited to that of the military areas alone – it has to be seen as having a social and economic basis as well.[62]

Many other reports, as I have shown above, agree in emphasising this point. This emphasis is more relevant than ever to the post-'9/11'and post-Madrid '3/11' world. The true 'war on terrorism' is primarily a war on poverty, a war on the gross disparities in living standards between rich nations and poor nations and between rich and poor within nations.

The Brandt Report declares:

> In the global context true security cannot be achieved by a mounting build-up of weapons – defence in the narrow sense – but only by providing basic conditions for peaceful relations between nations, and solving not only the military but also the non-military problems which threaten them.[63]

The problem of transferring resources, even rapidly, from arms production to development, are not insuperable. The Brandt Report states:

> An argument often heard (and as often overestimated) is that arms production and exports are essential to the North's economies and employment. This is a fallacy. While it is true that the arms industries have been a source of growth and jobs, they are certainly not irreplaceable. Conversion to civilian production could be achieved faster than is often assumed because the economic problems are easier to tackle than the political ones. Recent data from the United States and other studies .... confirm that investment in arms production creates fewer jobs than in other industries and public services. There is no reason to doubt that much of the capital and manpower presently employed in arms production or other military uses can be converted into producing peaceful equipment essential to development, including capital goods, as much research has shown:

All over the world, there are large unmet needs in health and transport or urban renewal which could expand to reduce any demand gap caused by reductions in arms production.[64]

Arms imports are directly associated with poverty and are linked with military repression. Arms exports are characteristic of the 'First World', namely the richer nations and primarily the United States and Western Europe. More than half a million scientists – some 50 per cent of all the scientists of the world – are involved in military-related research projects. For the period 1998-2002, the United States heads the list of arms exporting countries, with some 41 per cent of the market; Russia comes second, with approximately 22 per cent; France has about 9 per cent and Germany 5 per cent; while the UK has 4 per cent of the global market.[65] A dozen years ago it was estimated that Britain was exporting five billion dollars worth of military equipment to governments overseas, three-fourths of these being in poorer countries in the underdeveloped world. A dozen years ago Britain exported 150 million dollars worth of weaponry to Indonesia, some of it doubtless used for military repression of the people of East Timor. Large quantities were in the early 1990s being exported to Saddam Hussein's Iraq. Total world military expenditure in 2002 was estimated at 784 billion US dollars.[66]

Landmines are an obnoxious part of this trade. Unlike other military weapons, landmines or other anti-personnel-type bombs continue to kill long after wars have ended and soldiers have been withdrawn and peace officially restored. An estimated one hundred and fifty people are killed by landmines every week, nearly all of them civilians and most of them women and children. Fortunately, an Anti-Personnel Mines Convention (APM Convention) was agreed in 1997 under UN auspices and if enough nations, including the USA, endorse and implement it, these instruments of innocent death can eventually be brought under some semblance of control. Progress, however, is appallingly slow: stockpiles of these lethal devices were supposed to be destroyed; but 230 million of them in ninety-four states remain still stockpiled.[67]

Comparative figures show how much the expectation and the quality of life in poorer countries could be bettered if the priorities of both the exporting and the importing countries were changed. It costs more than 21,000 dollars to keep a B1 bomber in the air for one hour. This amount alone could set up maternal health units in ten African villages. One intercontinental Stealth bomber, or one Seawolf nuclear high-powered submarine, each costing some two-and-a-half billion dollars, would be enough to provide immunisation vaccines for all the children of the underdeveloped world and would save many hundreds of thousands of young lives. In some poorer countries, military expenditure exceeds the total expenditure on education and health combined.

Such figures show that the problems of poverty and hunger and disease could be resolved if there was the political will to do so. It is sad to reflect that very few individuals in the so called 'Great Power' nations question taxation for military purposes; but there is no political pressure for taxation to relieve poverty. One United States commentator remarked that 'governments are armed to destroy everything except poverty'. The truth is that the purchase and the use of arms by poor countries creates greater poverty. The Pontifical Council for Justice and Peace, in the 1994 document which I have referred to already, declared that the arms trade 'is one of the most gaping, if hidden, wounds that afflict the world today'.[68]

Disarmament and Development

The armaments race which dominated the 'Cold War' in recent decades has had grave consequences for the environment and for world poverty. Disarmament could create conditions favourable for a concerted international approach to ecological problems and to the problems of world poverty. I believe that Ireland has unique qualifications for giving leadership in this area. As a member state of the EU which is not militarily involved with NATO or with any military alliance, Ireland can have a unique mediating stance so far as the new member states of the EU and the countries which are outside any existing military alliance are concerned. In earlier times Irish representatives played a distinguished role in the field of disarmament, first at the League of Nations and subsequently at the United Nations. That experience can stand us in good stead now. There certainly is a right to legitimate self-defence, for nations as well as for individuals; and in today's unstable conditions, with terrorist threats from many sides, increased spending on military security can be a popular course. But this can bring an illusory sense of security and can be accompanied by neglect of non-military security measures, particularly the pursuit of a more just world order.

The counter-ecological thrust of the arms industry has been many-sided. It has entailed a vast diversion of personnel and funds away from environment-friendly concerns and activities. The research into and production of chemical and bacteriological weapons can only be called instances of human and ecological barbarism. The consequences of the stock-piling of nuclear missiles and of the prodigiously expensive 'Star-Wars' programme still carry frightening potential for nuclear holocaust and planetary catastrophe. Some progress has been made since the ending of the Cold War in the area of nuclear armaments reduction, but, with new states acquiring nuclear capability and with a black market in nuclear materials beginning to emerge, the danger of nuclear Armageddon remains frighteningly real.

Moral Influence

I wrote above about Trócaire's appeal to the Irish government to work during its EU Presidency for a more just EU in a more just world. This might seem much to ask from a small EU member state. Nevertheless, Ireland has a significant international image and an undoubted international prestige. Irish missionaries are found all over the underdeveloped world. Trócaire and Concern and similar Irish aid and development organisations are known and respected across that world. Many Irish men and women have been directly exposed to ethnic or tribal wars in such countries as the Congo, Somalia, the Sudan, Rwanda and Liberia, as well as in Bosnia. Irish Army and Garda peace personnel are known and respected in the councils of the United Nations and of Europe and most of all in the countries where they have been deployed. The PSNI are earning favourable recognition and respect in peacekeeping operations overseas. Irish government ministers and Irish officials are respected internationally for their diplomatic and negotiating skills. Previous Irish presidencies of the European Union have won respect for Ireland in other member states. Our own national experience of Famine enables us to have unique empathy with today's famine victims across the world. Ireland has a potential international influence far beyond its size. We could exert considerable moral influence in areas like world poverty, world debt, and the arms trade. We could make a significant contribution in helping to change that lack of political commitment, which, according to the 1997 UN Development Report, is 'the real obstacle to poverty eradication'. 'Extreme poverty', according to that report, 'can be banished from the globe by early next century', if the political commitment to do so is there. Ireland should keep pressing for that commitment.

Ireland's Role in the EU

Ireland's membership of the European Community gives this country an opportunity of making a positive contribution to the ecological process, promoting what the Pope calls 'a new ecological awareness' and developing this into 'concrete programmes and initiatives'. Ireland could usefully press for greater awareness of and support for the many reports and recommendations presented to the United Nations on care for the planet. It could press for institutional reform of international organisations and of the EU itself so as to make these more effective instruments of that world justice which is the only foundation for world peace. We can bring new vision to Europe; but we must remember the sobering words of the Brandt Report: 'new vision will not end hard bargaining'.

For the credibility of Ireland's stand in this regard it is essential that we face up honestly and energetically to our own ecological and social justice problems here at home. The rehabilitation of the inner cities, the conservation of our urban and rural heritage, the preservation of our rural way of life and of our scenic attractions from inappropriate housing development and from litter, the saving of our lakes and rivers and beaches from pollution and of our seas from sewage, the improvement of public transport, the elimination of urban air pollution, effective and environmentally-friendly measures for the disposal of waste – all of these are areas where we can and should take more effective action at home, at local parish and village and town and regional level as well as at national level.

Refugees and Asylum-Seekers

We need national soul-searching too on our attitude to refugees and asylum-seekers. As a nation whose history has been marked by long lines of Irish men, women and children waiting with their pathetic bundles to board boats and ferries on their way to being refugees and exiles in foreign lands, we have a special reason and a special responsibility to show understanding of the plight of refugees and a welcoming attitude towards them. As a people with a great missionary tradition, we have surely special ties with immigrants from countries and continents to which Irish people have sent men and women missionaries for more than a century. The Irish are the last people on earth who should be tainted with racism. The 1996 Refugee Act marked an important step forward, but there is constant danger in amendments which neutralise its import. A truly Christian immigration policy, worthy of our own history, requires a change in some racist attitudes in sections of the public. Debate about any aspect of immigration policy must be careful to exclude any semblance of racism and to avoid any hurt to immigrants already living amongst us or any hint that they are not welcome. Almost every Irish family has members or relatives who once were immigrants in other countries. Let us not forget Ireland's own emigrant past.

'Supplement of Soul'

Ireland's rich spiritual tradition gives us unique resources for the task of responding to the growing crisis of world poverty and injustice. The overwhelming economic and technical and military might of the United States and the European Union needs Bergson's 'supplement of soul'. Ireland should be better placed than most European countries to offer that supplement of soul. The inclusion or exclusion of reference to God and to Europe's Christian tradition in the proposed Constitution of the European Union has a direct bearing on all of these issues, particularly on the seriousness with which we view our and the EU's responsibility towards its poor and towards immigrants and refugees and towards world poverty.

Sadly, many of us seem at present to be so fixated on gaining the world of material things that we are in danger of losing our own soul. Pope Paul VI declared that greed 'is the most evident form of moral underdevelopment'. In countries which, like the Republic of Ireland, have become rich quickly, there is a tendency to attribute economic success to neo-capitalism, or liberal capitalism. This way of organising society, congenial to a globalised economic system, can indeed bring economic benefits; but unless controlled by a moral framework, it can also widen the gap between rich and poor and be the occasion of many grave social evils. Pope Paul VI, as I pointed out in my chapter on work, identified many of its false and morally flawed assumptions: such as, that profit is the key determinant of economic progress; that competition is the supreme law of economics; that private ownership of the means of production is an absolute right that has no limits and carries no corresponding social obligations. He declares that 'one cannot condemn such abuses too strongly'.

The alternative to liberal capitalism is commonly assumed to be socialism. The term 'socialism' has a variety of meanings and a diversity of historical exemplifications. Various attempts to embody doctrinaire socialist principles in political and economic structures have ended in inglorious failure. Soviet Russia was seen by many socialists as the model socialist state early in the last century. We now know the genocidal brutalities and the repressions of freedom by which it proposed to create the 'new socialist man and woman', and the economic and ecological mess which it left behind when it fell. Communist China later became the model, then Cuba; but each was repressive, China exceptionally and brutally so, and each in turn diluted its purist socialism by infusions of free market capitalism.

Pope John Paul II, who knew Soviet-style socialism from personal experience, and who knows liberal capitalism from his frequent pastoral visits abroad and his close contacts across the world, is well placed to analyse both, as he has done in various encyclicals, notably *Laborem Exercens, Sollicitudo Rei Socialis* and *Centesimus Annus*, which I quoted in an earlier chapter. In these documents, he has made an outstanding contribution to the corpus of Catholic social teaching. It is high time in Ireland for a radical critique of both liberal capitalism and doctrinaire socialism; and I am convinced that it is Catholic social teaching which provides the most thoroughly reasoned, while politically non-partisan, basis for that critique and for a coherent national programme of social justice. It is high time for all political parties to make social justice the paramount criterion for measuring economic progress and to make the elimination of poverty at home and in the underdeveloped world a primary and agreed aim of national policy.

Taxation, Tax-Evasion and Greed

Pope Paul VI asked governments to persuade people to 'accept necessary taxes on their luxuries and wasteful expenditures' so as to bring aid to poor countries. In contrast, one of the great scandals in modern Ireland is the systematic practice of tax evasion and even tax fraud by some of our wealthiest citizens. This results in an unfair distribution of tax across the population. It is responsible, in great part, for the widening of the gap between rich and poor in this country. In the end, it is the poor, at home and overseas, who pay the price. To add to the shame, banks and financial institutions have been complicit in facilitating this scandalous practice. Pope Paul VI declared:

> It is unacceptable that citizens with abundant incomes from the resources and activity of their country should transfer a considerable part of this income abroad, purely for their own advantage, without care for the manifest wrong they inflict on their own country by doing this.[69]

The words have extraordinary relevance to Ireland in the 1990s and early 2000s. Recent revelations regarding malpractice in the world of banking show what a creeping and corrupting moral evil is avarice or greed, and how ultimately self-destructive it is. It has a voracious appetite; the more it consumes, the more it demands. The Church rightly classed covetousness among the 'seven deadly sins', thereby indicating its propensity to spawn a host of other sins.

Globalisation abroad and social and class segregation at home can serve to distance richer people from the negative consequences for the poor of their decisions regarding their domicile, their citizenship, their investments and their profits and their tax compliance. In a globalised world the sin of greed can become depersonalised. Words written by Barbara Ward are applicable:

> Sin can be institutionalised and governments and corporations and unions can do a man's sinning for him.[70]

Christ, whose name we bear, warned that 'it is easier for a camel to pass through the eye of a needle than for a rich man to enter the Kingdom of heaven'. Could it be the same for a rich nation (such as Ireland must now be classed as being)? But the Lord added: 'For God all things are possible'.[71] We must pray, strive and hope that a rich Ireland may still bestir itself to pass that Gospel test.

Change of Lifestyle

This is a moral problem and a spiritual challenge for us all. Moral and spiritual conversion and change of lifestyle are demanded from all of us. It should put us all to shame that among the serious problems of our Western society are obesity, alcohol abuse, waste and waste disposal – all of them problems of superfluity; while a major part of the world's population suffers from malnutrition, disease, lack of educational opportunity – all of them linked to poverty. I have quoted Pope John Paul as asking us to take a serious look at our own lifestyle and pleading that moderation and a spirit of sacrifice become part of our everyday life. The season of Lent takes on a new meaning and an acute new relevance in our time. Indeed the slogan 'live simply that others may simply live', is a prescription for all-year-round living in today's consumerist world.

The Pope spoke of the urgent need for 'an education in ecological responsibility'. Excellent work is already being done in these areas in many of our schools, and great tribute is due to our school principals and teachers, religious and lay, in this connection. Tribute should also be paid to the Pontifical Commission for Justice and Peace and to Trócaire and other similar organisations for their great contributions to creating an ecological consciousness and an awareness of the related problem of world poverty. More young people should be encouraged and enabled to spend some time in underdeveloped countries, sharing the lot of the world's poor and at the same time learning from them something about the happiness that can come from living simply.

Covenant and Creation

It is sometimes wrongly suggested that the Genesis story of creation bears some responsibility for the ravaging of the planet and the reckless exploitation of its resources by science and technology. The word 'subdue' in some translations of the biblical injunction to mankind to 'fill the earth and subdue it', is sometimes misunderstood by critics as giving humans licence to treat the earth as their own, to do what they like with it, uncontrolled by any moral restraints. But, as I have tried to show, the Church has always taught that man's mandate from God in Genesis is a stewardship, to be exercised under the Law of God. Man and woman are stewards of creation, accountable to God for the exercise of their stewardship. The human person is the shepherd of creation, the gardener who is set by God in the garden of earth 'to cultivate and take care of it'.[72]

The Genesis creation account cannot be separated from the account of the covenant which God made with Noah after the Flood. In chapters 6 to 9 of Genesis we read that the earth itself had soon become corrupted because of human sin, and was 'full of violence of man's making', and this led to the destructive Flood. God commanded Noah to be careful to take two of every species of animal into the ark, so that the propagation of every species over the whole earth after the Flood might be ensured. During the Flood, God had thoughtfulness for the animals as well as for the humans:

> God had Noah in mind, and all the wild animals and all the cattle that were with him in the ark.

After the Flood, God established a new world order, making a Covenant with mankind, which extended also to 'everything that lives on the earth'. The Covenant had practical implications for the earth and its animals, as well as for the people of Israel. In Exodus and Leviticus we read that the Mosaic Law imposed on the Israelites a duty of care for animals and that the Sabbath was a 'day of rest' for farm animals and for the land, as well as for its human inhabitants; and also that one year in seven was to be a year of rest for the Israelites and also for their land and animals. The sign of this Covenant was the 'bow in the clouds', the rainbow, and this has become for us the symbol of hope.

> [God said]: When the bow is in the clouds, I shall see it and call to mind the eternal Covenant between God and every living creature on earth, that is, all living things.[73]

We can truly say that ecology as a moral and religious responsibility is firmly established in the Bible itself.

Pope John Paul II quotes a truly remarkable passage from the prophet Hosea, who declares that, because of people's sins:

> Therefore the land mourns and all who dwell in it languish and also the beasts of the field and the birds of the air and even the fish of the sea are taken away' [Hosea 4:3]

Written more than 2700 years ago, the words of Hosea strike a remarkably modern note.[74]

The Pope comments:

> If man is not at peace with God, then earth itself cannot be at peace.

Prayer Inspired by Creation

For the person of faith, creation is a reflection of God's bounty and beauty and an occasion for lifting up one's mind and heart to God in prayer and praise. The Bible has repeated examples of prayer inspired by wonder at the majesty and beauty of creation and contains many psalms and hymns of praise and thanksgiving offered to God for and on behalf of creation. Noteworthy examples are many of the Psalms and the Canticle of Creation, which we find in the Book of Daniel[75]. In this Canticle, as frequently elsewhere in the Bible, the person praying speaks in the name of created things. It is as though he or she were speaking to God in their place and saying to Him what created things of every species, if they could speak, would say to God in praise and thanksgiving to Him for their being and their beauty. This is a recurring theme throughout the history of Christian prayer. It is particularly the case in the old Irish tradition of prayer. Ascribed to St Patrick himself is the *Lúireac Padraig*, the Breastplate of Patrick, one verse of which runs:

> I rise up today
> strong in the strength of the heavens:
> the light of the sun
> the brightness of the moon
> the splendour of fire
> the speed of lightning
> the swiftness of the wind
> the profundity of the ocean
> the durability of the earth

the firmness of rock.
I rise up today
with the strength of God to guide me ...

Patrick, however, was confronted by a radically different 'spirituality' of the planet in the Celtic culture which he came to Ireland to evangelise. In this culture, veneration was given to the physical sun itself, which was given a divine status. Patrick vigorously rejected this, seeing in the sun only a reflection of the splendour of God its Creator and a symbol of Christ, the infinite and eternal sun, the true Light of the world. He pities the 'wretches' who adore the creature instead of the Creator. In his Confession Patrick writes:

> For this sun which we see rises daily for us because He commands so, but it will never reign nor will its splendour last ... We believe in and worship the true sun – Christ – who will never perish, nor will he who does His will; but He will abide for ever, who reigns with God the Father Almighty and the Holy Spirit before time and now and in all eternity. Amen.[76]

Examples of creation-based Christian prayer abound in the Irish-speaking oral tradition. We find many examples in the anthology of prayers from the Irish compiled by the late and lamented Father Diarmuid O'Laoghaire, SJ, a selection from which was translated by Father Stephen Redmond, SJ. One typical prayer reads:

> No flower in field
> No fish in stream
> No bird on wing
> No shape on shore
> No star in sky
> No living thing
> But is rich in Him
> And blessed in Him
> And sings of Him.
> Jesus, praise to you.[77]

Christian mysticism regularly sees nature as reflecting in its variety and pluriformity the limitless being and beauty and abundance which are enfolded in that 'ocean of infinite being' which is God. Gerald Manley Hopkins reflects biblical creation prayers when he gives 'glory to God for dappled things' in their endless variety, which 'He fathers forth whose beauty is past change'; and when he sings of the 'dearest freshness deep down things' which comes from the creative work of the Holy Ghost, who 'broods over the bent world with warm breast and with ah! Bright wings'.[78]

The New Creation

Hopkins is here celebrating also the radically new world order established by the incarnation and by the passion, death and resurrection of Jesus Christ. This is nothing less than 'a new creation'. The universe is revealed as having been created in Christ and for Christ, and as having been renewed, re-created, redeemed, reconciled and reunited with God in Christ.

In St John's Prologue, we learn that it was through Christ that all things came to be:

> Not one thing came into being except through him.[79]

This teaching is richly developed by St Paul. The great christological hymns in Ephesians and Colossians may well derive from the eucharistic liturgy of the Apostolic Church. The hymn in Ephesians praises

> the mystery of God's purpose,
> the hidden plan be so kindly made from the beginning …
> that He would bring everything together under Christ, as head,
> everything in the heavens and everything on earth.[80]

I have quoted the Colossians hymn already in this book; I hope I may be pardoned for quoting it again here, because of its relevance in this present context. In Colossians, St Paul hymns Christ as the one in whom

> God wanted all fullness to be found …
> and all things to be reconciled through him and for him,
> everything in heaven and everything on earth,
> making peace by his death on the cross.[81]

In Romans, St Paul speaks of the whole created universe as involved in redemption, 'waiting with eager expectation for God's sons and daughters to be revealed'.

> It was not for its own purposes that creation had frustration imposed on it, but for the purposes of him who imposed it – with

the intention that the whole creation itself might be freed from its slavery to corruption and brought into the same glorious freedom as the children of God. We are well aware that the whole creation, until this time, has been groaning in labour pains. And not only that: we too, who have the first-fruits of the Spirit, even we are groaning inside ourselves, waiting with eagerness for our bodies to be set free.[82]

This is adumbrated already in the prophet Isaiah's description of the reign of justice and universal reconciliation and cosmic peace which will be ushered in by the coming of the 'shoot from the stock of Jesse', the Son of David, on whom the Spirit of the Lord will rest:

> The wolf lives with the lamb,
> the panther lies down with the kid,
> calf and lion cub feed together
> with a little boy to lead them.
> The cow and the bear make friends,
> their young lie down together.
> The lion eats straw like the ox.
> The infant plays over the cobra's hole;
> into the viper's lair
> the young child puts his hand.
> They do no hurt, no harm,
> on all my holy mountain,
> for the country is filled with the knowledge of the Lord
> as the waters swell the sea.[83]

Ecology is linked to God's purposes for the salvation of mankind, and eschatology involves the transformation of the earth and the universe as well as of our human mortal bodies. The Second Coming will include 'a new heavens and a new earth' as part of the elevation of humanity to share in the glory of the Risen Christ.

The Cross: Symbol of Universal Reconciliation

This cosmic redemption and transformation are described by St Paul as an all-embracing reconciliation of all creatures with one another and with God through the saving work of Christ. This was made possible by Christ's death on the Cross, consummated by his Resurrection.

Very early in the Church's history, the Cross was seen as a symbol of universal reconciliation. St Irenaeus, early in the second century, wrote:

> The Son of God was crucified, putting his imprint on the world in the form of a Cross, in some way sealing the whole universe with the sign of the Cross; and the sign of the Cross, with its four dimensions, is the perfect sign that it is the *whole* universe that is so sealed ...; for he is the One who makes the height of heaven shine with what is born in the depths, under the earth, and stretches out to embrace the distance from east to west, and governs all the universe, calling creatures dispersed in every direction to a knowledge of the Father.[84]

Somewhat later in the same second century, Hippolytus of Rome wrote about the Cross of Christ as being like a cosmic tree. The text is quoted by Cardinal de Lubac at the end of his book, *Catholicism*. It runs as follows:

> This wood of the Cross is mine for my eternal salvation. ... This tree, which stretches up to the sky, goes from earth to heaven. Immortal plant, it stands midway between heaven and earth, a strong prop for the universe, binding all things together, supporting the whole inhabited earth, a cosmic interlacing which embraces the whole motley of humanity; the spirit holds it firm with invisible nails so that its contact with God may never be loosened as it touches heaven with its peak, keeps its base firmly on the earth, and embraces all the atmosphere between with its measureless arms. ...
>
> Alone and bare, [Christ] struggled against immaterial forces. When his cosmic battle came to an end, the heavens shook, the stars were near to falling, the sun was darkened for a time, stones were split open, and the world might well have perished, when Christ gave up his soul, saying: 'Father, into thy hands I commend my spirit'. And then when he ascended, his divine spirit gave life and strength to the tottering world and the whole universe became stable once more, as if the stretching out, the agony of the Cross, had in some way penetrated into everything.[85]

The ecological imperative is, therefore, not unknown to the early Christian theologians; the Passion of Christ restores and preserves the integrity of creation; the duty to respect and conserve the planet is already implicit in what St Paul terms the 'language of the Cross'. Cardinal Jean Daniélou suggested that the analogy between the Cross of Christ and the cosmic tree may have come to Hippolytus from India, whose culture was known in the Hellenistic world in the second and third centuries. In Hindu thought there is the idea of the cosmic tree, a symbolic tree planted in the centre of the world, 'which supports the sky, whose roots go deep into the earth, and which in some way unites the whole world in itself.'[86]

St Paul is very conscious of the cosmic dimension of the crucified, risen and ascended Lord, in whom 'all things were created [and who] holds all things in unity', and 'through whom and in whom all things [are] to be reconciled,'

> everything in heaven and everything on earth
> when he made peace
> by his death on the Cross.[87]

The Church, St Paul continues, is the 'fullness [of Christ] who fills the whole creation', for he 'rose higher than all the heavens to fill all things'[88]

The peace of Christ extends to all creation, but, of course, it is primarily offered to humankind, whom God has made stewards of creation. The Cross again is a symbol of that universal peace; for, as Daniélou puts it, 'it indicates the four points of the compass, so as to embrace all nations, those of the north and the south, of the east and the west'[89].The Cross represents 'the breadth and the length, the height and the depth' of the charity of Christ.[90] Christ transcends all human divisions, and in Christ all forms of human conflict are to be reconciled.

In the letter to the Galatians, St Paul notes three types of conflict between human beings; and these can be regarded as typifying all forms of human conflict. Through faith and baptism, St Paul says:

> there are no more distinctions between Jew and Greek, slave and free,
> male and female, but all of you are one in Christ.[91]

The conflict between Jew and Greek can stand for all inter-national and inter-racial conflicts; that between slave and free represents the class war and the exploitation of the poor by the wealthy, the weak by the strong, which marks so much of the history of nations and of the world; the conflict between male and female represents the continual struggle for domination of women by men, for power over women by men, the struggle for greater empowerment of women. Daniélou remarks that this text of St Paul is an extraordinary text, for it 'seems to apply quite exactly to all the problems of today'. 'It is most interesting', Daniélou observes, 'that St Paul could describe so long ago the state of the world we now live in'.[92] This book, *Advent*, was published in 1949. Daniélou's words seem even more relevant now, more than half a century later, than they were at the time.

The Eucharist and Ecology

The sacrifice of Christ on the Cross and his resurrection from the dead are present sacramentally in our Eucharist. The Eucharist, like the Cross, has relevance to ecology. In the Eucharist, the risen and glorified Body of Christ is already truly and really and substantially present. The bread 'which earth has given and human hands have made' and the wine which is 'fruit of the vine and work of human hands' are changed into the very substance of that crucified but risen and glorified Body. In the Eucharist the transformation of the material universe into the glory of the risen Christ has already begun. As we are reminded in the Easter liturgy of the Eucharist, 'the joy of the resurrection renews the whole world.' And from the Eucharist, on the day which is the end of all days and the beginning of *The Day*, the day of Christ's Second Coming, the Parousia will break forth upon the whole universe in an explosion of cosmic glory.

St Francis of Assisi and Ecology

Pope John Paul in 1979 pronounced St Francis of Assisi, the twelfth-century saint, as heavenly Patron of those who promote ecology. In his 1990 New Year Message he presented St Francis as an example for all 'of genuine and deep respect for the integrity of creation'. The Pope concludes his message with these words:

> It is my hope that the inspiration of St Francis will help us to keep ever alive a sense of 'fraternity' with all those good and beautiful things which Almighty God has created. And may he remind us of our serious obligation to respect and watch over them with care in the light of that greater and higher fraternity that exists within the human family.[93]

St Francis' wonderful 'Canticle of Brother Sun' is an outstanding example of creation prayer. It should be familiar to all who are concerned about ecology:

Most high, all powerful, all good Lord!
All praise is Yours, all glory, all honour and blessing.
To You, alone, Most High, do they belong.
No mortal lips are worthy
To pronounce Your name.
All praise be yours, my Lord, through all that you have made,
And first my Lord Brother Sun,
Who brings the day: and light You give to us through him.
How beautiful is he, how radiant in all his splendour!
Of You, Most High, he bears the likeness.
All praise is Yours, my Lord, through Sister Moon and Stars;
In the heavens You have made them, bright
And precious and fair.
All praise is Yours, my Lord, through Brothers Wind and Air,
And fair and stormy, all the weather's moods,
By which You cherish all that You have made.
All praise be Yours, my Lord, through Sister Water,
So useful, lowly, precious and pure.
All praise be Yours, my Lord, through Brother Fire,
Through whom You brighten up the night.
How beautiful he is, how gay! Full of power and strength.
All praise be yours, my Lord, through Sister Earth, my mother
Who feeds us in her sovereignty and produces
Various fruits with coloured flowers and herbs.

I have referred already to Teilhard de Chardin's prose-poem, *Hymn of the Universe,* as a contemporary expression of cosmic praise, in the spirit of St Francis' Canticle, but set in a context of contemporary science.

Ecology and Mary, Mother of the Lord

A Catholic approach to ecology could scarcely be complete without reference to Mary, Mother of God, whom the Church salutes as *Regina Coeli*, Queen of Heaven, and as Queen of the Universe. There is in the Prophet Isaiah, a depiction of a great national disaster described in terms of what we might now call ecological catastrophe; it is, I believe, the background to St John's account of the miracle at Cana. Here are some verses from that chapter of Isaiah:

See how the Lord lays the earth waste,
makes it a desert, buckles its surface,
scatters its inhabitants …
Ravaged, ravaged, the earth,
Dispirited, despoiled …
The earth is mourning, withering,
the world is pining, withering,
the heavens are pining away with the earth.
The earth is defiled
under its inhabitants' feet,
for they have transgressed the law, violated the precept,
broken the everlasting covenant.
So a curse consumes the earth ..
The wine is mourning, the vine is pining away
all glad hearts are sighing.
The merry tambourines are silent,
the sound of revelling is over,
the merry lyre is silent.
They no longer sing over their wine …
The city of emptiness is in ruins,
the entrance to every house is shut.
There is lamentation in the streets: no wine,
joy quite gone.[94]

At Cana, it is Mary alone who notices that the couple 'have no wine'. With the support of a number of biblical scholars I believe that we have here an implicit recall of the above Isaian chapter, with its phrase, 'no wine, joy quite gone'. It is at Mary's request that Jesus turns the water into wine. The overflowing abundance of the wine and the excellence of its quality are emphasised in the Gospel. Human sadness and mourning and earth's ravaging are overcome by the unbounded joy of the eternal messianic banquet, of which Cana is the foreshadowing.

    That messianic banquet, the wedding feast of the Lamb, is described in the Book of Revelation:

Then I saw a new heaven and a new earth: the first heaven and the first earth had disappeared now, and there was no longer any sea … God will wipe away all tears from their eyes; there will be no more death, and no more mourning or sadness. The world of the past has gone.[95]

Ecological disaster is transformed into a new world of glory, radiating from the Risen Lord, who, as St Paul says,

> in the order of the Spirit, the Spirit of holiness that was in him, was proclaimed Son of God in all his power through his resurrection from the dead.[96]

Cana was the first manifestation of that glory in the public ministry of Jesus, as St John tells us:

> This was the first of the signs given by Jesus: it was given at Cana in Galilee. He let his glory be seen, and his disciples believed in him.[97]

The miracle at Cana has ecological application. And it happened through the mediation of Mary, Mother of the Lord. We can confidently entrust to Mary's motherly care and to her prayers the task of human caring for the earth, 'our common and only, fragile and beautiful, home.'

So, in spite of all 'the portents – the cold statistics, the burning realities' – of which Barbara Ward wrote and which so many ecological reports substantiate, I end this chapter and this book on a note of hope. When the Apollo XI astronauts started on their historic space flight to the moon they brought with them recorded messages from the Heads of State of all the states across the world. These they deposited on the surface of the moon before their return to earth. Pope Paul VI, as Head of the Vatican City State, was included. He chose as his message the text of the eighth psalm. These words, recorded on a small disk of indestructible metal, are now embedded in the surface of the moon, like a 'faithful witness in the skies.'[98] They are a reminder to us, at the dawn of the space age, that God's word does not pass away. They can stand as a sign of our indestructible hope, whatever the future may hold. The words are:

> O Lord, our God, how wonderful is your name
> over all the earth …

When I see the heavens, the work of your hands,
the moon and the stars which you arranged,
what is man? – Yet you keep him in mind.
Mortal man? – Yet you care for him.

O Lord, our God, how wonderful is your name
over all the earth.[99]

APPENDIX
BEHOLD YOUR GOD

A meditation on the relevance of the Bible for modern scientific man*

> 'Lift up your voice with strength, lift it up, be not afraid, say to the cities of Judah, *Behold your God*'.

But is it possible for us today to lift up our voice with the strength of conviction conveyed in Handel's majestic music and, unafraid, to say to the secular cities of the 2000s; 'Behold your God'? One is tempted to think: it was so much easier in Handel's time. But now the world might seem to get on very well without God. Bishop John Robinson asked, 'Can a contemporary person *not* be an atheist?'[1]

Science and the sense of human power and self-sufficiency it brings, on one hand; the problem of evil and man's moral revulsion from pointless suffering, on the other hand, are powerful thrusts of modern atheism. Religion, in face of them, can seem on the defensive, unsure of itself, frightened.

Sometimes people answer by saying that this is only because my grandmother's religion is being confronted by my father's science. I do not like this way of putting it. My grandmother's religion was in many ways so much better than mine. God was far more real to her than He is to me. Her sense of God was far more able to cope with both cosmos and catastrophe than mine is.

It would be a great mistake to think that people were being childish and pre-scientific when they spoke of God as 'high above', 'up there' in heaven, or 'out there', 'beyond' outer space. They knew very well that this language

---

*The original of this text was broadcast in the BBC Northern Ireland Home Service in 1967. The broadcast was introduced by excerpts from Handel's *Messiah*. The text was published in *The Irish Ecclesiastical Record* in August 1967. There are some duplications with passages in the main body of the book, but I hope these may be forgiven, since I wished to respect the integrity of the broadcast text (although I have added my references in footnotes). I have retained the style of the spoken word.

wasn't to be taken literally. It was only a way of acknowledging God's immensity and majesty and mystery. And people remembered to say at the same time that God is nearer to me than I am to myself, that God is in the depths of my soul and my experience. Traditional language about God is tied to no 'three-decker model' of the universe and is as relevant in the age of astrophysics as it was in the days of 'celestial spheres'. The biblical and Christian God was never thought to be in space or time at all. He is reached by love, not levitation.

Listen to the robust no-nonsense words of a fourteenth-century English writer, the author of *The Cloud of Unknowing*, who raps the foolishness of people who take the word 'up' literally in respect of God:

> For if it so be that they either read or hear read or spoken, how that men should *lift up their hearts unto God*, at once they stare in the stars as if they would be above the moon, and hearken as if they should hear any angels sing out of heaven. These men will sometimes with the curiosity of their imaginations pierce the planets and make a hole in the firmament to look in thereat. These men will make a God as they like and clothe Him full richly in cloths, far more curiously than even was He depicted on this earth ... And therefore they say that we should have our eyes upwards. I grant well that in our bodily observance we should lift up our eyes and our hands. ... But I say that the work of our spirit shall not be directed neither upwards nor downwards, nor on one side nor on the other, nor forward nor backward, as it is with a bodily thing. Because our work should be ghostly, not bodily, nor on a bodily manner wrought.[2]

Later on the same writer declares that Christ did ascend into heaven' but that this was only 'for seemliness'.

> But else than for this seemliness, He needed never the more to have gone upwards than downwards; I mean for nearness of the way. For heaven ghostly is as near down as up, and up as down, behind as before, before as behind, on one side as on other. Insomuch, that who had a true desire for to be at heaven, that same time he were in heaven ghostly. For the high and nearest way thither is run by desires, and not by paces of feet ... And surely as verily is a soul there where it loveth, as in the body that liveth by it and to the which it giveth life.[3]

That was long before science revealed to us the vastness of astronomical space and geological time. If we had kept that adult and mature idea of God which many pre-scientific Christians had, science would never have intimidated faith. But what happened was that the soul contracted as science expanded, instead of expanding with it. We badly need for this scientific age, as Bergson put it, a 'supplement of soul'. The soul in us is a name for our capacity for God. It's because our God has become too small, too vague, too vacuous, that our soul, in this age of science, has become like the Emperor Hadrian's 'poor wee wisp of a thing, nebulous and vanishing'. The soul can't be science-size unless it feeds on a God who is Big enough – Big enough *to be God*. The God who is big enough for men of the science-age is the God of the Bible and of Christian faith. The supplement of soul we need will come only from a supplement of diet of the true and living , creative and loving God, made real for us in faith and prayer and praise.

It is sometimes said, for example, that religion is discredited by what science has shown us of the vast meaningless enormities of manless space and mindless time. Man and his planet are reduced to insignificance. His philosophy and his religion are shown up as presumptuous irrelevance.

But what, then, of science itself? It too is earth-based, man-made and human-shaped. If man's thoughts are held vain in a scientific universe, then science too must be held vain in the scientific universe it has itself unveiled. And this is plain self-contradiction.

And what is science itself but the extension of man's thinking, man's measuring, man's mathematics, man's mental categories and techniques, endlessly out into space, endlessly down into matter, endlessly back into time? The probes of science are all manned-probes. And wherever science has gone with its manned-probes, it has found mind-like structures, mathematical and therefore mental patterns in matter. Mind was everywhere throughout the universe before man's mind caught up with it. And science is just man's mind discovering, at the end of our giant telescopes and electron microscopes, presences of mind where man's mind never penetrated before, patterns of mind that man's mind never designed.

Who can account for this better than the person who knows that an Infinite Mind created the universe and that science is the discovery of God's mindfulness in it? Nobody expressed the scientific attitude to the cosmos better than the ancient Hebrew who wrote the eighth psalm. He felt, as crushingly as modern man feels, the overpowering immensity of space and the insignificance of man beneath the stars.

When I see the heavens, the work of your hands,
the moon and stars which you arranged,
what is man? ...

But then he reflected that man alone in nature shares reason with God, and can recognise in nature the working of God's mind. He recalled that in man alone the cosmos can become conscious that it is created; and can speak its Maker's name and sing His praise. For man is nature's priest and through him nature fulfils itself by singing its Creator's glory. Creation, become conscious of itself in man, is prayer, is liturgy. So the author of the psalm went on:

What is man – that you should keep him in mind?
mortal man, that you care for him?...
O Lord, our God, how wonderful is your name through all the earth.

What is man? – Yet God is mindful of him! Science is the discovering of God's mindfulness of man and of cosmos. Science is possible because God made nature and nature bears upon it the patterning of His mind. God made man's mind also, in the image of His own, and thereby made man capable of understanding and explaining nature and capable of being 'reminded' by nature of the God who made it. And therefore science and technology can be man's instrument for the 'minding' of nature and the shaping of it more and more to the Mind of its Maker and the purpose of its making.

The eighth psalm expresses man's vocation from God to understand and control nature. It repeats the great charter of science and technology given by God to man at the moment of man's appearance on the earth, as described in the Book of Genesis: 'Be fruitful, multiply, fill the earth and conquer it. Be masters of the fish of the sea, the birds of heaven and all living animals on the earth'.[4] Indeed, this is part of what is meant by man's being made in the image of God: 'God said, Let us make man in our own image, in the likeness of ourselves, and let them be masters of the fish of the sea, the birds of heaven ... and all the beasts ...'[5]

But it is not primarily science as power which makes man like to God; but science as power at the service of love and justice. The Book of Wisdom prays:

> God of my fathers, and Lord of mercy,
> you have made all things by your word
> And by your wisdom you have appointed man,
> that he should have dominion over the creature that was
> made by You
> that he should order the world according to equity and justice,
> and execute justice with an upright heart.[6]

Bertrand Russell long ago warned the modern world of the dangers of power without love, and said even that 'what the world needs is Christian charity, love or compassion' to control the terrifying power of science.[7] St Paul had put it better long before when he said:

> If I have all the eloquence of men or of angels, but speak without love, I am simply a gong booming or a cymbal clashing. If I have the gift of prophecy, understanding all the mysteries there are, and knowing everything, and if I have faith in all its fullness, to move mountains, but without love, then I am nothing at all ... it will do me no good at all.[8]

It is only science at the service of love which gives to creation the meaning God intended it to have. For, as Mother Julian of Norwich said, in that same wonderful English fourteenth century, 'Love was His meaning'.

> Wit it well: Love was His meaning. Who shewed it to thee? – Love. What shewed He thee? – Love ... Thus was I learned that Love was our Lord's meaning. And I saw full surely in this and in all, that ere God made us He loved us; which love was never slacked, nor ever shall be. And in this love He hath done all His works; and in this love He hath made all things profitable to us; and in this love our life is everlasting. In our making, we had beginning; but the love wherein He made us was in Him, from without beginning: in which love we have our beginning.[9]

If love was God's meaning in the making of us, then love must be our meaning in the making of our lives. 'Charity unmade is God', said Mother Julian, 'Charity made is our soul in God; Charity given is virtue.'[10]

For as verily as we have our being of the endless Might of God and of the endless Wisdom and of the endless Goodness, so verily we have our keeping in the endless Might of God, in the endless Wisdom, and in the endless Goodness. For though we feel in us wretches, debates and strifes, yet are we all-mannerful enclosed in the mildness of God and in his graciousness. For I saw full surely that all our endless friendship, our stay, our life, and our being, is in God ...

Thus saw I that God is our very Peace, and he is our sure Keeper when we are ourselves in unpeace, and he continually worketh to bring us into endless peace. And thus when we, by the working of mercy and grace, be made meek and mild, we are full safe; suddenly is the soul oned to God when it is truly peaced in itself; for in him is found no wrath.[11]

Love was His meaning and peace His ending. Man is most God-like when he turns knowledge into love and power into peace. It is then that the fitful fever of man's life, the toil and anguish of his history, have the meaning meant by God.

In a splendid poem, 'God's Grandeur', Gerald Manley Hopkins wrote:

The world is charged with the grandeur of God.
It will flame out, like shining from shook foil;
It gathers to a greatness, like the ooze of oil
Crushed. Why do men then now not reck his rod?
Generations have trod, have trod, have trod;
And all is seared with trade; bleared, smeared with toil;
And wears man's smudge and shares man's smell: the soil
Is bare now, nor can foot feel, being shod.
And for all this, nature is never spent;
There lives the dearest freshness deep down things;
And though the last lights off the black West went
Oh, morning, at the brown brink eastward, springs –
Because the Holy Ghost over the bent
World broods with warm breast and with ah! bright wings.

The poet feels that man's industrial presence mars the fresh beauty God gave to unspoiled nature; but God restores it in the bright glow of morning, before the factory chimneys black the sky again. This is beautiful as poetry. But theologically, we must insist that industry too can and should charge the world with the grandeur of God. The Holy Spirit must be implored to brood with the warmth of love and the brightness of justice over the bent world of industry and trade. And when He does, the smear and smudge and smell of man the worker can become a space of freedom and love around the globe in which people can serve their fellow humans and find God. Christ, who came amongst men to work and to serve and to give His life as a ransom for many, is the first to whom the Holy Spirit was given. Work done for Him, service given to Him in His brothers and sisters, can, by the same Holy Spirit, bring good news to the poor, proclaim liberty to captives, give sight to the blind and set the downtrodden free.[12]

Never was love more brutally jack-booted by power than in Auschwitz, Belsen, Dachau, and Buchenwald. But even here the Holy Spirit brooded, amid the smell of decomposing bodies, and His love warmed men's shattered lives and rose up to God in irrepressible praise.

Father Joseph Müller, awaiting death in his prison cell in Brandenburg-Görden, in 1944, prayed:

> There is nothing here that brings joy or warmth. I only know that you are here my God, you whom I have made God in my temple of suffering, companion of my solitude, my confidant in all my thoughts and desires. Thoughts and desires! Here in your creation stands a portion of your omnipotence, given me by you as part of my life, which I am to bring with me on my journey to you – man. You inhabit his spirit; you look at me through his eyes; he stands on every road I take – your creation, man ... Through you, we are full of joy, warmth, and love towards one another. When you rejoice, the light of it shines out to me from their eyes. Then all the comfort, all the joy, all the light that comes from you spreads over the bond of brotherly love ... We saw one another in storm and ascent, in love and struggle, when the will was lame and the soul numb, and when the body was weary and ill ... For, in order to come to you completely, one must always first traverse a zone of silence and weeping, for you are to be found only on the paths of compassion and charity ... It is your will, then, that among brothers and sisters each – the one thanks to the other – should grow beyond himself and be led onward to those eternal powers and truths for which, indeed, a human being lives. Whoever has not seen your light shining above brothers and sisters has never in his life seen your most beautiful light.[13]

It is not power which has the last word, but love; and its word is forgiveness and peace among men, and prayer and praise to God. It was for man's prayer that the world was made. St Francis de Sales said: 'All things have been created for the sake of prayer'. Science, technology, industry, politics, all find their final meaning in prayer. Never had man better cause for prayer as praise and adoration and thanks than today. Never had man more need for prayer as repentance and intercession than today. And what better prayer for contemporary man than the 138th psalm? For however far down we go into the proto-particles of matter or into the depths of the unconscious or the ultimates of human concern and commitment, however far back we go in time, however far out in space, we will everywhere and always be encountering God.

> O Lord, you search me and you know me,
> you know my resting and my rising
> you discern my purpose from afar.
> You mark when I walk or lie down,
> all my ways lie open to you …
> O where can I go from your spirit,
> or where can I flee from your face?
> If I climb the heavens, you are there.
> If I lie in grave, you are there.
> If I take the wings of the dawn
> and dwell at the sea's furthest end,
> even there your hand would lead me,
> your right hand would hold me fast …
> For it was you who created my being,
> knit me together in my mother's womb.
> I thank you for the wonder of my being,
> for the wonders of all your creation.

NOTES

Chapter I: SCIENCE AND FAITH

1 Johann Hari, *The Sunday Tribune*, 15 February 2004

2 Some of the writing popular in the 1960s about 'religionless Christianity' assumes as a premise the truth of the theory that copernican astronomy definitively destroyed the religious picture of the cosmos. See the Bishop of Woolwich's *Honest to God*, SCM 1963, and *The New Reformation* SCM 1965; John Wren-Lewis, 'Does Science Destroy Belief? in *Faith, Fact and Fantasy*, Fontana Books, 1964, pp. 11-44. These draw extensively on Barth, Bonhoeffer and Tillich. See Dietrich Bonhoeffer, *Letters from Prison*, Fontana Books, 1959, pp. 90-95, 106-10; *Ethics*, Fontana Books, p. 75-78, 88-109; Paul Tillich, *The Shaking of the Foundations*, Penguin Books, 1962, pp. 11-21, 59-70, 99-108; *The New Being*, SCM Press, 1963, p. 63-91; *Theology of Culture*, A Galaxy Book, Oxford University Press, New York, 1964, pp. 43-51; *The Courage to Be*, Fontana Books, 1962, pp. 114-34; 176-83, E.L. Mascall was a penetrating critic of this thesis: see his *The Secularisation of Christianity*, Darton, Longman and Todd, 1965, especially pp. 107-40, 190-212; see also his *Christian Theology and Natural Science*, Longmans, London, 1956, especially pp. 1-31, 91-104, 132-55. Cf. Daniel Jenkins, *Beyond Religion*, SCM Press, London, 1962.

3 Hume's *Dialogue Concerning 'Natural Religion'*, (edited with an Introduction by Norman Kemp Smith), Nelson (1935), 1947, p. 148.

4 A.C.B. Lovell, *The Individual and the Universe*, Oxford, 1959, pp. 8, 11. Compare Alexander Koyré, *From the Closed World to the Infinite Universe*, Harper Torch Books edition, New York, 1958. Koyré speaks of the copernican revolution as a spiritual revolution or crisis. He writes (p. 29): 'I need not insist on the overwhelming scientific and philosophical importance of copernican astronomy, which, by removing the earth from the centre of the world and placing it among the planets, undermined the very foundations of the traditional cosmic world-order'. Koyré however, a philosopher of Jewish birth and secular education, came gradually closer to a Christian and Catholic world view as his life advanced. He was at one time a friend of Edith Stein.

5 James Jeans, *The Mysterious Universe*, Cambridge, 1937, pp. 2-3.

6 Reprinted in *Mysticism and Logic*, 1918; my edition is that by Penguin Books, 1953.

7 pp. 51, 59. The same theme is developed, in less Miltonic prose, as if it were the intelligent man's guide to the history of science, in Russell's *Religion and Science*, Home University Library, Oxford (1935) 1949; see especially pp. 19-48.

8 *Portraits from Memory*, Allen and Unwin, London, 1956, p. 196; see also Alan Wood, *Bertrand Russell, The Passionate Sceptic*, Allen and Unwin, 1957, p. 232.

9   C.E.M. Joad, *Guide to Modern Thought*, Faber, London, 1933, pp. 39-40.

10 This aspect is particularly evident in Bertold Brecht's play, *The Life of Galileo* (English translation by Desmond I. Vesey, published by Methuen, London, 1963). The play is in large part a brave-new-world-ish propaganda tract in praise of science and technology. But it falsifies the historical perspective, projecting into Galileo's time the thought-patterns widespread in our own.

11 Book ii, *Prosa*, vii.

12 Collingwood, *The Idea of Nature*, Oxford, 1945, pp. 96-97

13 *The Almagest*, Book 1, Chatper 5. See C.S. Lewis, *Essay Collection and other Short Pieces*, ed. Lesley Walmsley, Harper Collins, London 2000, p. 145. Annibale Fantoli says Ptolemy's astronomical system remained for more than 1400 years the Alpha and the Omega of theoretical astronomy'. See Fantoli, *Galileo, For Copernicanism and for the Church*, Vatican Observatory Publications Rome, 1994, p. 8. I draw copiously on Fantoli's work in the next chapter.

14 *S. Theol.*, I, 32 ad 2.

15 James Brodrick, *Robert Bellarmine*, Vol. II, pp. 360-1. Brodrick quotes the great French scientists, Henri Poincaré and Pierre Duhem, in support of this view. Duhem's 'instrumentalist' view of science was, however, eccentric and is now discredited. (See Fantoli, *Galileo*, Vatican Observatory Publications, pp. 15-16 and n. 18; and Fantoli 2002, pp. 4-9 and 30).

16 *In 8 libros Physicorum Aristotelis Expositio*, III, 1, 8, 4, (ed. P.M. Magiolo, Marietti, Rome, 1954, 352)

17 cfr. *S. Theol.*, 1, 7; 46, 2, and 7.

18 *S. Theol.*, I, 46, 1.

19 *S. Theol.* 1, 46, 2: 'the temporal origin of the cosmos cannot be demonstrated from the nature of the cosmos itself' cfr. *De Potentia*, III, 14-5 and 17; *Opusc, De Aeternitate Mundi*, in *Opuscula Omnia*, ed. J. Perrier, Lethielleux, Paris, 1949, pp 53-61; *Quodlibetum* III, a, 31 in *S. Thomae Aquinatis Quaestiones Disputatae*, etc., (ed. R.M. Spiazzi, Mariette, Rome, 1959); S.C.G., II, 31-38.

20 Koestler, op. cit., pp. 94. seq. Koestler's suggestion that Copernicus 'let in the destructive notions of infinity and eternal change, which destroyed the familiar world like a dissolvent acid' (p. 216) is disproven by the reading of the texts; and with it falls another sub-theory, namely that 'This meant, among other things, the end of intimacy between Man and God. Homo sapiens had dwelt in a universe enveloped by divinity as by a womb; now he was being expelled from the womb. Hence Pascal's cry of horror' (p. 218).

21 cf. E.L. Mascall, *Existence and Analogy*, Longman, London, 1949, pp. 73-74.

22 Philip McNair; see *The Listener*, 1st July, 1965.

23 In a broadcast on 'The World and the Observer' see *The Listener*, 6th February, 1958

24 cf. Emil Brunner, *The Word of God and Modern Man*, Epworth Press, London, p. 33.

25 See John Polkinghorne *Belief in God in an Age of Science*, Yale University Press. New Haven and London, 1998, pp. 5-11.

26 H. Bondi, 'Some Philosophical Problems in Cosmology', in *British Philosophy in the Mid-Century*, ed, C.A. Mace, Allen and Unwin, London, 1957, pp. 195-201; the reference is to p. 197.

27 *The Nature of the Universe*, Blackwell, Oxford, 1950, p. 5; cf. his *The Frontiers of Astronomy*, Mercury Books edition, London (1955), 1961, pp. 342-7.

28 Thus Bertrand Russell, in 'On Scientific Method in Philosophy' (1914) (*Mysticism and Logic*, Penguin Books edition, pp. 96-97): 'In the days before Copernicus, the conception of the 'universe' was defensible on scientific grounds: the diurnal revolution of the heavenly bodies bound them together as all parts of one system, of which the earth was the centre. Round

this apparent scientific fact many human desires rallied: the wish to believe Man important in the scheme of things, the theoretical desire for a comprehensive understanding of the whole, the hope that the course of Nature might be guided by some sympathy with our wishes. In this way, an ethically inspired system of metaphysics grew up, whose anthropocentrism was apparently warranted by the geocentricism of astronomy'. Professor J.J.C. Smart of Adelaide wrote: 'In the Middle Ages the aristotelian view that man stood at the centre of the cosmos prevailed. There was a spherical earth around which the various sublunary and superlunary spheres rotated. This cosmology was clearly very congenial to Christian theology ... (which) ... gave to man a unique place in the cosmos ... No wonder that there was resistance against the non-anthropocentric cosmologies of Copernicus and later scientists. Modern cosmology is even less anthropocentric'. (*Philosophy and Scientific Realism*, Routledge and Kegan Paul, London, 1927, p. 254)

29 *Ethical Studies*, Oxford, 1927, p. 254.

30 *Pensées*, Everyman's Library Edition, J.M. Dent, London, 1943, nos. 205, 206

31 *Pensées*, nos. 347-8.

32 Thus, in Bertrand Russell's *Why I am not a Christian* (edited by Paul Edwards, Allen and Unwin, London, 1957), we read on p. 17: 'We want to stand on our own feet and look at the world ... see the world as it is and not be afraid of it, conquer the world by intelligence and not merely by being slavishly subdued by the terror that comes from it. The whole conception of God is a conception derived from the ancient Oriental despotism. It is a conception quite unworthy of free men. When you hear people in Church debasing themselves and saying that they are miserable sinners, and all the rest of it, it seems contemptible and not worthy of self-respecting human beings.' But on p. 32, only 15 pages later, we read: 'Religion has, however, other appeals, especially to our human self-esteem. If Christianity is true, mankind are not such pitiful worms as they seem to be; they are of interest to the Creator of the universe. This is a great compliment.'

33 *Orthodoxy*, John Lane, The Bodley Head, London, 1912, pp. 160-2.

34 *The Listener*, 28th November, 1963.

35 Cambridge, at the University Press. My edition is the Pelican Books edition, published in 1938.

36 Op. cit. pp. 7-19.

37 *An Essay on Metaphysics*, Oxford (1940) 1962, pp. 2123-21.

38 Op. cit. p. 226.

39 See his *Mystery and Philosophy*, SCM Press, London, 1957, for an excellent critique of some aspects of British analytical philosophy in his time.

40 *Mind*, vol. XLIII (1934), pp. 446-68.

41 Op. cit., p. 465. It is relevant at this point to recall studies (such as those of C.G. Hasking, Charles Singer, Lynn Thorndike, Pierre Duhem, G. Sarton), which show that there is more continuity than has been commonly assumed between medieval natural philosophy and the origins of modern science. A.C. Crombie argues that the combination of logical coherence with experimental confirmations which are the basis of Western science, 'was brought about by the interests and genius of the peoples who entered into the classical intellectual inheritance during the so-called Dark Ages and Middle Ages', and shows 'how the interests and methods then established are essentially continuous with those in evidence since the seventeenth century'. (Preface to *Robert Grosseteste and the Origins of Experimental Science*, 1100-1700, Oxford, 1953).

42 I have discussed some of these questions more fully elsewhere. See an essay entitled: 'Metaphysics and the Limits of Language', published in *Prospect for Metaphysics*, ed. Ian Ramsey, Allen and Unwin, London, 1961, and reprinted in *New Essays on Religious Language*, ed, by

Dallas M. High, Oxford University Press, N.Y. 1969. See also my essay, *The Knowableness of God*, published in *Philosophical Studies*, Vol. IX, December 1959.

43 See *The Irish Times*, 15 February 2003. The book from which the extract is taken is *The Devil's Chaplain*, published by Weidenfeld and Nicolson, 2003. The thirteenth-century manuscript I have referred to is reproduced on the cover of Umberto Eco's work, *Le problème esthétique chez Thomas d'Aquin*, Presses Universitaires de France, 1993.

44 *A Devil's Chaplain*, pp. 242-8. Here too, however, Dawkins ruins his case by presenting a risible caricature of the reasons which Christians give for believing as they do.

45 H.A. Reason, *The Road to Modern Science*, Bell, London, 1944, pp. 207-9. Wightman comments on the incident: 'The light of Neptune is thus a reflection of the light of Newton's thought which shone with such power as actually to bring new material bodies within the range of human ken'. (*The Growth of Scientific Ideas*, Oliver and Boyd, London, 1951, p. 108).

46 *The Nature of the Universe*, p. 5.

47 *Man and Materialism*, Allen and Unwin, London, 1957, pp. 155-7.

48 See the *Irish Times*, 18 July 2002. Professor Reville is a regular contributor on matters of science for the *Irish Times*.

49 *The World As I See It*, The Thinker's Library, Watts, London, (1935) 1949, p. 5.

50 cf. J. Walton, *Six Physicists*, Oxford, 1941, p. 26.

51 See E. Schrödinger, *Science and Humanism, Physics in Our Time*, Cambridge University Press, 1951.

52 The article was published in *Spirituality*, Dominican Publications Dublin, in the issue of September/October 2003.

53 Wisdom: 7-9. The writer of the Book of Wisdom saw all categories of knowledge as forming a unity and as deriving from one source, the Eternal Wisdom of God the Creator. His enumeration of types of knowledge, based on those pursued in the Greek culture of the last century BC, included 'the structure of the world and the properties of the elements, ... the solstices and the succession of the seasons, the revolution of the year and the position of the stars, the nature of animals and the instincts of wild beasts ...'. In other words, what we now know as the sciences would have been included in his list and would have been seen as a reflection in nature of the Creator's Eternal Wisdom. Science itself would have been seen as the result of man's being made in the image of God. The writer knew the 'gladness and joy' of such knowledge. He would have had some experience akin to the excitement of scientific experimentation and the thrill of scientific discovery.

54 A.D. Lindsay or Lord Lindsay of Birker, was Professor of Moral Philosophy at Glasgow University, then Master of Balliol College, Oxford, and Vice Chancellor of Oxford University. He was appointed principal of the new University College of North Staffordshire at Keele in 1949, and died in 1952. The books by Lindsay on Christianity and democracy to which I refer here are the following: *The Moral Teaching of Jesus*, Hodder and Stoughton, 1938; *The Modern Democratic State*, Oxford University Press, 1962; *The Two Moralities*, Eyre and Spottiswoode, 1940. See also his *Christianity and Economics*, Macmillan, 1934.

55 *The Modern Democratic State*, p. 58.

56 From the *Acta Procunsularia*; see J. Stevenson, *A New Eusebius*, SPCK, 1995, pp. 249-250.

57 *The Modern Democratic State*, pp. 58-62.

58 Ephesians, 4: 23-4.

59 *The Moral Teaching of Jesus*, especially pp. 35-6. This volume is sub-titled; *An Examination of the Sermon on the Mount*. See also *The Two Moralities*, especially pp. 41-70. Interesting also is Lindsay's chapter on St. Paul's teaching on slavery. See *op. cit.*, pp. 71-90. There are echoes here of Bergson's *Les Deux Sources*, on the two sources of morality. Lindsay wrote also on Bergson, by whom he was doubtless influenced.

60 *The Moral Teaching of Jesus*, p. 47.

61 *Op. cit.*, pp. 47-9.

62 *The Modern Democratic State*, pp. 62-3. The quotation is from D'Entrèves, *The Medieval Contribution to Political Thought*.

63 H. de Lubac, *Sur les chemins de Dieu*, Aubier, Paris, 1956, p. 202.

64 Will Hutton, *The Observer*, 9 February, 2003.

65 *Beowulf*, A New Translation, Faber, 1999.

66 cfr. *2 Corinthians*, 4:6.

67 *Summa Contra Gentiles*, ii, 2 (translation by James F. Anderson, Image Books, Doubleday, New York, 1956). *Op. cit.*, p. 48.

68 *Waiting on God*, English translation by Emma Craufurd, Collins. Fontana Books, (1951) 1974, pp. 113-135. Strangely, she suggests that 'the beauty of the world is almost absent from the Christian tradition' (p. 116). This remark may be due in part to her apparent assigning of the Old Testament to Israel; whereas Christianity has always refused to separate the two Testaments, regarding the New as the fulfilment of the Old.

69 *The Complete Works of St. John of the Cross*, translated and edited by E. Allison Peers, Vol. II, p. 26.

70 *Op cit.*, p. 48.

71 *De Potentia*, III, 10, 3 and 4. It is interesting to compare this passage from Aquinas with the views of two great scientists, Albert Einstein and Erwin Schrödinger, on the man-oriented purpose and humanist value of all science. Einstein begins his book, *The World as I See it*, with the words: 'What is the meaning of human life, or of organic life altogether? To answer this question at all implies a religion. Is there any sense, then, you ask in putting it? I answer, the man who regards his own life and that of his fellow-creatures as meaningless is not merely unfortunate, but almost disqualified for life' (*op. cit.*, p. 1). (*The World as I See it*, The Thinker's Library, Watts, London, 1949. p. 1). I have quoted a comparable passage from Schrödinger already (see p. 45 above).

Chapter II: THE GALILEO CASE

Bibliographical Note
There is a voluminous library of studies on the Galileo affair. I have consulted mainly the following:

Brodrick, James, SJ, *Galileo, the Man, his Work, his Misfortunes*, Chapman, London, 1964.

Brodrick, James, SJ, *Robert Bellarmine*, 2 volumes, (1928) 1950. The role of Bellarmine in the Galileo case is discussed in Volume II, pp. 326-373. Bellarmine died in 1621.

Drake, Stillman, *Discoveries and Opinions of Galileo*, Doubleday, New York, 1957.

Paschini, Pio, *Vita e Opere di Galileo Galilei*, Herder, Rome, 1965.

McMullin, Ernan, ed., *Galileo Man of Science*, Basic Books, New York, 1967, edited by Ernan McMullin and with an important chapter by Professor McMullin.

Santillana de, Giorgio, *The Crime of Galileo*, Mercury Books edition, Heineman, London, 1961.

Koestler, Arthur, *The Sleepwalkers*, Hutchinson, London, 1959.

Dictionnaire de Théologie Catholique, Letouzey, Paris, s.v. Galilée.

Dictionnaire Apologétique de la foi Catholique, Letouzey, Paris, s.v. Galilée.

Fantoli, Annibale, *Galileo, for Copernicanism and for the Church*, Vatican Observatory Publications, distributed by Libreria Editrice Vaticana, Vatican City. My copy is the second English language edition, 1996. It is translated by George Coyne, SJ, Director of the Vatican Observatory, who also writes a foreword. This detailed and exhaustive study of Galileo seems likely to be the classical book of reference on Galileo and on Galilean research for many years to come. I refer to this work simply as 'Fantoli'.

Fantoli, Annibale, brings the story right up to date in a paper with the title, *Galileo and the Catholic Church. A Critique of the 'Closure' of the Galileo Commission's Work.* This is published in English, translated by George Coyne SJ, by Vatican Observatory Publications, Vatican City, 2002. I refer to this work as 'Fantoli 2002'.

Sobel, Dava, *Galileo's Daughter*, Fourth Estate, London, 1999

The Cambridge Companion to Galileo, edited by Peter Machamer, Cambridge University Press, 1988. This is a valuable collection of recent studies on Galileo by leading British and American scholars. It includes an important chapter by *Ernan McMullin, 'Galileo on Science and Scripture'*, op. cit., pp. 271-347.

1   *Galileo's Daughter*, by Dava Sobel, Fourth Estate, London, 1999.

2   Ibid., p. 366

3   *Galileo and Freedom of Thought*, by F. Sherwood Taylor, Rationalist Press Association, London, 1938, p. 19.

4   Sobel, *op. cit.* p. 55.

5   *Galileo, For Copernicanism and For the Church*, by Annibale Fantoli.

6   Fantoli, pp. 173-5.

7   Fantoli, p. 181.

8   Brodrick, *Galileo*, pp. 77-9, 97; Fantoli, pp. 173-5.

9   Brodrick, *Galileo*, pp. 93-5; cfr Brodrick, *Robert Bellarmine*, Burns and Oates, London, 1961, vol. II, pp. 326-373.

10 Brodrick, *Galileo*, p. 92; *Robert Bellarmine*, pp. 357-8.

11 cfr. Fantoli, pp. 189-208. In his reference to St Augustine, Galileo is quoting from *De Genesi ad Litteram* l.11, 9.

12 Fantoli, pp. 205-205. Fantoli treats extensively of the important *Letter to Christina* (see pp. 189 foll.).

13 Fantoli, pp. 204-5.

14 See Ernan McMullin in *Cambridge Companion to Galileo*, pp. 289-314. Brodrick, in his study of Bellarmine, remarks on 'how near in many places Galileo came to the very words' of Pope Leo XIII. See *Robert Bellarmine*, vol. II, p. 351. Compare also Stillman Drake, *op. cit.*, pp. 145-216.

15 There were eleven consultors, one of whom was Peter Lombard, a Dominican priest, who had been named Archbishop of Armagh but was impeded by penal law from taking possession of his see. See Broderick, *Robert Bellarmine*, vol. II, p. 371.

16 Fantoli, p. 263.

17 Fantoli, pp. 219-220.

18 Fantoli, pp. 226-8.

19 Fantoli, p. 290.

20 Fantoli, pp. 289-298.

21 Fantoli, pp. 293-5.

22 Fantoli, pp. 321-2.

23 Fantoli, p. 352.

24 Fantoli, pp. 357-8.

25 Fantoli, pp. 425, 431.

26 Fantoli, pp. 431-6.

27 Fantoli, pp. 442-3.

28 Fantoli, pp. 444-6.

29 Fantoli, pp. 446, 451-2.

30 Fantoli, p. 448

31 Fantoli, p. 216, quoting the Holy Office ruling of 1616; Ernan McMullin has thoroughly explored Galileo's position on Science and Scripture; in the *Cambridge Companion to Galileo*, pp. 271-347.

32 Sobel, pp. 300, 332.

33 See James Brodrick, *Robert Bellarmine*, Vol I, p. 304.

34 See Sobel, pp. 375-6.

35 See Sobel, pp. 360-2.

36 See Sobel, p. 371.

37 See Sobel, p. 377.

38 Fantoli, p. 512.

39 Fantoli, pp. 503-5. The extent and nature of the changes are detailed by Fantoli; see pp. 503-5 together with footnotes on pp. 524-8.

40 Fantoli, pp. 505-6. It was signed, among others, by Father Dominique Dubarle, a Dominican priest and scientist, who was one of my teachers at the Institut Catholique in Paris in the early 1950s. I remained in contact with him afterwards until his death some years ago. He attended my ordination as bishop in Longford in 1967.

41 Constitution on the Church in the Modern World, *Gaudium et Spes*, par. 36.

42 *Gaudium et Spes*, par. 59. The quotations within this paragraph are from the *Constitution on the Catholic Faith* of the First Vatican Council.

43 Fantoli, pp. 507-8.

44 Annibale Fantoli, as I pointed out in my bibliographical note, has published an article on this Commission; I refer to it as Fantoli 2002.

45 Fantoli 2002, pp. 4-12.

46 See the Apostolic Letter, *Tertio Millennio Adveniente*, 1994, pp. 42-8.

47 In Chapter I, I quoted Erwin Schrödinger, who spoke in a similar sense in *Science and Humanism*, being the text of four lectures delivered in the Dublin Institute for Advanced Studies, published by Cambridge University Press, 1951, p. 4. See my p. 45 and chapter 1 footnote 71.

48 See *Origins*, published by the United States Conference of Catholic Bishops, vol. 22, no. 22, 12 November 1992.

49 St. Augustine, Ep. 143, 7.

50 See *Origins*, as in n. 47 above.

51 *Tertio Millennio Adveniente*, p. 48.

52 *Dei Verbum*, 12.

53 Newman, in *The Idea of a University*, Longmans Green and Co., London, 1901, pp. 466-7. This is taken from an 'occasional lecture in School of Science at the Catholic University of Ireland, Dublin; the lecture had the title: 'Christianity and Scientific Investigation'.

54 See for example Thomas S. Kuhn, *The Structure of Scientific Revolutions*, University of Chicago Press, 1962. Wittgenstein, both in the *Tractatus* and in *Philosophical Investigations*, has illuminating insights on this theme. See also *Metaphysical Beliefs*, by Stephen E. Toulmin, Ronald W. Hepburn and Alasdair Macintyre, SCM Press, London, 1957, which features three studies respectively, of 'contemporary scientific mythology', 'poetry and religious belief', and 'the logical status of religious belief'. The writers collectively acknowledge indebtedness to Wittgenstein.

55 *Cambridge Companion*, pp. 348-366.

56 *Cambridge Companion*, pp. 367-387.

57 *Fides et Ratio*, Vatican Press, Rome, and Veritas, Dublin, 1988, p. 3.

58 Ludwig Wittgenstein, *Tractatus*, 6.52.

59 *Tertio Millennio Adveniente*, 33.

Chapter III: CHURCH AND WORLD

1 *Thus Spake Zarathrustra, The First Part ... Of Otherworldlings*; my edition is the Everyman Edition, London, 1950. The reference is to pp. 23-5. Nietzsche's dates were 1844-1900.

2 Ibid., p. 6.

3 See K. Marx and F. Engels, *On Religion*, Foreign Languages Publishing House, Moscow, 1957, pp. 41-2. (The second extract is from Marx's *Contribution to the Critique of Hegel's Philosophy of Right.*) cfr. *Theses on Feuerbach*, esp. IV; see ibid., pp. 70 seq.

4 The passage from St Augustine's *Confessio* is so beautiful it deserves to be quoted in full:

> O eternal Truth and true Love and beloved Eternity, you are my God and I long for you day and night. When first I came to know you, you lifted me up just far enough to see that there was something to be seen, but that I was not yet fit to see it.

The Latin original is still more beautiful:

> *O aeterna Veritas et vera Caritas et cara Aeternitas, tu es Deus Meuus, tibi suspiro die ac nocte. Cum te primum cognovi tu me assumpsisti ut viderem esse quod viderem et nondum me esse qui viderem. (Confessions VII 10).*

5 See Norman Malcolm, *Ludwig Wittgenstein: A Memoir*, Oxford University Press, 1958, p. 71.

6 See especially his *Saint Genet, Comédien et Martyr.* Gallimard, Paris, p. 177; cfr. P. 211. This work is, I suggest, in effect the volume on morality which Sartre promised in *L'Être et le Néant*, but never formally wrote. Interestingly, Gustave Thibon, in his book *Back to Reality*, (Hollis and Carter, 1955), wrote:

> 'The thing that amazes me in every project for reform – individual, social or international –is the ever sharper convergence of the necessary and the impossible'. (p. 145)

A.D. Lindsay wrote something similar in *The Two Moralities*, (Eyre and Spottiswoode, London, 1940), pp. 41 foll.

7 *Thus Spake Zarathustra*, Everyman, ed. pp. 256-7.

8 *De Trinitate* VIII, 14

9 Romans 14: 8-9.

10 *The Mystery of Easter*, transl. By Alan Neame, The Liturgical Press, Collegeville, Minn., USA, 1993, p. 120.

11 cfr. Acts 1: 9-11.

12 cfr. Luke. 18:8.

13 cfr. Marx, *Theses on Feuerbach*, XI; op. cit., p. 72.

14 *Gaudium et Spes*, 21

15 cfr. John 17:3

16 Hebrews 11: 1.

17 Anscar Vonier, *The Victory of Christ*, in *Collected Works*, London, 1952, Vol I, p. 325.

18 cfr. 1 Corinthians 9:26-7

19 cfr. Romans 8: 24-5

20 Colossians 3:2-4.

21 1 John 4: 20.

22 cfr. Hebrews 2: 16.

23 Matthew 25: 31-46.

24 Revelation 1:8
25 cfr. Luke 24:28.
26 cfr. John 17:15.
27 *Gaudium et Spes*, No. 39.
28 John 6:55
29 Hebrews 3:13
30 Hebrews 4:11.
31 *J'entre dans la vie*, Cerf, Paris, 1973, p. 85.
32 *Thus Spake Zarathustra*, p 288.
33 *Le Mystère pascal*. Cerf Paris, 1950, pp. 35-6.
34 *La Messe sur le Monde*, in *Hymne de l'Univers*, Edits du Seuil, Paris, 1961.
35 My edition is dated 1919 and was published in New York and Dublin. It has reflections and prayers by Bishop Challoner appended to each chapter. I slightly adapt the spelling to modern usage. Thomas à Kempis was born in 1380 at Kemp near Cologne and became an Augustinian monk. A contemplative, he remarked, near the end of his life, somewhat like Pascal, that he had 'sought for rest everywhere, but found it nowhere except in a little corner with a little book'. (The 'little book' was, of course the Bible) He died at age 90, in 1471.
36 Book I chapter 1: 3.
37 cfr. St Paul, Ephesians, 5:28-32
38 cfr. John 3: 16 and 12: 47; contrast 15: 18-19 and 17: 14-16.
39 II 4: 1.
40 III 38: 1.
41 The text I am using is the Fontana Books edition, published by Collins, London, 1964. The dedication of Teilhard's book is 'For those who love the world', and this subtends the words from St John's Gospel: *Sic Deus dilexit mundum*, 'God loved the world so much.' The present citation is from p. 120.
42 pp. 72-3.
43 Book III 54: 4, 7, 9, 10, 13, 14.
44 *The Mystery of Easter*, Liturgical Press, Collegeville, Minn., 1993, p. 97; cfr. *op. cit.* p. 106. The 'world' as used by Cantalamessa at the end of this quotation is, of course, understood as that world whose values are at variance with God's Kingdom.
45 cfr. Eucharistic Prayer III.
46 cfr. *Tectio Millennio Adveniente*, nos. 31-2, 40-41; *Novo Millennio Ineunte*, nos. 29-31.
47 Matthew 6: 33
48 Philippians 4: 8
49 2 Corinthians 6: 1-20.
50 1 Corinthians 7: 29-31 (Knox translation).
51 See *On Being the Church in the World* pp. 17-18, quoting the anonymous *Epistle to Diognetus* (5-6).
52 See especially his novel, *La Peste*, Gallimard, Paris, 1947.
53 cfr. Matthew 4: 4, Hebrews, 3: 13-15.
54 See *Edith Stein*, by Sister Teresia ODC, transl. by Cecily Hastings and Donald Nicholl, Sheed and Ward, London, 1952, p. 160.
55 Hans Urs von Balthasar, *Prayer*, Transl. by A.V. Littledale, Chapman, London, 1961 p. 160.
56 *Sacrosanctum Concilium*, 12.
57 *Imitation* III. 38: 2.
58 *Le Milieu Divin.* pp. 65-6.
59 Ibid. p. 133.
60 Revelation 8:8.

61 Archbishop A.M. Ramsey, *Sacred and Secular*, Longmans 1965, pp.43-4, quoting from Gregory, *Moralia XXX,8*.

62 St Vincent de Paul, *Letters 25,46*.

63 Wisdom 9: 1-3.

64 Bertrand Russell, *The Scientific Outlook*, Allen and Unwin, London, 1954, p. 241.

65 Bertrand Russell, *Human Society in Ethics and Politics*, p. 9.

66 1 John 3: 17-18.

67 Ephesians 4: 28

68 *Gaudium et Spes*, 43

69 *The Work of Justice*, Veritas, Dublin, 1977, pp. 4-5

70 *Novo Millennio Ineunte*, Vatican Press, 2001, par. 29

Chapter IV: THE CHRISTIAN AND WORK

1 *Rerum Novarum* was published in English translation by the Catholic Social Guild of Oxford, in 1910, with the title, 'The Workers' Charter', and printed by the Catholic Truth Society of England in 1930 and 1960. My references are to numbers 2, 37-39, as numbered in this latter edition.

2 *Quadragesimo Anno* was translated into English and published by the Catholic Truth Society of England with the title: *The Social Order*. The passages quoted are nos 107 and 109.

3 *Op. cit.* no 135.

4 *Mater et Magistra* was translated into English and published by the Catholic Truth Society of England with the title: *New Light on Social Problems*. The passages quoted are from no. 254-6.

5 *Op. cit.* no 259.

6 *Op. cit.* no 125.

7 *Op. cit.* no 127.

8 *Op. cit.* no 140.

9 *Op. cit.* no 20-21.

10 *Op. cit.* no 28.

11 *Op. cit.* no 32.

12 *Op. cit.* no 34.

13 *Gaudium et Spes*, 68.

14 *Laborem Exercens*, Vatican Press, 1981, p. 32.

15 See *Easter Vigil and Other Poems*, translated by Jerzy Peterkiewicz, Hutchinson, London, 1979 pp. 32-33.

16 *Laborem Exercens*, pp. 41-44.

17 *Op. cit.* pp. 60-67.

18 *Op. cit.* p. 52.

19 *Centesimus Annus*, pars 41-43.

20 *Op. cit.* pp. 50-51.

21 *The Work of Justice*; Veritas, Dublin, 1977, p. 31.

22 *Christian Faith in a Time of Economic Depression*, A Statement from the Irish Catholic Bishops, June 1983, p. 7.

23 *Op. cit.* pp 70-71

24 See *Reconciliatio et Paenitentia*, Vatican Press, 1984, no 16.

25 *Sollicitudo Rei Socialis*, no 37.

26 *Op. cit.* no 36.

27 *Centesimus Annus*, p. 75.

28 *Centesimus Annus,* p. 84.

29 *Populorum Progressio,* no. 27.

30 *Centesimus Annus,* pp. 73-4, 80.

31 See K. Marx and F. Engels, *On Religion,* Foreign Languages Publishing House, Moscow, 1957, and Lawrence and Wishart, London, 1958, p. 15. Marx wrote the words in Berlin in 1841.

32 Genesis 1:26-8.

33 Genesis 2:8-15.

34 Exodus 5:8 and 9: 17-18.

35 Edmund Leach, *A Runaway World,* published by the BBC, 1967.

36 John 5:17.

37 Philippians 2:6-7.

38 Luke 12:49.

39 Mark 10:32.

40 Luke 12:48.

41 Matthew 3:11.

42 *Lumen Gentium* 34.

43 *Lumen Gentium* 32-38

44 Philippians 2:14-16.

45 See the collection, *Hymme de l'Univers,* published by Editions du Seuil, Paris, 1961.

46 Pope Paul VI, *Ecclesiam Suam,* published in English by the Catholic Truth Society of England; see p. 23.

47 John 6:51.

48 Revelation 20: 4-6.

49 *Gaudium et Spes,* 39.

50 Psalm 113:16.

51 Ben Sirach 17:1-4.

52 1 Peter 4:11.

53 Philippians 1:27 (Knox translation).

54 1 Corinthians 15:57-8 (Knox translation).

55 *Op. cit.* Routledge, London, 1933/1961, p 264.

56 Thomas Aquinas, *Summa contra Gentiles,* IV 97.

57 Philippians 3:12-14.

58 Colossians 1:15-20.

59 cfr. footnote 68 below.

60 Ephesians 2: 20-1.

61 Romans 8: 18-25.

62 *The 1916 Poets,* edited by Desmond Ryan, Allen Figgis, Dublin, 1963, p. 192.

63 Gerard Manley Hopkins, from the poems, 'Godhead, I adore thee', 'The world is charged with the grandeur of God', 'Pied Beauty', and 'Hurrahing in Harvest', in *G.M. Hopkins, Oxford Poetry Library,* Oxford University Press, 1995.

64 Patrick Kavanagh, 'The One', from *Patrick Kavanagh, Collected Poems,* Martin Brian and O'Keefe, London, p. 159.

65 cfr. *Gaudium et Spes,* 39.

66 *Laborem Exercens* no. 27.

67 *Gaudium et Spes,* 57.

68 *Ecclesia in Europa,* Vatican City, 2003, p. 102.

69 Ephesians 3: 20-1.

Chapter V (1) and (2): THE MINDING OF PLANET EARTH

1   See *NASA and the Exploration of Space*, Stewart, Tabori and Change, New York, 1998 and James Irwin, *To Rule the Night*, A.J. Holman, Philadelphia, 1973; *More than earthlings, an astronaut's thoughts for Christ-centred living*, Pickering and Inglis, Basingstoke, 1984. *Destination Moon*, Multnormah, Portland, Oregon, 1989.

2   See John Passmore, *Man's Responsibility for Nature*, Duckworth, London, 1974, cfr. pp. 28 foll. And p. 195.

3   Constitution on The Church in the Modern World, *Gaudium et Spes*, p. 57.

4   *Gaudium et Spes*, p. 69.

5   *Gaudium et Spes*, p. 57.

6   This phrase is commonly referred to by the initials JPIC. The complete text issued from this WCC convocation is to be found in the collection, *The Ecumenical Movement: an Anthology of Key Texts and Voices*, edited by M. Kinnamon and B.E. Cope, WCC/Eerdmans, 1997

7   *Mater et Magistra*, Catholic Truth Society of England edition, London 1961, pars, 157, 158, 161.

8   *Pacem in Terris*, CTSE edition, London, 1963.

9   *Populorum Progressio*, pars 22, 32-4.

10 *Sollicitudo Rei Socialis*, par. 34. Father Sean McDonagh relates the Pope's latter paragraph to the problems of genetic engineering and the 'patenting' of life. These issues and the question of genetic modification of seeds and crops certainly require rigorous ethical scrutiny. Assuredly, before any legislation on or any official support for patenting were to be decided by the Irish government, a thorough public debate on all the relevant issues is required. Pope John Paul calls for 'careful ethical reflection' and 'adequate legal norms', in this domain, particularly where human life is concerned. [World Day of Peace Message 1999]. The subject is too complex to be discussed adequately here. On the question of ecological ethics in general, Father McDonagh has written extensively. The following are among his titles: *To care for the Earth*, a call to a new theology, Geoffrey Chapman, London, (1988) 1989; *The Greening of the Catholic Church*, Orbis Books NY and Chapman, London, 1990; *Greening the Christian Millennium*, Dominican Publications, Dublin, 2000; *Passion for the Earth*, Chapman, 1994; *The Scramble to Patent Life*, Columban Faith and Justice Office, 1999. *Patenting Life! Stop!* Dominican Publications, 2003; *Dying for Water*, Veritas, 2003. By his writing and research Father McDonagh has made a great contribution to reflection and discussion on ecological issues.

11 *Centesimus Annus*, Vatican City, 1991, nos. 37-39.

12 *Gaudium et Spes*, 9, 29.

13 *The Angry Seventies*, by Barbara Ward, a Study Paper prepared at the request of the Pontifical Council Justice and Peace, Rome 1970, p. 63.

14 All of these published by the Pontifical Academy of Sciences, Vatican City.

15 The text is reproduced in full in *The Ecumenical Movement*, edited by Kinnamon and Cope, WCC/Eerdmans, 1997.

16 Vatican City, 1989.

17 *Peace with God the Creator, Peace with all Creation*, p. 3.

18 *Peace with God the Creator, Peace with all Creation*, p.6.

19 *Peace with God the Creator, Peace with all Creation*, pp. 6-9.

20 *Peace with God the Creator, Peace with all Creation*, p. 6.

21 My copy is the second printing, published by the MIT Press, Cambridge, Mass., 1980.

22 *The Brandt Report*, p. 13.

23 *The Brandt Report*, p. 19.

24 *The Brandt Report*, p. 19-20.

25 *The Brandt Report*, p. 12.

26 *The Brandt Report*, p. 16.

27 *The Thorsson Report*, par. 28.

28 *The Thorsson Report*, pars. 44, 72-3-4.

29 *The Thorsson Report*, par. 51. Cfr p. 7 above.

30 My copy is the Penguin Books edition, Harmondsworth, Middlesex, England, 1982. This is a single volume, printed in double-column pages. Volume I outlines the major findings and conclusions of the study; Volume II is in two parts, and includes the technical detail on which the findings and conclusions are based. The study is supported by a copious array of maps, graphs, statistical tables, etcetera.

31 *Global 2000 Report*, p. 4.

32 *Global 2000 Report*, p. 39-42.

33 *Global 2000 Report*, pp. 32-35.

34 *Global 2000 Report*, pp. 32-33.

35 *Global 2000 Report*, p. 37.

36 *Global 2000 Report*, p. 38.

37 *Global 2000 Report*, p. 36.

38 *Global 2000 Report*, pp. 27-29.

39 *Global 2000 Report*, p. 356.

40 *Global 2000 Report*, p. 26-9, 40.

41 *Global 2000 Report*, pp. 105-115.

42 Stanislas Fumet, *L'impatience des Limites*, Fribourg, Geneva, 1942. This book was reprinted in 1999.

43 Barbara Ward, *A New Creation*, p. 68. See footnote 47 below.

44 *The Brandt Report*, p. 23.

45 *SIPRI Yearbook 2003*, pp. 33-43. See footnote 58 below.

46 *Peace with God the Creator, Peace with all Creation*, 1989, pp. 12-13.

47 Barbara Ward, *A New Creation*, Pontifical Commission for Justice and Peace, Vatican City, 1973, p. 59.

48 *Thorsson Report*, par. 66.

49 See *The Tablet*, 17 January 2004.

50 Nick Cohen in *The Observer*, Sunday 7 March 2004.

51 *At the Service of the Human Community*, Vatican City, 1986, p 30.

52 *Tertio Millennio Adveniente*, Vatican City, 1994, no. 51

53 *At the Service of the Human Community*, An ethical reflection; Vatican City, 1986, p. 25.

54 *At the Service of the Human Community*, p. 17.

55 *From Promise to Action*. A development agenda for the EU Presidency in 2004, a Briefing Paper by Dr Lorna Good, July 2003.

56 Dr Jan Pronk, *Collateral Damage or Calculated Default?*, a lecture at the Institute of Social Studies, The Hague, 11 December 2003, p.21.

57 For facts and figures relevant to the sections on 'The Arms Trade' and 'Disarmament and Development', I refer to the *Brandt Report*; to Pauline Eccles, *Disarmament and Development*, Irish Commission for Justice and Peace, 1987; to *Peace and Disarmament*, Documents of the World Council of Churches and the Catholic Church, published by the Pontifical Council, Justice and Peace, 1982; to Ruth L. Sivard, *World Military and Social Expenditures*, edition 1982, World Priorities Inc., Leesbury, Virginia; and to *SIPRI Yearbook 2002*, sub-titled: *Armaments, Disarmament and International Society*; Stockholm International Peace Research Institute, Oxford University Press, 2003.

58 *The International Arms Trade*, An ethical reflection; Vatican City, 1994, p. 5.

59 *The Brandt Report*, p. 14; cfr. Pauline Eccles, *Disarmament and Development*, pp. 11-12.

60 *The Brandt Report,* p. 117.

61 *The Brandt Report,* p. 16.

62 *The Brandt Report,* p. 124.

63 *The Brandt Report,* p. 124.

64 *The Brandt Report,* p. 123.

65 *SIPRI Yearbook 2003,* pp. 439-445.

66 *SIPRI Yearbook 2003,* pp. 302-3.

67 *SIPRI Yearbook 2003,* pp. 712-5; cfr. *The International Arms Trade,* p. 30.

68 *The International Arms Trade,* p. 5.

69 *Populorum Progressio,* no. 24.

70 Barbara Ward, *A New Creation,* Vatican City, 1973, p. 65.

71 cfr. Barbara Ward, *The Angry Seventies,* Vatican City, 1970. p. 61.

72 Genesis 2:15.

73 Genesis 8:1 and 9:16-17, see also Exodus 23:10-12, Leviticus 25: 6-7, Deuteronomy 5:12-15 and 22:10, 25:4. A scholarly and profound study of the biblical account of God's covenant with the entire creation is found in Father Robert Murray's *The Cosmic Covenant,* Sheed and Ward, London 1992.

74 Pope John Paul II *Peace with God the Creator, Peace with all Creation,* 1989, no. 5.

75 Daniel 3: 31-90.

76 *The Works of St Patrick, Confession,* Translated and annotated by Ludwig Bieler, Longmans Green, London, 1`953, pp. 39-40.

77 *Prayers of Two Peoples,* translated by Stephen Redmond SJ, Veritas, Dublin.

78 Gerard Manley Hopkins, 'God's Glory', and 'Glory be to God for dappled things', in *Selected Poems,* The Oxford Poetry Library, 1995, pp. 114 and 117.

79 John 1: 2-3.

80 Ephesians 1: 91-10.

81 Colossians 1: 15-20.

82 Romans 8: 21-25.

83 Isaiah 11: 6-10.

84 See Jean Daniélou, SJ, *Advent,* English translation by Rosemary Sheed, Sheed and Ward, London and New York, 1950, pp. 127-9.

85 Henri de Lubac, *Catholicism,* English translation by Lancelot Sheppard, Burns, Oates, London, 1950, pp. 282-3. cfr. Daniélou, *Advent,* pp. 127-8, 137-8.

86 See *Advent,* p. 137.

87 Colossians 1: 15-20.

88 Ephesians 1: 23; 4: 10.

89 Daniélou, *Advent,* p. 127.

90 cfr. Ephesians 3: 17-19.

91 Galatians 3: 28.

92 *Advent* p. 134.

93 *Peace with God the Creator, Peace with all Creation,* no. 16.

94 Isaiah 24: 1-11.

95 Revelation 21: 1-4.

96 Romans 1:4.

97 John 2: 11.

98 cfr. Psalm 88: 38.

99 Psalm 8.

Appendix: BEHOLD YOUR GOD

1   John A.T. Robinson, Bishop of Woolwich; see the lecture with this title printed as Appendix I in *The New Reformation,* SCM Press, London, 1965. His question was, of course, a rhetorical one and his answer was an emphatic affirmation that a contemporary person can believe in God when the concept 'God' is properly grasped and the arguments for God's existence correctly stated.

2   *The Cloud of Unknowing,* revised, edited and introduced by Abbot Justin McCann, Burns, Oates, London, 1952, pp. 77-8.

3   *Op. cit.* pp. 82-3.

4   Genesis, 1:28.

5   Genesis, 1:26.

6   *Wisdom,* ix, 1.13.

7   *Human Society in Ethics and Politics,* Allen and Unwin, London, 1954, p.9. Compare *The Scientific Attitude,* Allen and Unwin, London, 1931, pp. 241, 260.

8   1 Corinthians xiii, 1-3.

9   *Revelations of Divine Love,* edited and introduced by Dom Roger Huddleston, Burns, Oates, London, 1952, p. 169.

10 *Op. cit.* p. 167.

11 *Op. cit.* pp. 88-9.

12 cf. Isaiah, lxi, 1-2; Luke iv, 18-19.

13 *Dying we Live,* edited by H. Gollwitzer and others, foreword by Trevor Huddleston, Fontana Books, London, 1958, pp. 240-2.

INDEX

A

Acts of the Apostles 151
Adams, astronomer 41
Advent 219
Africa 198, 200-1, 205-6, 207
AIDS, and poverty 194
Almagest 24, 31
Angelico, Fra 26
Angry Seventies, The, 174
Anthropic Principle 28
Anti-Personnel Mines Convention 205
Aquinas, St Thomas 20, 53, 54, 56, 91-2, 101-
   2, 103-4, 170
   Summa contra Gentiles 160
   Summa Theologica 24-6
Aristotle 29, 48, 60-2, 73, 88
   and aristotelian philosophers 63, 66
Armagh 51
arms trade 202-6
arms exporting countries 205
   landmines 205
   and poverty 202
Asia, religious traditions of 35
Assayer, The 70-2
astronomy 19, 23-5, 29
astronauts 169, 222
   planets 32, 41-2
Athanasian Creed 36
atheism 224
atheistic humanism 95, 97
   and work 149-50
atomic bomb 42
attachment-detachment 120-3
Augustine, St 55, 100, 103, 113, 115-16, 118,
   126

and mystery of Blessed Trinity 44-5
quoted by Galileo 67-9
quoted by Pope John Paul II 85
Austrian National Library 39

B

Babel, tower of 150, 157
Balthasar, Father Hans Urs von 124-5
baptism 109-10, 112
and work 152-5
Barberini, Cardinal Maffeo 70-1
Barcelona 200
Baronius 85
Bartholomew, Ecumenical Patriarch, joint
   declaration on human stewardship of
   the environment 178-9
BBC Reith Lectures 20, 150
Bea, Cardinal Augustine 86-7
Bellarmine, Cardinal Robert
   and Foscarini 65-7, 77
   and Galileo 25, 63, 70, 83, 93
   and the pope 78, 85
Belloc, Hilaire 35
Benedict, St 35
Benedict XIV, Pope 81
Beowulf 51
Berdyaev 131
Bergson 130, 209, 226
Bible
   Daniel 54, 213
   Ecclesiastes 31
   Exodus 53, 178
   Genesis 30, 149, 150, 157, 167, 172-3,
   212, 227
   Isaiah 32, 63, 216, 221

Hosea 213
Joshua 63
Judges 63
Leviticus 132, 197, 212
Psalms 3, 51-3, 109-12, 129, 213, 222-3, 226-7, 231
Wisdom 46, 129, 227
Hebrews 111
Revelation 57, 126, 156, 222
and science 224-31
and work 148-9
Blackwell, Richard 90
Boethius 23, 24, 31, 101
Bono 198
Bosnia 207
Bouyer, Father Louis 112
Bradley, F.H. 29
Bradley, General Omar 137
Brahe, Tycho 41
Brandenbug-Görden 230
Brandt, Willi 181-3, 189, 203-4, 208
Braun, Dr Herbert 189
Breslin, Sister Dr Carol 127
Brodrick, James 25, 65-6
Byzantines 33

C

Caccini, Tommaso 69
Caesar Augustus 47
Cambridge Companion to Galileo 90, 91
Cambridge University 36, 41
Camus, Albert 106-7, 122
Cana miracle 221-2
Cantalamessa, Raniero 106, 119
capitalism 135-6, 143-4, 209-10
Carter, President Jimmy 184-5
Casey, Michael 165
Castelli, Benedetto 79
    Galileo's letter to 63-4, 85
Catholicism 217-18
Central National Library, Florence 58
charity, politics and science 129-31
Chernobyl 189, 192
Chesterton, G.K. 17, 22, 33, 35
children 177-8, 194
China 34, 187, 209-10
Christ
    coming 106-7
    kingship over matter 154-5

and peace 156-7
and work 150-1, 155-6
Christian Democrats 50
Christian terminology, semantic difficulties in 98-9
Christianity
    and democracy 46-50
    and nature's beauty 50-7, 163-6, 213-6, 229-230
    and time 104-6
    and work 135-66
Christina, Countess, Galileo's letter to 67-9
Christus Rex 140
Church
    and ecology 169-75
    and science 77-8, 93-4
    social teaching 135-66, 171
    and the world 95-134
Ciampole, Father Giovanni 66
Claudel, Paul 51
Clemenceau 123
Clinton, President Bill 198
Cloud of Unknowing, The 225
Cold War 206-7
Collingwood, R.G. 23-4, 26, 34, 36-7
Communion, First 194
communism 144
concentration camps 230
Concern 207
Congregation of the Index 70
Constitution on the Church in the Modern World 133
contemplation and action 123-9
Copernicus, Nicolaus 19-20, 24, 29, 60-3, 80
compatibility of copernican system with Holy Scripture 65-8, 84
copernican system condemned 69-77, 80
    and Galileo's Dialogue 73-4
Cosimo II, Grand Duke of Tuscany 58, 67
cosmology
    and the human mind 27-30
    steady state theory 28
Council of Trent 68
creation
    and covenant 212-13
    new 158-62, 215-17
    prayer inspired by 213-14
    and work 157-8

cross, symbol of universal reconciliation 217-19
Cuba 209-10
Cullen, Father Shay 127
Cyprian, St 47

D

Daniélou, Cardinal Jean 127, 218-19
Dante 26
Dawkins, Richard 17, 38-40, 89
Dawson, Christopher 35
De Consolatione Philosophiae 23
de Valera, Eamon 45
debt, and poverty 197-9
Del Monte, Cardinal 66
democracy
    and Christianity 46-50
    and science 46-7
Descartes 78
development, and disarmament 206-7
Devil's Chaplain, A 39
Diable et le bon Dieu, Le 97
Dialogue, The 72-7
Dialogues Concerning Natural Religion 20
Diognetus, epistle to 121, 130
Dirac, theory of electron 43
disarmament, and development 206-7
Disney 193
divine creation, and work 157-8
Divino Afflante Spiritu 86
Dublin Institute of Advanced Studies 45
Duggan, Sister Dr Miriam 127

E

East Timor 205
ecology 167-95
    acid rain 188
    Brandt Report 181-3
    and the Catholic Church 169-75
    ethical principles 178-9
    and the Eucharist 219
    extinction of species 187
    floods, famine and disease 186
    forests, soil erosion and desertification 185-7
    Global 2000 Report 184-90
    greed 193-5
    individual responsibility 191-2

    joint declaration on human stewardship of the environment 178-9
    and Mary, Mother of the Lord 221-3
    non-renewable resources 182, 184-8, 191-2
    nuclear energy 188, 192
    and the other Churches 174, 177
    ozone layer and greenhouse effect 180, 184, 188, 191
    pollution 182, 186-7, 191-2
    and St Francis of Assisi 219-20
    Thorsson Report 183-4
    waste 191-2
    water 188
    World Charter for Nature 184
education, access to 177
Einstein, Albert 14-15, 38, 44, 59, 82
    equation 42
    principle of relativity 29
Elchinger, Monsignor 81
Elsom, John 131
Emmaus Communities 127
encyclicals
    Centesimus Annus 144, 147, 173, 210
    Ecclesiam Suam 156
    Fides et Ratio 92
    Laborem Exercens 141-3, 145, 165-6, 210
    Mater et Magistra 137-8, 139
    Pacem in Terris 171-2
    Populorum Progressio 138-9, 146, 147, 172
    Quadragesimo Anno 136
    Rerum Novarum 135-6, 141, 144, 171, 173
    Sollicitudo Rei Socialis 146, 172-3, 210
Enlightenment 17, 35, 49, 50, 59
Enron 118
environment see ecology
Essay on Metaphysics 36
eternity 104-9
    Last End 102-3
    last things are now 107-9
Eucharist 110-11
    and ecology 219
European Union 200, 201, 202
    Constitution 50, 209
    and disarmament 206-7, 209
    Ireland's role in 207-8
Evidence for Christianity 39-40

F

faith, and science 13-15, 17-57, 89-93
famine 186
    in Ireland 198, 207
Fantoli, Annibale
    paper on Galileo Commission 83
    study of Galileo 61-2, 68, 70-1, 76-7, 79,
    81, 91, 94
Foscarini, Antonio 65-7, 70, 77
Foster, M.B. 34, 37
Foyers de Charité 127
France, arms exports 205
Francis of Assisi, St 219-20
Francis de Sales, St 231
French Revolution 49
Fumet, Stanislas 188-9

G

Galileo 18-20, 25, 26, 28-9, 58-93
    beginning of dispute 63
    'First Trial of Galileo' (1616) 69-70
    condemned by Holy Office (1633) 75-8
    could there be another Galileo case?
        89-93
    daughter Maria Celeste 58, 62, 72, 79
    fervent faith 62-3
    last years and death 79-80
    letter to Castelli 63-4, 87
    letter to Christina 67-9, 87
    summary of life 58-60
    and the telescope 39, 59, 62
    theory of tides 66
    under house arrest 78-9
    vindication of 80-3
    visits to Rome 63, 69-70, 71, 72, 74-6
Galileo's Daughter 58
Gamba, Marina (mother of Galileo's
    children) 58
Geldof, Bob 194
Gemelli, Father Agustino 81
German Ideology, The 97
Germany, arms exports 205
Global 2000 Report 184-90
Goethe 20
Gorbachev, Mikhail 142
Gospels 115, 150-1, 215, 221
Greece 34, 47, 201
greed
    and the environment 193-5

and capitalism 136, 146-7, 194-5, 210-1
and tax evasion 210-11
Gregory the Great, Pope 35, 126

H

Hadrian, Emperor 21, 226
Hague, The 202
Handel 224
Harding, Abbot Stephen 128
Hayes, Canon John 139
Heaney, Seamus 51
Heidegger 30, 119
hermeneutics 86-7
Herschel 41
Hilary, St 105
Hindu thought 218
Hippolytus of Rome 217-18
Hiroshima 184, 192
Hopkins, Gerard Manley 53, 164, 165, 215,
    229
Horace 190
Hoyle, Fred 29, 42-3
human centrality 26-31
human rights 175-8
    and poverty 176, 196
    see also women's rights
Hume, David 19-20, 27
Hussein, Saddam 205
Huxley, Aldous 128
Huxley, Julian 17
Huxley, T.H. 17

I

iconographic tradition 163
Ignatius Loyola, St 111, 120
Ignatius of Antioch, St 132
Ilychev Report 132
Imitation, The 114-20, 125
immigration 208-9
immortality 101-2
Impatience with Limits 188-9
Independent Commission on International
    Development 181-3
Index of Prohibited Books 70, 80
India 34, 187
Individual and the Universe 20
Indonesia 193, 205
industry 180-1
Inquisition 59-61, 75-7, 87, 93

Institute of Social Studies, the Hague 202
International Monetary Fund 197, 198
Ionesco 56
Iraq 205
Ireland
    aid to low-income countries (ODA) 201
    and disarmament 206-7
    famine in 198, 207
    and immigration 208-9
    and Millennium Development Goals
      200
    role in EU 207-8
    tax evasion in 210
    and wealth 194, 209-11
    and world poverty 209
Irenaeus, St 217
Irwin, James 169
Israel 212

J

Jaspers, Karl 119
Jeans, Sir James 20
Joad, Professor C.E.M. 22
John of the Cross, St 55-6, 126
John Paul II, Pope 93-4, 120, 166
    address to Pontifical Academy of
      Sciences 14-15, 82
    Apostolic Letter for the new millennium
      134
    Centesimus Annus 144, 147, 173, 210
    and ecology 178-81, 189, 192, 208, 211,
      213, 219-20
    Fides et Ratio 92
    and Galileo 62, 82-9
    on human rights 196
    joint declaration on human stewardship
      of the environment 178-9
    Laborem Exercens 141-3, 145, 165-6, 210
    poems 142
    on poverty 194-5
    Reconciliation and Penance 146
    Sollicitudo Rei Socialis 146, 172-3, 210
    on work 135, 141-7
John, St 108, 115, 152, 215, 221
John XXIII, Pope 184
    Mater et Magistra 136-8, 171
    Pacem in Terris 171-2
Jubilee of the year 2000 94, 197-8
Julian the Apostate 132

Julian of Norwich, Mother 228
Jung, C.G. 159-60
justice, and peace 177
Justinian 35

K

Kant 31, 102, 103 4, 116
Kavanagh, Patrick 165
Kennedy, President John Fitzgerald 130
Kepler 41, 66
Kierkegaard 101, 119

L

La Pira, Georgio 131
labour, and popes 135-40
Lagrange, Jean Louis 87
landmines 205
L'Arche communities 127
Larkin, Philip 109
Leach, Dr Edmund 150
Leo XIII, Pope 69, 87, 135-6, 140-1
    Rerum Novarum 135 6, 141, 144, 171, 173
Leverrier, astronomer 41
Lewis, C.S. 24
lifestyle, change of 211-12
Lindsay, A.D. 47-9
Lovell, Sir Bernard 19-20, 25
Lubac, Cardinal de 49, 91, 127, 217-18
Luke, St, Gospel 151
Luther, Martin 61, 77

M

McNamara, Robert S. 181
Madrid 204
Makarov, Oleg 169
Malebranche 101
Malone, Professor Jim 45-6
Man and Materialism 42
Man's Responsibility for Nature 170
Marcel, Gabriel 45, 123
Maria Celeste, Sister (Galileo's daughter)
    58, 62, 72, 79
Maritain 131
Mark, St, Gospel 151, 152
Mars, landing of probe 32
Marx, Karl 95-8, 106-7, 109, 148, 149
    and Marxism 60, 144, 150, 157
Mary, Mother of the Lord, and ecology
    221-3

Maxwell, theory of light 42
Medici, Don Cosimo de, Grand Duke of
    Tuscany 58, 67
medieval Christian thought, and science
    34-5, 170
Melanchthon 77
Merbold, Ulf 169
metaphysics 19, 36, 98-9
Michelangelo 23, 58, 59
Middle Ages
    medieval Christian thought 34-5, 170
    medieval philosophers 39
    myth about 19-26
Milieu Divin, Le 116, 125
Millennium Development Goals
    199-200, 202
    countries meeting target 200
    and Ireland 200
Milton, John 21, 59-60, 79
Modern Man in Search of a Soul 159-60
monastic settlements 128-9
Monterey, Mexico 200
moon, first landing on 168-9, 222
Moral Teaching of Jesus, The 48-9
Mosaic Law 212-13
Mount Wilson Observatory 42
Muintir na Tíre 139-40
Müller, Father Joseph 230
Mysterious Universe, The 20
Mystery in Science 38-9, 42-5

N

nature, reason in 41-6
Nature of the Universe, The 42
Nazis, and genetic experimentation 50
New Creation, A: Reflections on the
    Environmental Issue 175
New Testament 150-1, 161-2
Newman, Cardinal 87, 162
Newton, Isaac 41, 42, 44, 80
Nietzsche 95-9, 106-7, 109, 111, 160-1
Noah and the Flood 212-13
Notre Dame cathedral 49
nuclear energy 188

O

O'Faolain, Nuala 193
O'Laoghaire, Father Diarmuid 214-15
Orthodox Church 178-9

other-wordliness 95-8
Overseas Development Aid 199-202

P

Pascal 30-1, 119
Paschini, Monsignor Pio 81, 90
Passmore, John 169-70
Pastoral Letter on Justice 134
Patrick, St 213-14
Paul, St 105-6, 108, 114-15, 217
    Colossians 161, 215-16, 218
    Corinthians 120-1, 228
    Ephesians 132, 166, 215-16
    Galatians 218-19
    Philippians 120, 151, 154, 158, 160-1
    Romans 106, 163, 216, 222
Paul V, Pope 63, 68, 70
Paul VI, Pope 81-2, 93, 173, 194, 209, 210,
    222
    Ecclesiam Suam 156
    Populorum Progressio 138-9, 146-7, 172
    peace 156-7
    and justice 177
Péguy, Charles 111, 156
Pera, Marcello 91-2
Persia 34
Peter, St 158
Pharaoh 149-50
Philippines 127
Piccolomini, Archbishop Ascanio 79
Pierre, Abbé 127
Pius X, St 128
Pius XI, Pope 81, 136, 140
Pius XII, Pope 69, 86, 136, 140
Plato 44, 48, 99-102, 115
Plotinus 92
Plunkett, Joseph Mary 164
politics, science and charity 129-31
Polkinghorne, John 28
Pontifical Academy of Sciences 14, 81, 82,
    83, 175
Pontifical Council for Justice and Peace
    173-5, 197, 199, 203, 206, 211
Pope, Alexander 100
popes, and labour 135-40
population growth 190-1
Poupard, Cardinal 83
poverty
    world poverty 176-9, 201-2, 207-8

and AIDS 194
and arms trade 202
and debt 197-9
gap between rich and poor 194-5
and human rights 176, 196
impact of economic development on
    183-4, 194-5
and Overseas Development Aid 199-202
and population growth 190-1
and social justice 209-10
and social partnership 145
and war 182-4
power, exercise of 176
prayer, and creation 213-14
profit 144-5
Prejean, Sister Helen 127
Prometheus 148-9
Pronk, Dr Jan 202
Protestant Reformation 78
Psalms 3, 51-3, 109-12, 129, 213, 222-3,
    226-7, 231
PSNI 207
Ptolemy 23-4, 31, 60-1

R

racism 176, 208
Radical Orthodoxy movement 36
Ramsey, Archbishop Michael 126
Ranke 104
Rationalist Press Association 60
reason in nature 41-6
Redmond, Father Stephen 214-15
refugees and asylum-seekers 208-9
religious communities 189
Reville, Professor William 43-4, 55
Robin, Marthe 127
Robinson, Archbishop 51
Robinson, Bishop John 121, 224
Roman Empire 47, 190
Russell, Bertrand 17, 20-3, 26-8, 56, 89,
    129-30, 228
Russia 188, 209
    arms exports 205

S

sacraments 109-13
Sartre, Jean-Paul 30, 97, 102
Schödinger, Erwin 45, 92
science

and the Bible 224-31
and the Church 77-8, 93-4
and democracy 46-7
developments in 88-9
and faith 13-15, 17-57, 89-93
and medieval Christian thought 34 5
and mystery 38-40
politics and charity 129-31
role of hypothesis in 24-5
and technology and industry 180-1
theology as preparation for 33-7
Science and the Modern World 34
Sellafield 192
semantic difficulties in Christian
    terminology 98-9
Sermon on the Mount 48-9
Shanghai conference 200
Sharpe, Sister Dr Ursula 127
Short, Clare 194
sin, structures of 146-8
social sin 146
social justice 131-4, 209-10
socialism 209-10
Socrates 100
SODEPAX 174
solar eclipse 32
Soviet Union 132, 150, 209
Stein, Edith 124
Summa Theologica 24-5
Sunday Times 18
Switzerland 190
Synge, John Lighton 45
Synod of Bishops 175

T

tax evasion 210-11
Taylor, Dr F. Sherwood 60
technology 180-1
Teilhard de Chardin 90-1, 116-17, 120-2, 125,
    160, 220
    Mass on the World 112-13, 155
Teresa of Calcutta, Mother 122, 127
Teresia Benedicta, St 124
theology, as preparation for science 33-7
Thérèse of Lisieux, St 17, 111-12, 119
Thomas à Kempis 117-18, 120
Thorsson Report 183-4, 194
Thus Spake Zarathustra 95-7, 111-13
Tibetans 33

trade unions 140-1, 154-5
transfiguration 163-6
Trevor-Roper, Professor 33-4
Trinity College, Dublin 45
Trócaire 198, 200-1, 207, 211

U

UK, arms exports 205
United Nations 174, 183, 199, 206, 207, 208
    Millennium Development Goals 199-200
    Universal Declaration of Human Rights
    196
    University in Hiroshima 192
    World Charter for Nature 184
United States 184-5, 200, 209
    arms trade 204-5
    Conference of Catholic Bishops 198
Urban VIII, Pope 71-6

V

Vanier, Jean 122, 127
Vatican Council, First 78
Vatican Council, Second 13, 69, 93-4, 110,
    114, 119, 124-5, 156-7, 165
    Constitution on Church in Modern
    World 132-3, 153, 166
    Dei Verbum 86-7
    and ecology 170-1
    and Galileo 81-2
    Gaudium et Spes 32-3, 153, 166
    and the Mass 110, 155
    on peace and justice 173-4
    and trade unions 140-1
    and women's rights 174
Vatican Observatory 94
Vincent de Paul, St 126
Virgil 105
Viviani, Vincenzio 80
Voltaire 18, 59
Vonier, Abbot 108

W

Wallace, Sister Vincent 141
war
    and nuclear weapons 183-4
    and poverty 182-4
Ward, Barbara 174-5, 189, 193, 211, 222
Weil, Simone 55
Wells, H.G. 17
Whitehead, A..N. 34-5
Wittgenstein 93, 102
Wojtyla, Karol 141
Wolfensohn, James 200
women's rights 174, 176
    and work 145-6
    see also human rights
work
    atheistic theories of 149-50
    and baptism 152-5
    and the Bible 148-9
    and Christ 150-1, 155-6
    and Christianity 135-66
    and creation 157-62
    family aspects of 145-6
    and popes 135-40
    and women 145-6
Work of Justice, The 144
world
    and the church 95-134
    contempt for 113-14
World As I See It, The 44
World Bank 181, 197, 198, 200
World Charter for Nature 184
World Convocation in Seoul 175-8
    affirmations 176-8
WorldCom 118
World Council of Churches 174-8
World Day of Peace 179
World Health Organisation 203

The Minding of
Planet Earth

CARDINAL CAHAL B DALY

The Minding of
Planet Earth

VERITAS

First published 2004 by
Veritas Publications
7/8 Lower Abbey Street
Dublin 1
Ireland
Email publications@veritas.ie
Website www.veritas.ie

ISBN 1 85390 579 8

Cover design by Bill Bolger
Printed in the Republic of Ireland by Criterion Press, Dublin

Veritas books are printed on paper made from the wood pulp of managed forests. For every tree felled, at least one tree is planted, thereby renewing natural resources.